JAMES BRYCE

(VISCOUNT BRYCE OF DECHMONT, O.M.)

VOLUME II

THE MACMILLAN COMPANY
NEW YORK · BOSTON · CHICAGO · DALLAS
ATLANTA · SAN FRANCISCO

MACMILLAN & CO., LIMITED
LONDON · BOMBAY · CALCUTTA
MELBOURNE

THE MACMILLAN CO. OF CANADA, LTD.
TORONTO

PRINTED IN THE UNITED STATES OF AMERICA

CONTENTS

VOLUME TWO

LIST OF ILLUSTRATIONS

JAMES BRYCE

(VISCOUNT BRYCE OF DECHMONT, O.M.)

VOLUME II

JAMES BRYCE

VOLUME II

CHAPTER XIX

WASHINGTON

The corner stone of this Republic, as of all free government, is respect for and obedience to the law. When we permit the law to be defied or evaded, whether by rich men or poor men, by black men or white, we are by just so much weakening the bonds of our civilisation and increasing the chances of its overthrow.

T. Roosevelt.

On the eve of entering upon his official career in America, Sir Henry Campbell-Bannerman sounded Bryce as to his willingness to take a peerage. Neither Bryce nor his wife cared about a title, and apart from any sentiment of personal reluctance, Bryce suspected that a peerage might hamper him in America, where he was already well-known as a commoner, besides affronting the strong sentiment of equality which prevails among the American people. His friend, Mr. Choate, whom he consulted privately, was of the same opinion. "By the name of James Bryce," he replied, "you have been so long known and so much beloved and honoured by the American people, that it would be a mistake to disguise yourself under a new title." The peerage then was respectfully declined, not so, however, the Order of Merit which King Edward was pleased to confer upon him "on his own account and not as ambassador." Three years later the offer of a peerage was repeated and again declined. "Had I returned to England," wrote Bryce to Mr. Asquith, December 4th, 1912, "I should have considered it carefully and asked the advice of yourself and one or two old friends as to whether there was such a prospect of my being useful in the House of Lords as would be sufficient to overcome the reluctance which both my wife and I have always felt towards taking a title. But it is clear to me that I ought not to take one while in service here. As you know, I declined the late King's suggestion of it when I came out here and have reason to be glad that I so decided. It would have hampered me in many ways."

When Bryce was appointed to the Embassy at Washington, the general sentiment in Britain was that no better choice could have been made. It is true that he was no professional diplomatist and that hitherto the American Embassy had been regarded as one of the prizes of the diplomatic profession, but it was felt that now, if ever, there was an excuse for going outside the charmed circle, and that Bryce, with his wide knowledge of American affairs, his numerous American friendships, and his known sympathy with American life, would be likely to make a greater contribution to good feeling between the two nations than the most experienced member of the diplomatic corps.

These anticipations were fully realised. Bryce regarded himself as being not so much an ambassador to the State Department at Washington as an emissary of Great Britain to the American democracy. "He set himself," said President Lowell of Harvard University, "to charm a people." Though there was important work to be carried through in the Chancery, and though many difficult and thorny negotiations were brought to a happy conclusion under his régime, it is not this which gives to Bryce's mission to America its singular importance. It is rather that, for the first time, the British representative in Washington was felt by the American people to be an understanding friend, a wise man who, though a foreigner, had established his right to offer counsel, and an orator whose addresses upon many historical and educational topics were always welcomed and generally forthcoming on demand, in quite surprising profusion. It is usual, and no doubt salutary, for ambassadors to be discreet. Bryce was in the fortunate position of being able to talk at large on a vast variety of topics quite disconnected from current political controversy to a great audience which knew him already by reputation and was anxious to hear his message on any topic under the sun. It is hardly an exaggeration to say that his speeches were, for a period of six years, an important addition to the general stock of intellectual pleasure at the disposal of the American public. Everyone had heard of him; few people could have escaped reading him. He became for the time being an American institution. The professors, the politicians, the lawyers knew him. The rest of the world knew of him. Two American miners once got on to a railway car in Nevada. After a long pause one observed to the other, "Ole man Taft is all right." To which, in due course, the answer came, "Yes, ole man Taft is all right." "And old man Bryce is all right," resumed the first speaker. "Yes, old man Bryce is all right." And having thus exhausted the world of politics, the two speakers relapsed into silence.

A friend once said of Bryce that he was a "natural American." Certainly none of the barriers which obstruct the easy flow of communication between some Englishmen and the average American citizen existed for him. Of pomposity or class feeling there was not the smallest grain in his composition. He was the same to everybody, simple, modest, courteous, interested in all that might be told him, and himself copious in discourse. When I was staying with him in Washington in 1909, it was our custom in the afternoons to drive out into the country and take a walk on the high ground, whence a view of the blue mountains of Virginia could be obtained. Once, as we stepped out of the smart ambassadorial car, a poor ragged fellow came out to Bryce, holding out a coin. "Ambassador Bryce," he said, "will you please identify this coin for me?" And Ambassador Bryce at once rose to the occasion and delivered a neat little lecture on the career of Charles III of Spain, to the delight, though not the surprise, of the unknown enquirer.

Such accessibility is, in a country like America, where men of importance are permitted far less privacy than in the old world, an almost indispensable element of political success. All this Bryce thoroughly understood. Though he was the servant of his British Majesty, he was altogether at the disposition of the great American public, "a good mixer," more at ease, no doubt, with professors and lawyers than with others, but from his wide experience and zest in life moving quickly into an unembarrassed communion with all sorts and conditions of men.

As a small illustration of the courtesy which he showed to all, it was noted that if he was driving out with ladies, however young, he would insist on exchanging places, as soon as the car had passed through the principal thoroughfares of Washington, and sitting with his back to the chauffeur for the remainder of the journey.

It was no small part of Bryce's equipment for the part which he was called upon to play in the United States that he was of the Scoto-Irish race, which has given at least five Presidents to the Republic, not to speak of men like John Marshall and Patrick Henry and John C. Calhoun. It is true that Ulstermen form a very small proportion of the American population, but the number of leading figures in American public life who have family affiliations with the North of Ireland is surprising, and Bryce found in America that many of the influential men with whom he was brought into contact came of the stock from which he was himself sprung and shared the simple puritanical outlook upon life which he had inherited from his forbears. Moreover, the less ecclesiastical forms of Christianity are common in America and the aversion from sacerdotalism very widely spread. Here again Bryce was in sympathy with the genius of American Protestantism.

To such Americans as had followed with any attention the course of British politics, Bryce was also commended by his liberalism. The three causes with which he had been principally identified as a Parliamentarian were matters upon which many Americans felt deeply, even if their information might leave something to be desired. For Armenia, for the Boer Republics and for Ireland there

Secretary of State everything went easily, for the Secretary of State was not only an able, cultivated, high-minded man, with whom it was a pleasure to deal, but he was skilful in his handling of the Foreign Affairs Committee of the Senate, a body peculiarly susceptible of offence at the merest suspicion of neglect and always able to interpose a fatal obstacle to the progress of negotiations, however well devised to achieve an important object. That a number of important arbitration treaties were signed during the rule of President Roosevelt was due to the skill and tact of the Secretary of State.

The functions of an ambassador are to observe, to report, to negotiate, and throughout to safeguard the interests of his own country and of those of his countrymen who may have relations with the State to which he is accredited. For the discharge of these various and responsible tasks Bryce was fitted by knowledge and sympathy, as well as by his wide social gifts; but he was also fortunate in his opportunity. A considerable part of the diplomatic work which comes to the British Embassy at Washington is concerned with Canadian questions, matters of trade, of boundary, of fisheries, of tariff. Now Bryce noted that there was not only a great change for the better since his earlier travels in the States in American feeling towards Great Britain, but that the improvement extended to Canada as well. The Dominion of Canada no longer excited a sense of disparagement among the citizens of the Republic. "It is noticeable," he observes, "that when Canada is now mentioned, it is with a tone of respect."

And as the material development of Canada had

impressed the inhabitants of the United States, so conversely the leaders of Canadian public opinion were less averse than formerly from improving their neighbourly relations with the Republic on their Southern border. In Sir Wilfred Laurier, the gifted Liberal Prime Minister of the Dominion, the spirit of intelligent conciliation was fully developed.

A good deal of circumspection was required in handling questions which affected the interests of the young, proud, and susceptible nation. For in the few settlements which had already been secured, such as that of the Alaska boundary, Canadians believed that the vital interests of the Dominion had been sacrificed to British world policy. The Canadian movement for independent diplomatic representation was consequently already strong and could only be countered by a clear demonstration that the British Ambassador at Washington understood Canadian needs and studied Canadian susceptibilities. The British Ambassador had then to be careful not to interfere in any matter of domestic concern to Canada, and yet so to employ his opportunities that Canada should have no reason to regret that she was not directly represented in Washington. In every negotiation it was his duty to press Canadian interests on the Government of the United States and to remind the Canadian Government of British or Imperial interests whenever they might be affected. The judicious compound of helpfulness, watchfulness, and abstinence from undue interference was not very easy to arrive at. When the skeins of diplomacy became tangled Bryce adopted a procedure hitherto almost unprecedented. He either put himself into a train and rushed

putting up against the Republican bosses in New York. Public opinion too was ranging itself behind the men who, like Roosevelt and Hughes, were fighting the demons of corruption. There were movements for purer city government in Chicago, in Boston, in San Francisco. "One always comes back to the same feeling," he observes, "that the nation is much sounder than anyone who did no more than note the evils which it tolerates would have believed."

When Bryce first came to Washington as Ambassador, the Spanish War was a very recent memory. Nevertheless it was curious to note how faint was the reverberation of that event and how swiftly America had fallen back upon her traditional attitude of isolation, attending little to these new dependencies save for the purpose of putting a tariff on their products, and often in private expressing regrets that the Philippines had been annexed. The subjects which interested opinion were domestic. How should the Senate be chosen? Should the Federal Government extend its powers? Should women have votes? In what way should the capital resources of the nation be preserved? The President indeed was in favour of a large army and a navy without, however, obtaining much response from Congress. So powerful still remained the ghost of George Washington, counselling non-intervention in the affairs of the old world.

The British ambassador was deprived by his official position from expressing in public any opinion upon these high matters of policy. His view, however, was strong and definite. He held that it was not to the interest of the United States to acquire or to maintain an empire overseas. The tasks which confronted the American government at home were sufficiently complex and formidable without the additional burden of foreign possessions. The vast area of the United States government, the mixture of European races, the presence upon American soil of a numerous coloured population only recently emancipated from slavery, the urgent necessity of developing and conserving the natural resources of the continent, these were factors which counselled a concentration of political energy upon domestic problems. It was, in his view, a wild paradox to maintain that the American Union required additional territory. The area covered by the United States was big enough and perhaps exceeded the capacity of any single body of men, however able, adequately to administer. Walking once in Washington with Professor Wrong of Toronto, he waved his arm towards the Capitol exclaiming "If Canada did not exist, it would be to the advantage of the United States to create her."

It may be questioned whether there is in the world any purely artificial city so beautiful as Washington. It rises, like a casket of stainless ivory, into skies of turquoise. Beside it flow the sparkling waters of the Potomac, which, eighteen miles above the city, dash over an intricate medley of rocks in a hundred enchanting and delicate cascades. A noble cluster of public buildings, the great Congressional Library, said to be the largest repository in the world of political and legal literature, an extensive park cleft by picturesque ravines and retaining, despite the ample curves of the level roads which interesect it, much of the primitive savour of the wilderness, give dignity and charm to the political metropolis of the Republic. Yet with all these attractions something is lacking to Washington. There is business, there is intrigue, there is movement; but one misses in this gleaming white city the large and variegated pattern of American society and the throb and pulsation of American life. There is in Washington something of that desiccating official atmosphere which pervades the artificial capital of India.

In Connecticut Avenue, a wide but undistinguished thoroughfare, stands the British Embassy, an unsightly building which, in a competition for defective planning and exposure to noise and publicity, would have outdistanced most rivals even in a strong field. Here, amid many discomforts, the Bryces kept open house to their English visitors and to a wide circle of American friends and acquaintances, justifying for their home, by the exercise of a generous and catholic hospitality, M. Jusserand's nickname, "L'hôtel des Anglais."

An observant visitor cannot live a year in London without learning a very great deal about England. A similar proposition would scarcely be true of Washington, where a society exists of a peculiar character and very unlike that which is to be met with in other great American cities. Here is an assemblage of diplomats, congressmen, and state officials, of *nouveaux riches* undergoing a social apprenticeship among the diplomats before passing on to the glittering society of New York, of journalists on the hunt for copy, of financiers and business men come to push their interests with the legislature, together with a smaller number of genuine residents, who live in Washington not because of its social or financial prizes, but because the city is to their taste. The Bryces enjoyed all that was best of Washington society and made several close friends among the residents. The Ambassador, however, did not regard it as a sufficient discharge of his duties to divide his time between Washington and the summer resort of the Mission, whether at Intervale among the New Hampshire Hills, or on Mount Desert. Apart from his own delight in travel, he considered that, having the honour of representing Great Britain in America, he should use his opportunities to explain English ideals and thought to the American people, by accepting invitations to speak in different parts of the country, and by showing that his sympathies and interests were not limited to diplomatic and political circles. Thus, even in his first year of office, despite the critical importance of the work which was going forward in the Chancery, he took part in a number of important functions in widely scattered parts of the Union. In March he spoke at the Pilgrims' Dinner in New York, which was held under the Chairmanship of his old friend Mr. Choate a popular master of genial postprandial eloquence. In April he was at Jamestown, Virginia, for the Tercentenary Celebration of the First English settlement. In May he appears in St. Louis, in June in Chicago, for the commencement celebration of the University, in August he is in Provincetown (Cape Cod) for the Foundation Stone ceremony of the Puritan movement, and in Portland (Maine) for an address to the American Bar Association. In October he is the guest of President Woodrow Wilson at Princeton (New Jersey) for the dedication of a sundial in the gardens of the Graduate College.

The speech which he delivered on the last of these occasions may be taken as a sample of the occasional oratory, light, graceful, and erudite, in which he excelled, and with which he delighted American audiences of every sort and description from the Atlantic to the Pacific. The occasion was the dedication of a sundial, a facsimile of the dial in the Corpus College, Oxford, and presented to the beautiful Graduate College at Princeton by Sir William Mather, a well-known and much beloved English pioneer in educational reform.

"I am here to-day to present to you, in behalf of my old and valued friend, Sir William Mather, this Sun-dial, which, as you know, is a reproduction of a very ancient dial which stands in the quadrangle of Corpus Christi College, a college in which I have had very many dear friends, and which is separated only by a narrow street from Oriel College, to which I myself belong. Corpus Christi is celebrated for the many illustrious men it has produced and which it produces even down to our own time, of whom I will only mention two. One is well-known to you as Dr. Thomas Arnold, who was a scholar of Corpus Christi and afterwards of my own college of Oriel; and one eminent scholar, who is a dear friend of mine, and who is known to all of you who pursue classical studies, Henry Nettleship. But I might easily enumerate many men whom Corpus Christi has given to the world and whom I hope you will remember in connection with this dial.

You have very properly thought, Mr. President, that it was not necessary to unveil the dial, because, after all, it is not the dial that does the work; it is the sun that does the work. And the sun has unveiled himself with a brilliance which beats all we could have desired. You have asked me to offer a few remarks, and they must of necessity be few; because though the sun, as all the poets from Homer down have told us, is unwearied, we are capable of weariness and most so when we are standing. I need not dilate on the importance and dignity of sun-dials, because some of you may remember an eminent philosopher in the early part of the nineteenth century who, in writing a treatise on the sun and the purpose which the sun served in the universe, culminated by saying that the sun runs the sun-dial, and without the sun there would be no sun-dial. That was the teleological view of the sun. Nor need I dilate upon the antiquity of sun-dials — the earliest method of measuring time, which, I think, man invented. Herodotus says the sun-dial was invented by the Chaldeans, and we may easily believe him, because it is just the kind of thing that the Chaldeans would have done, and we know from the Scriptures that there was a sun-dial in Jerusalem in the reign of Ahaz. It is hard to realise how man could have made such progress as he has made without such aid as the sun-dial affords. At the same time it must be remembered and admitted that the sun-dial is not to be compared with the more modern instruments which man has invented for recording time. The sun-dial was superseded in the Athenian law courts by the water-clock, by which they limited the length of the speeches delivered by the plaintiff and defendant. In England, where we are often not privileged to see the sun for many days at a time, we use in the House of Commons a sand-glass — a comparatively primitive contrivance, but which is in keeping with our conservatism. It is used to mark when a division is called and when a division is taken. I notice that in Congress you adopt a method of enabling bills to be passed in the last hour of the session which would not be possible if you had to depend on the sun. Someone unostentatiously turns back the hands of the clock. You could not get the sun to go back on his dial.

Nor need I dilate on the moral lessons which our ancestors used to draw from the sun-dial. They were lessons of a very sombre character — not much sunshine about them. There are attached to sun-dials mottoes reminding us of the shortness of time and the necessity of using it. I remember one that stands in the quadrangle of All Souls College, Oxford: "Pereunt et imputantur." But of course that is an idea which the constant passage of the shadows naturally suggests to one, that every hour of sunshine is to be used; and it is a reflection which comes back painfully to many of us in the later hours of life, when we think of the many hours we might have spent in acquiring knowledge, which we have neglected. I shall not dilate upon these melancholy aspects, hoping that every Princeton man uses his time to the best advantage, and that Princeton graduates, when they reach the age of sixty or seventy, have no such reflections to make.

This dial will, I hope, stand here for many ages. It will stand here when all of us have been forgotten. It will stand here when even our memories have been forgotten, though Princeton, I hope, will be even greater with even a wider range of influence that she has now. Let us hope that it will always be remembered that this dial was the gift of a large-hearted Englishman who loved America as he loves England, and who desired to commemorate, to typify, not only the union of learning and work, but also the union of the heart of the two peoples."

Washington and Whitehall were at first inclined to question the amount of time which Bryce spent in these academic divagations. But the Ambassador knew what he was about. The real capital of the United States is not Washington but the American Electorate. Neither public opinion nor even official policy was or is created in Washington. Owing to the Treaty Power of the Senate, the Middle West through Knox and Beveridge, and New England through Lodge and Crane, could upset or recast international agreements, however delicate, however painfully and laboriously arrived at by the process of official bargaining. Provincial, or even private, interests could in this way prevent settlements desired by both governments. There were politicians who looked with suspicion on all diplomatic deals, there was a section of the Press very susceptible to the German and Irish vote and a public still influenced by Anti-British literature and legends. In a city like Washington, standing in a certain isolation, these influences could readily be mobilised to secure the defeat of arrangements which, for one reason or another, were favoured by Great Britain. What was wanted was a more general will to peace, and the spirit of general accommodation, and this will Bryce set himself to create by establishing a direct contact with the vast numbers of plain-dealing, unpolitical citizens who were scattered all over the territory of the Union. His voyages, irrelevant as they seemed, were in effect an act of faith in the essential soundness of American democracy.

Nor should we forget that he was greatly assisted in his task by the beneficent reforms which President Roosevelt had instituted in the State Department. During the Behring Sea arbitration on more than one occasion forged documents had been used. Such unworthy practices were henceforward unthinkable. The morals and the machinery of the Department had been raised on to a higher plane by a great reformer, and the men in the State Department with whom Bryce was called upon to deal, were in respect of their ability, their integrity, and their excellent spirit, worthy representatives of a great State.

An important public man in America must be prepared to live in the continuous and unsleeping searchlight of the Press. Night and day, in the privacy of his home or amid the toils of his office, the glare of the public eye is turned upon him. With pressmen at large, Bryce was characteristically reserved. He neither invited nor accorded interviews. Though, like all persons of any public importance in America, he was beset by journalists in search of copy, he declined in his commerce with pressmen, which was genial and frequent, to gratify any curiosity but his own. Nor did he pose to the photographer. All that side of modern political life which consists in the effort to be continually read about and talked about was repellent to his taste. Moreover he had a deep moral aversion from the vulgarity and lack of scruple which characterised much American journalism, holding that the extravagance and laxity of thought of many widely read newspapers was undoing much of the admirable work of the American schools and colleges. It is fair to add that he did not suffer from the austerity of his standards; but received from the American Press, as a whole, a full measure of appreciation and support from the beginning of his mission to the end. More particularly was he grateful to the pressmen of Washington, of whom he used to say that in all his experience of them they had never betrayed a confidence.

Another trait in his character was his inability to sympathise with the annual celebration of Independence Day. So far from being a legitimate occasion for rejoicing, the rupture between Britain and her colonies in the eighteenth century appeared to him as one of the great misfortunes of world history. He was not concerned about the rights and wrongs of this historic quarrel. It was a sufficient source of chagrin for him that the Republic owed its origin to a domestic quarrel in which there was not much statesmanship or width of view on either side, but on the contrary many sordid and painful incidents. He did not think that a severance between Britain and America was, as has often been alleged, inevitable. That it should have been allowed to occur at all was in his eyes a calamity and that it should have been brought about by a quarrel leaving so much bad blood behind it and poisoning quite needlessly, for many generations, relations which otherwise might have remained sweet and wholesome, was an added misfortune.

With the Embassy Staff Bryce was always on the best of terms in work times and holiday times alike. Everybody about him realised that there was important work to be done under a chief who was a miracle of energy himself and quick to realise ability and hard work in others, so that the whole mission responded to the stimulus and provided the ambassador with many occasions, in writing home to the Foreign Office, to allude to the skilled and loyal service which he had received from this or that member of the Staff. The experienced help of Mr. Esmé Howard, Counsellor to the Embassy, and now himself ambassador in Washington, was specially valuable during the first year, but quite apart from the assistance of older diplomats, like Mr. Howard or Mr. George Young, the First Secretary, Bryce was fortunate in having round him a number of younger men of quite exceptional promise and ability. One of these, Lord Eustace Percy, who was Third Secretary from 1910 to 1913, is now (1926) President of the Board of Education, others were cut short by the stroke of destiny in the Great War. H. Beresford Hope, a very able young man, died in Constantinople, W. C. G. Gladstone, the grandson of the great statesman and the owner of Hawarden, was killed in France.[1] Hugo Charteris, another Honorary Attaché of singular charm, fell in Egypt. Of the naval Attachés Horace Hood, a splendid sailor, bearing an historic name, went down in the battle of Jutland, as did Captain Sowerby. But the "rough clouds of war" were not yet apparent in the stainless American skies. The Mission was a happy family, well occupied, well interested, and well content.

The impression which he made as Ambassador upon a trained member of the Diplomatic Service is thus recorded by Mr. George Young.

" Bryce had a fine instinct for personal character and for political conditions, but in business he was professorial rather than practical. More than one cherished baby was thrown away with the bath water before the present day procedure of Round Table diplomacy was evolved and the backs of the Ambassadorial armchairs at critical conferences screened anxious secretaries ready to twitch their chiefs' coat tails or slip notes under their elbows. . . . His simplicity of manner and sense of humour made such devilling for him a pleasure rather than the penance that it can be in the case of a lesser man. . . . It was, indeed, soon found that this new procedure of settlement by symposium had peculiar dangers. Through it ill-devised and ill-drafted decisions may become as immutable, as pernicious. . . . Bryce, curiously enough, in the case of so lucid a writer, was a bad draftsman, but he never allowed a bad draft, whether his own or another's, to become a *fait accompli*.

" His foreign colleagues, professional plenipotentiaries,

[1] Bryce's eloquent tribute to young Gladstone is printed in Appendix I.

untrained in this sort of committee work, came plentifully to grief at it. Diplomatists of that day, always on their dignity, became under such conditions positively dangerous. Thus, at the critical meeting of the Pelagic Sealing Conference, the Russian was pressing the Japanese for assent to a clause. The Oriental had not been able to follow and didn't know where he was, so in the courteous manner of his nation, he laughed brightly and gave no reply. The Russian, after a crescendo of cross-examination had resulted in nothing but gentle ripples of laughter, lost his temper. The pelagic fur was about to fly when Bryce rose, mildly observing, 'I should like to consider this point in its various aspects.' By the time he had dealt with the seventeenth aspect, the Japanese had been posted by his secretaries, the Russian pacified by his, and all was again peace.

"It was often difficult to know when the Ambassador's divagations were deliberate policy and when they were just intellectual diversions. Just as he never, when on a walk, could pass a byway or a hill without wanting to get to the bottom or top of them, so his accurate memory and active mind made association with him in business always entertaining and often exhausting. A detail in some dull draft would lead to an excursion into remote regions of history or geography which often ended in indefinite suspension of the whole despatch, and one never knew whether this was the object in view or not. On the other hand, he sometimes could dispose of a difficulty by a touch of genius. For example, public opinion at home had become greatly excited over atrocities in the Putumayo rubber industry. Whitehall had sent out

Roger Casement to report, and pressed Peru for reforms. Peru appealed to Washington, then very Pan-American. Casement started home with a dossier that would have given our stunt press material for a month, while the shade of President Monroe began to loom large in the American yellow Journals. 'Get Casement up here,' said the Ambassador, and he was accordingly intercepted and brought north on a cruiser. President Taft was lured to dinner in the Embassy and led away into a quiet corner where Casement was let loose on him. A queer picture they made — the tall Celt haggard and livid from the Putumayo swamps, fixing with glittering black eyes the burly rubicund Anglo-Saxon. It was like a black snake fascinating a wombat. But Putumayo gave no further trouble in Washington.

"Such unconventional short circuits and short cuts helped a great deal; but all the same it was a marvel, in view of his methods, how Bryce put to his credit such a record output of treaties, conventions, and arbitrations. But then it was a daily miracle how he got through his day's work. Besides his official despatches and a regular correspondence, that was voluminous as it was valuable, he had his literary work and his lectures. On top of that a swelling flood of correspondence that seemed entirely unimportant to anyone of less comprehensive human sympathies. It really seemed as though every young literary aspirant in a population of ninety million all earnestly cultivating their minds, was applying to him for advice and getting a kindly answer in his own hand. He had no private secretary and these letters, which he could not bear to destroy, were put back into their envelopes, which he minuted on the outside, and then accumulated round his study in Alps until they descended in avalanches and were swept away by Lady Bryce.

"He owed not a little of his influence to his success as a speaker, and his power of adapting himself to an audience probably accounted for his popularity as much as the wit and wisdom of what he said. Thus on one occasion, when he was making notes for an address at a Boston function, a secretary offered him a quotation from Emerson, very apt to the occasion. 'They will get that from one of the others,' said he, 'there are three New Englanders speaking before me.' Sure enough the first New Englander got it, to the embarrassment, no doubt, of the other two.

His relations with his official staff were as novel as the rest of his diplomatic atmosphere. He knew nothing of the old relationship, then dying and now dead, which made the Staff members of the Chief's household. But he was so human that a merely formal relationship was impossible and his secretaries, trained in a tradition under which they were treated as pages in a princely household, acquired a real affection for him in the wholly unfamiliar relationship of pupils to a professor. That they profited by what they learnt from him is suggested by their subsequent careers. His Counsellor has now succeeded him as Ambassador in Washington, his first Head of the Chancery left diplomacy for Labour politics, his second is now in the Conservative Cabinet, and his secretaries have all become Ambassadors or Ministers. He associated himself with their activities as one of themselves, whether it was for the building of a Fives Court in the

Embassy area in which, in his seventies, he was one of the most active players, or whether it was presenting a Petition of Rights to the Foreign Office, calling for reforms in the Diplomatic Service. This last movement, which eventually led to the realisation of most of the reforms demanded, is a good example of the penetrating influence of his inspiring personality."

The Bryces were both hospitable and catholic in their hospitality. It had not been customary for scientific experts to be asked to the parties at the British Embassy; but under the new régime the doors of the big house in Connecticut Avenue were open wide to interesting men, whether they were young or old, famous or obscure. The new Ambassador would not infrequently go geologising or botanising along the banks of the Potomac with members of the Geological Survey, and at his general receptions the savants of the Smithsonian or Carnegie Institutes would mingle with the world of diplomacy and fashion. Among the corps diplomatique itself Bryce found in M. Jusserand, the French Ambassador, an old and valued confederate in historical knowledge and research, but new friends and acquaintances were rapidly made and it was noticed that the British Ambassador took special pains to establish cordial personal relations with the representatives of the South American States, who, since they had been somewhat neglected of old, were the more flattered by his attentions and by the sincere interest which he evidenced in all South American affairs.

Living in Washington, Bryce was actively concerned with the preservation of the amenities of the city and its environment. He was never tired of insisting on the singular beauty of the capital and of the danger that assailed it from the inconsiderate appetite of the speculative builder. The planning and development of the city itself, the preservation of the wild and noble park, which is one of its present glories, were to him matters of the keenest concern. Had he been the oldest inhabitant and sprung from Colonial stock, he could not have been more emphatic in his desire to arouse and sustain among his neighbours a genuine sense of responsibility for the safeguarding of the natural and architectural beauties of the capital of the United States. Such solicitude in the representative of a foreign power might have been misunderstood, but the city, so far from resenting the intrusions of a stranger, welcomed with open hands the advice and exhortations of a friend. It was perhaps significant of the feeling which he inspired that, whenever the British Ambassador attended Divine Service in the Old Presbyterian Church, he was, as a matter of course, ushered into Abraham Lincoln's pew.

CHAPTER XX

CLEANING THE SLATE

There are a large number of ambassadors and ministers who belong to what I call the pink tea type, who merely reside in the Service instead of working in the Service, and these I intend to change whenever the need arises.

T. ROOSEVELT.

THE first year of Bryce's mission to Washington was marked by a signal triumph. Though the feeling between Canada and the United States had improved, there still existed among the Canadian people a widespread conviction that the interests of Canada weighed very lightly with the British Foreign Office in comparison with the good graces of the Government in Washington. Earl Grey, the Governor General of Canada, put this to the new Ambassador with the frankness which one old friend employs in writing to another. "The idea," he wrote, "that Canada has been sacrificed again and again by John Bull in his desire to cultivate the friendship of Uncle Sam is rooted so deep in the conviction of Canada, that nothing that I can say, nothing that you can say, nothing that any Englishman can say, can uproot it." But if Canada could not be persuaded to modify her judgment of past events, she might at least be led to believe that Great Britain was determined to change her course in future. From this point of view Bryce's visit to Ottawa in April 1907, for the purpose of establishing cordial relations with the Canadian ministers, was amply rewarded. The mere fact of the visit was felt to be significant. "Mr. Bryce," said Sir Wilfred Laurier, "has done something new in connection with British diplomacy in Canada — he has visited Canada." And the speech to the Canadian Club confirmed the good impression.[1] The Ambassador opened on economics — the striking progress of Canada since his first visit thirty-seven years before, the great field for the investment of British capital, the need for more advertisement; and then he told his audience how much he had been impressed by the improved relations between the United States and the Dominion, how, in place of the old feeling of hostility and suspicion, there was now in the United States a very real sentiment of friendship to Canada. Finally he touched upon the relations of Great Britain and the Dominions, how in Britain the great Colonies were regarded as sister states entitled to complete self-government, so that, if there was to be any closer connection between the Mother Country and the Dominions, it must be on the basis of equality and copartnership. Two days later he told a Toronto audience that he regarded it as his paramount duty to obtain "justice for Canada."

On all hands his Ottawa speech was regarded as a triumph. If it did not remove outstanding difficulties, it created an atmosphere in which they could be removed. The Canadian ministers were delighted with him and felt that they had found a friend. The Governor General,

[1] Toronto Globe, April 2nd, 1907.

who was out of Ottawa at the time gave expression to the general opinion. "Your speech has won the confidence and heart of Ottawa. Sir Frederick Borden told me that he preferred your speech even to Root's, the previous 'record.' You have dissipated, I hope for ever, the fear that the British Ambassador at Washington will not jealously protect the rights and interests of Canada." [1]

America is a country which likes to do her thinking for herself. She was content to listen to James Bryce, the scientific publicist, because she felt that there was no suspicion of condescension in his manner and that he had taken exceptional pains to arrive at impartial conclusions, but there is a wide difference between accepting advice from a private individual and listening to the commentary of a British Ambassador. Of this difference Bryce was fully aware. He realised from the first that the freedom which was permitted to the individual was no longer possible to the official representative of a foreign country, and he was careful, therefore, to abstain from any public reference to the political controversies of the day.

It was for this reason a matter of great annoyance to him to read in the newspapers a report that, on the occasion of a visit (May 1907) to St. Louis and the State of Oklahoma, he had expressed his approval of the new Oklahoma Constitution. An enterprising journalist in Oklahoma, operating in that field of pure imagination in which everything which is plausible becomes true and everything which is copy becomes legitimate, had published the fiction in a local newspaper. Thence it was

[1] April 6th, 1907.

copied in the larger American Dailies, and thence in due course transmitted to the Press in Britain, where it at once excited the animadversions of Bryce's political adversaries. Wiseacres wagged their heads over a grave indiscretion, impossible, of course, to the trained diplomatist, and drew the moral that radical professors should never be sent abroad on diplomatic missions, for what true-blue Tory would have expressed an opinion on the Oklahoma constitution, or even have heard of Oklahoma? The great American papers, out of affection for Bryce were more indulgent, but nevertheless noted an indiscretion. It was all extremely annoying for, though a prompt and emphatic contradiction of the fiction prevented any spread of the mischief, temporarily some harm had been done. Then, as afterwards, Bryce had much reason to regret the disregard for accuracy which characterised many of the less reputable organs of the Press in the United States.[1]

It is not to our purpose to write the diplomatic history of Bryce's mission to America. For many of the questions upon which he lavished most care and in the solution of which he discovered most difficulty, there now survives but the faintest scintilla of interest, and were the fortunes of nations always governed by great principles and portentous issues, we might afford to neglect them altogether. It is not so, however, that history is made. Disputes about small things have a way of dragging on for years, sometimes even for centuries. The parochial quarrels of a simple but limited society may infect with their

[1] In this instance the man was made to confess that he had never been within 50 miles of the Ambassador and had invented the speech himself.

characteristic obstinacy the attitude of statesmen who, if left to themselves, would practice the charitable accommodations which come with a larger perspective. The mere fact that the matter of a dispute is of secondary importance is sometimes among the reasons for not concluding it. And thus it comes about that the relations between two great countries may be clogged and envenomed by an accumulation of rotten and festering diplomatic detritus which no one has had the courage or energy to clear away.

So it was with Britain and America. Friendly as were the relations between the two peoples, there were a number of old controversies arising out of the relations between Canada, Newfoundland, and the United States, which urgently called for settlement. Bryce came to Washington charged with the mission of cleaning the slate of these hoary but harassing dissensions, and with the hope that, when this purpose had been achieved, it might be possible to place the relations of the two Anglo-Saxon communities upon a basis of mutual understanding so secure that it could not thereafter be disturbed.

Under the Roosevelt administration all went prosperously. A Boundary Waters Treaty, signed by Root and Bryce on 11th January, 1909, after discussion between Bryce and Laurier at Ottawa and a conference with the Canadian ministers at Washington, secured the two great principles for which Canada had always contended; that is, that the water of the boundary streams should be divided equally and that the interests of navigation should be preferred to those of the use of water for industrial or agricultural purposes. Moreover it set up an International Joint Commission for the purpose of settling any disputes which might arise in future between Canada and the United States with reference to the waters which divided the two nations. With the attitude of the chief officials of the State Department Bryce was entirely satisfied. "Mr. Root and Mr. Bacon behaved all through in a most fair and reasonable way. One could not have wished for more honourable and straightforward negotiators." The Senate, however, was less tractable and an obscure rider, inserted into the Treaty by a Senator from Michigan, aroused alarm in Canada and led to further difficulties and delays.

Older and more inveterate were the quarrels dating back to the Treaty of 1783 about the respective rights of American, Canadian, and Newfoundland fishermen in North Atlantic waters. Here again, after passing through many vicissitudes, an agreement was signed on the very day (January 27th, 1909) on which Mr. Root quitted office, in accordance with which all disputes arising out of the exercise of the liberties granted to fishermen in North Atlantic waters under the Treaty of 1783, which closed the war of American Independence, were to be referred to the Court of International Arbitration at the Hague. This was a source of great satisfaction on two grounds, not only as closing an ancient wound, but also because, as Bryce observed, "no arbitration of recent years has been wider in scope or has dealt with matters more thorny or which had been for a longer period a theme of controversy." The historian knows that wars have often proceeded from the quarrels of fishermen.

Here, then, after many difficulties (for the susceptibilities of Newfoundland were not easily appeased) a possible source of conflict between Britain and the United States was satisfactorily removed.

On a minor scale of importance was the adjustment of a large number of pecuniary claims, some of ancient date, others recent, made by citizens of the United States against the Governments of Britain or Canada, and conversely by British or Canadian subjects against the Government of the United States. These it was agreed should be sent to arbitration, but what claims should be admitted and what excluded from the scope of the proposed arbitration was a matter which led to prolonged and intricate negotiation. The question had, however, been nearly settled when a change of government came and with it a batch of new officials, who, being ignorant of what had previously passed, required to be instructed from the beginning.

It was not till August 1910 that the Pecuniary Claims Agreement was finally signed and settled.

Diplomacy was comparatively easy when a matter could be settled between the British Ambassador and the Secretary of State, without the intervention of the Senate. There are few more important and few more delicate understandings than that which was effected by a mere exchange of notes in 1807 for the limitation of naval armaments on the great lakes which intersect the frontier of Canada and the United States. The Rush-Bagot Agreement, as it is called, imposed a limit of four armed vessels, not exceeding a hundred tons, but though there was no difference of opinion between the two Governments as to the value of an arrangement which had secured a century of peace, and averted a ruinous competition in armaments between Canada and the United States, the necessity of providing training ships for the State militias had gradually led to requests being preferred to Canada to place additional armed ships on the Upper Lakes. Such a request was preferred in 1908 and caused some uneasiness in Ottawa. Fortunately, at a hint from Bryce, Mr. Root withdrew a proposal which, while entirely devoid of sinister intention, might, if persisted in, have caused friction in a matter in which it was specially desirable to avoid the shadow of a dispute.

Three other diplomatic instruments were signed during the second year of Bryce's mission to America. The first was a Treaty to fix the International boundary line between the United States and Canada; the second a Convention for the protection, preservation, and propagation of food fishes in the waters contiguous to the United States and the Dominion, according to which an International Fisheries Commission was to be set up to prepare a system of uniform and common regulations of the protection of fish in the prescribed waters, while the third, an Arbitration Convention, signed on April 4th, 1908, provided for the submission to the International Court of the Hague of such differences between Britain and the United States as it may not have been possible to settle by diplomacy provided that "they did not affect the vital interests, the independence or the honour of the two contracting States nor concern the interests of a third party."

It is no exaggeration to say that all these measures

taken in combination were calculated to give to the continent of North America a degree of security such as had never hitherto been attained. Boundary disputes, fishery disputes, disputes as to the interpretation of treaties, were removed into an atmosphere of peaceful discussion.

When it is realised that there were no less than thirteen States along the International boundary, that each State had its own system of fishing laws, that on Lake Erie alone, one of the best fresh water fishery areas in the world, there were no less than six different sets of laws, no two being precisely alike, and that the Canadian and American fishermen were in constant conflict on account of the different regulations which were applied to the portions of the Lake belonging to these two countries, the advantages of the Fishery Treaty of 1908 will be readily apprehended. A code of uniform regulations was clearly the true cure for a chronic and dangerous malady.

Thus happy and prosperous were the opening stages of Bryce's American mission. "I heard from an independent American source the other day," wrote Sir Edward Grey, the British Foreign Secretary, "that the British Embassy at Washington had never been so well done as it is now and the Americans are delighted with you and Mrs. Bryce and speak of you both in the most gratifying way." [1] Sir Charles Hardinge, the permanent Under-Secretary of the Foreign Office, was no less complimentary. "I think it is the first time," he wrote, "that one of our Ambassadors has been really able to obtain the confidence of the Canadians. It has entailed upon you a great deal

[1] December 25th, 1908

of travelling and hard work, but you must be very satisfied with the result." [1]

The Presidential Election of the autumn of 1908 resulted in another Republican victory. The democratic candidate, W. J. Bryan of Nebraska, "the peerless hero," as he was termed by his admirers, was a sincere lover of peace and quite friendly to Britain and Canada; but his political gifts appeared to be limited to a fine presence, a mighty voice, and a torrential flow of emotional eloquence, and his associates failed to inspire confidence. He was beaten, as many a showy candidate for Presidential honours had been beaten before him, by that shrewd estimate of personal character which is characteristic of the American people. The choice of the nation fell upon the bluff and portly Mr. Taft, who was commended by his personal integrity, his legal knowledge, his friendship for Mr. Roosevelt, his public services in the Philippines, and in Cuba, and, perhaps above all, for his engaging smile and sunny good humour. Mr. Knox, a clever corporation lawyer, became Secretary of State under the new administration.

The new Secretary of State was an agreeable, upright man, entirely free of unworthy motives, who brought to the conduct of international affairs the shrewd, keen intellect of a business lawyer "eager to force circumstances rather than to guide and use them as they came." To Bryce he gave the impression of having cared little, known little, or thought little of foreign politics till he became a minister, and as being, partly from a lack of diplomatic or historical preparation, partly from a certain impatience

[1] May 12th, 1908.

of temperament, inclined to be autocratic and rapid in his decisions. In contradistinction to his predecessor, who had been studious to adopt an attitude of friendly equality towards the Southern neighbours of the United States, Mr. Knox sometimes failed in due consideration for the feelings of the weaker nations. He was all for a spirited foreign commercial policy, descrying in China a new and illimitable field for American enterprise, and in the Latin States of Southern America a group of commercial vassals who should obey the nod of a Protecting Power. Thus, by certain minor faults of manner and method, the new Secretary of State impaired the influence which the wise policy of Mr. Root had painfully secured for the United States among the Governments of the Southern hemisphere.

Bryce was from the first on excellent terms with the new administration. He liked the simplicity and directness of the genial President, and appreciated the ability of the Secretary of State. Of their complete integrity and friendliness to Great Britain he had not, for a moment, the slightest doubt. His only source of anxiety was the fear lest the new administration might not possess the power and the drive, coupled with the indispensable measure of influence with the Senate, without which the long list of questions outstanding between Britain and the United States could not be liquidated.

The good work of "cleaning the slate" proceeded not without some difficulties and disappointments during the remaining years of Bryce's American mission. A controversy with respect to the Passamaquoddy Bay boundary (between New Brunswick and the State of Maine) was happily settled (Aug. 20th, 1910) on the lines of a compromise suggested by the British Ambassador, who, with characteristic energy, had personally inspected the *locus in quo*. A more difficult matter was the framing of a treaty for the cessation of pelagic sealing in the North Pacific, since, though it was a good bargain for Canada and much needed for the preservation of free sealing, many of the ministers at Ottawa were reluctant to enter upon an agreement which might seem to derogate even for a limited period of years from the right of free sealing. Even after an agreement had been signed, murmurs of dissatisfaction reached Bryce from Ottawa. It was urged that at least Japan and Russia should pay compensation to Canada for her self-denying ordinance, in consenting to abstain from free sealing for a period of fifteen years.

Bryce wrote in some concern to Earl Grey:

"I gather that your Ministers are not so much anxious for money compensation from Russia or Japan as to assert the principle that Canada has a right to pelagic sealing everywhere, and ought not to forego it except on having an acknowledgment of that right from the other Powers as well as from the United States. Sensitiveness as to that right is natural when we remember the extravagant claims formerly made by the United States to exclude Canada. But the right is now incontestable. It was affirmed by the Paris Award. It was admitted by the United States when they offered the recent agreement. All that is now asked is that Canada, which has agreed to suspend its exercise for fifteen years in the Eastern part of the North Pacific, should agree to its suspension for a like period in the Western part in consideration of a like suspension of their similar rights by the other powers concerned. Canada would receive compensation during that period in the immunity from capture by the subjects of any Power of the Pribyloff seals in which she is now interested, and at the end of the period her full rights would revive.

"If four nations, all of which have an interest in a land catch, agree to forego their undoubted rights of pelagic sealing for fifteen years, is not the equality of rights duly recognised, and does not each receive a compensation in the increased value of its land catch?

"Japan having suggested that there should be some sort of pooling of the land catches on the various islands, and the United States, having asked if Canada could contribute something to enable them to meet the demand of Japan for compensation, it occurred to Pope[1] that perhaps your Ministers might agree to a plan by which Canada, in return for giving up some small part of her share of the Pribyloff Isles land catch, would get a share in the land catches on the Japanese and on the Russian islands. He is preparing an outline of their scheme, which will be sent to you. It seems to deserve consideration.

"I feel some difficulty in writing more without knowing exactly what the views of your Ministers are, but may say that it would be a misfortune if the Conference were to break down, for that would mean: —

(1) Canada would lose her one-fifth of the Pribyloff seals, a share which may amount before long to some hundreds of thousands of dollars a year.

(2) The seals themselves would altogether perish as a species, because it is agreed on all hands that nothing but the stopping of pelagic sealing can save them.

(3) The London trade in preparing sealskins, which quite lately employed 10,000 workers, would disappear.

"In comparison with these evils the loss of any result from the four years we have spent in negotiating the Agreement with the United States would, though regrettable, be a small matter.

[1] Sir Joseph Pope, Under Secretary of State for External Affairs, Ottawa, and H. M. Plenipotentiary at Pelagic Sealing Conference, Washington.

"I gather that those of your Ministers who are now in Ottawa are deemed unfriendly to the whole Agreement with the United States. Still, it has been signed, and ought to be carried out loyally. It is a good bargain. It is only for fifteen years, so why should it be supposed that it sacrifices a natural and national right? That right is admitted, though suspended, and revives in full force after fifteen years.

"I gather that the Ministers at Ottawa are sensitive as to the right of free sealing everywhere. Why? The right was declared by the Paris Award. It is incontestable. To waive it *for fifteen years* does not weaken it. Why should it be essential to Canada to get compensation from Japan and Russia as well as from the United States? They have just as much ground for asking compensation from anyone interested in the Pribyloff Island seals, for by agreeing to the plan now proposed, they also would suspend their natural and national right of pelagic sealing.

"I confess myself unable to understand why your Ministers should stand out against the United States proposal that the four nations should agree to a fifteen years suspension, now that Canada has had her right admitted and a substantial interest. If I am missing any of the real issues, will you have me enlightened? If you agree with the views here stated, could you influence your Ministers to forego the claim of compensation against Japan and Russia and enter the quadripartite agreement proposed?

"I have written at this great length in order to try to convey the arguments which Pope tells me are influencing your Ministers. It is a great pity I had not known of their attitude when I was in Ottawa, so that the matter might have been thoroughly discussed.

"To break up the Conference without any result would be too serious a matter to let happen without consulting Sir Wilfrid and Brodeur[1] and the Foreign Office, and Colonel Office, for it would have a very unfortunate effect here — besides losing

[1] Hon. Louis Philippe Brodeur, Minister of Marine and Fisheries, Ottawa, 1906–11.

all we have accomplished — two years' negotiation over this question."

An arrangement satisfactory to all the parties concerned was eventually reached on July 6th, 1911, after a conference of the four interested Powers, the United States, Japan, Russia, and Great Britain. "The settlement of this very troublesome question," wrote Bryce, "which has occupied diplomacy for many years in a manner which all the Powers recognise as fair and which promises to preserve the fur seal species and to maintain an industry of considerable importance to England, has a value which is much greater than might be judged from the comparatively slight attention which it has caused."

The award of the Hague Tribunal on the questions submitted to it did not cover all the ground of the North Atlantic Fisheries dispute. There were still three questions left over, which demanded settlement. Were the existing fishery regulations in Canada unfair? What is a bay within the meaning of the Treaty of 1918? How should future fishing regulations of the United States, of Canada, or of Newfoundland deemed to be unfair, be dealt with? Agreement on the first two questions was easily reached, but the third, which was intrinsically more delicate, gave rise to a regrettable dispute between the United States and Canada, the Americans maintaining and the Canadians denying that certain assurances were given at the Hague by Sir Charles Fitzpatrick, the Canadian Minister of Justice. The merits of the issue do not concern us here so much as the method of settlement. Bryce believed in personal interviews rather than in an exchange of letters, which is only too often calculated to protract, to complicate, and to envenom a controversy. Taking advantage of an invitation from the Duke of Connaught, the new Governor General of Canada, he went to Ottawa in December 1910 and discussed the question with Sir R. Borden, who had just risen to power on the defeat of Sir Wilfrid Laurier at the autumn elections. To the new Prime Minister he unfolded a line of accommodation and suggested that a Canadian Minister should be sent to Washington to carry the negotiation to a conclusion. His advice was accepted and before long an arrangement was reached, satisfactory to Canada and the United States.

It will be seen that Bryce was not a little assisted by the addition of arbitration to the catalogue of diplomatic expedients. A settlement, essentially diplomatic, in that it consisted of mutual concessions, was found to be obtained more easily when presented in the form of an arbitral award. In reality, however, the judicial procedure was, in many cases, little more than an imposing façade. The awards which settled such controversies as the North Atlantic Fisheries were determined not by anything in the nature of a legal pronouncement, but by diplomatic negotiation, and were drafted by diplomatists. Yet arbitration, though costly, was invaluable, for two Anglo-Saxon peoples will always be more prone to respect a procedure, however expensive, which carries with it the authority of a court with its bench of judges and array of counsel, than one which consists only of the naked clash of diplomatic argument. Bryce then was wisely inspired in the plentiful use which he made of judicial or semi-judicial methods to decide international disputes.

CHAPTER XXI

A SOUTH AMERICAN HOLIDAY

I can hardly think of any greater misfortune for the United States than to be obliged to set up a Government which it would have to maintain, or to become directly responsible for the administration of any South American country.

BRYCE to WOODROW WILSON.
Dec. 19th, 1913.

By the rules of the diplomatic service an Ambassador is allowed two months leave in the year. These periods may however be doubled in exceptional circumstances, and having purposely omitted to quit his post in 1909 Bryce applied for double leave in the following year in order that he might visit South America.

The plan commended itself to Sir Edward Grey. To the Foreign Secretary as to his Ambassador such a visit seemed to offer a useful opportunity of making the South American States, whose importance in the world was steadily increasing, more generally known to Englishmen. The information on political, commercial, and social topics which might be gained by so alert and well-trained an observer even in the space of a hurried journey could not fail to be useful to the British Foreign Office. The conclusion of commercial treaties might be helped, the weight and quality of German competition in the South African markets more accurately determined. As for Bryce, who had a passionate desire to see the whole world before he died, here was a chance of exploring a very important segment of the world's surface with a minimum of time wasted in ocean travel.

The plan of campaign was ambitious and so contrived as to extract the utmost value out of every moment of the holiday. It is indicative of the care and accuracy of the staff work expended upon the time-tables of steamship and railway companies that the travellers sailed into New York harbour on January 1st, 1911 after a voyage of 17,500 miles and having accomplished all that they had set out to do, upon the very day upon which the ambassador's leave expired. In the months which succeeded his return Bryce consigned his impressions of South America to paper and so rapidly despite the calls of official duty did the work proceed that a volume of nearly six hundred pages was issued to the public in 1912. The intellectual and physical energy implied in such a performance are remarkable in a man well over seventy years of age.

Many and respectable as might be the political and economic arguments for a South American holiday, it was romance which counted most with Bryce. "It had been," he writes, "a main object of our journey to see the Straits of Magellan, that great sea highway from ocean to ocean, the finding and traversing of which was an achievement second only to the voyage of Columbus." This sentence is very characteristic of its writer. The great events of history, and there are few greater than the voyage of the Portuguese explorer which finally proved not only that the earth was round and that the western sea route to India really existed but also that the earth was immensely larger than was supposed, were not with him formal propositions which lay idle in the mind, but emotions stirring the blood and kindling a strong desire to visit the scenes which these high transactions had made immortal. Besides, there were the memories of early reading about the vanished civilisation of the Incas and the primitive American peoples, and the conquest of Pizarro, and the wonderful Lake Titicaca spreading its waters high among the snows of the Andes, the scenery of which had so often tantalised his imagination. To the romantic historian and the mountaineer the very names Peru and Bolivia sounded with a magical attraction. Not all the material opulence of the Argentine plains with their network of railways and their hundred millions of invested British capital counted in comparison.

The Bryces sailed from New York on September 1st, in the United Fruit Company's boat "Santa Marta" for Kingston, Jamaica where they spent twenty-four hours on shore, being entertained by the Governor (Sir S. Olivier) at the King's House. Thence they voyaged to Colon, the Atlantic port of the Isthmus of Panama, arriving alongside the wharf early on September 9th. The great task of piercing the Isthmus was in full swing, and under the skilled guidance of Colonel Goethals, the head of the Canal Commission, the Bryces spent two days travelling up and down the Isthmus, and inspecting the stupendous engineering works which were in process. "We are staying," wrote Mrs. Bryce on September 11th, "with Colonel Gorgas, the Chief Medical Officer, who lives in the suburb of Ancon, the hill just above Panama, from which there is a most lovely view over the Bay with its picturesque islands, bounded on either hand by distant hills; and inland over the beautiful rolling country of the Isthmus — hills crested with tropical forests, dense jungle of all kinds of tropical trees, palms, rubber, bread fruit, mangoes, bananas and orchids, and climbing vines, with openings of green grass slopes, here and there, streams."

In an admirable chapter of his *South America*, Bryce describes the impressions made upon his mind by the marvellous triumph of modern science over the reluctant earth implied in the piercing of the Panama Canal, "the greatest liberty man has ever taken with nature." The huge dam at Gatun and the great Culebra Cut, "the deepest open cutting anywhere in the world," and therefore of peculiar interest to the geologist, are carefully described; as also the measures taken by the American medical staff against yellow fever and malaria.

"Never before on our planet have so much labour, so much scientific knowledge, and so much executive skill been concentrated on a work designed to bring the nations nearer to one another and serve the interests of all mankind. . . . To have made one of the pest houses of the world, a place with a reputation like that of the Pontine Marshes or Poti on the Black Sea, or Sierra Leone itself, as healthy as Boston or London is an achievement of which the American medical staff and their country for them may well be proud."

These reflections, which are both true and important might have occurred to many travellers. Of more unusual quality is the following piece which fixes the whole image of the Canal voyage in the mind, so that once established there it can easily and readily be recalled.

"The voyager of the future in the ten or twelve hours of his passage from ocean to ocean, will have much variety. The level light of the fiery tropic dawn will fall on the houses of Colon as he approaches it in the morning, when vessels usually arrive. When his ship has mounted the majestic staircase of the three Gatun locks from the Atlantic level, he will glide slowly and softly along the waters of a broad lake which gradually narrows towards its head, a lake enclosed by rich forests of that velvety softness one sees in the tropics, with vistas of forest-girt islets stretching far off to right and left among the hills, a welcome change from the restless Caribbean Sea which he has left. Then the mountains will close in upon him, their slopes of grass or brushwood rising two hundred feet above him as he passes through the great Cut. From the level of the Miguel lock he will look southward down the broad vale that opens on the ocean flooded with the light of the declining sun and see the rocky islets rising, between which, in the twilight, his course will lie out in the vast Pacific. At Suez the passage from sea to sea is through a dreary and monotonous waste of shifting sand and barren clay. Here one is for a few hours in the centre of a verdant continent floating on smooth waters, shut off from the sight of the ocean behind and the ocean before, a short sweet present of tranquillity between a stormy past and a stormy future."

On the afternoon of September 11th, the travellers set sail for Panama in the Pacific Steam Navigation Co.'s steamer Guatemala, reaching Callao, the port of Lima, after a spell of cold cloudy weather early in the afternoon of September 17th. Here they were allowed three and a half hours on shore, none too long a time for what had to be accomplished. A special electric car whisked them up to Lima, seven miles inland, where "James in top hat and frock coat was taken off to call on the President and the Foreign Minister and after that was allowed to see as much of the town as was possible." What he saw in the time and the reflections which his impressions provoked are recorded in seven instructive pages of *South America*, and afford a pretty sample of the art of effective travel. The Spanish Americans, he observes, are not very communicative to strangers but whoever speaks their language can learn a good deal from them about minerals and revolutions — the two chief products of the northwest coast. It is needless to add that Bryce spoke Spanish and when required to do so could make a speech in the language.

A new steamer, the Oropesa, carried the travellers to the little seaport of Mollendo, "standing," writes Mrs. Bryce, "on its bare cliff on the edge of the desert," which was the starting point for the inland voyage to the mountain regions of Peru. The journey was one of astonishing interest and beauty, for after two hours of steady climb to a height of over four thousand feet the train reached the rim of a tableland and as it emerged on to level ground passed out of mist into dazzling sunshine disclosing a view the like of which even Bryce had never seen before.

"In front looking eastward was a wide plain of sand and pebbles with loose piles and shattered ridges of black rock rising here and there from its surface, all shimmering in sunlight. Beyond the plain thirty miles away is a long line of red and grey mountains, their sides all bare, their crags pierced by deep, dark gorges, so that they seem full of shadows. Behind these mountains again and some fifty or sixty miles distant three gigantic mountains stand up and close the prospect. . . . This was our first view of the Andes."

On a still higher shelf of the Peruvian tableland stands Arequipa, the second city of Peru, and a great ecclesiastical stronghold, with the great snow mass of Chachani and the majestic cone of El Misti and Pichu Pichu with its long grey line of precipices mounting guard over it. Here the Bryces spent a day and two nights in the pleasant airy house of Mrs. McCulloch, the wife of one of the railway officials, tasting this oriental looking city, with its dry keen air, its flat roofs on which people sit in the evening, its deep and pungent dust, its absence of wheeled vehicles, its scantily dressed Indians "wild-looking as Bedaween," its llamas in place of camels — all set in a mountain landscape amid snow fields and majestic towers of rock which brought back memories of the Swiss highlands. And here Bryce picked up a local romance — of a nun who ran away with a young doctor, the telling of which loses nothing in transmission and should find a place in any selection of his writings.

The next object of interest was Cuzco, the sacred city of the sun, the ancient Inca capital of Peru and the metropolis of an Empire which stretched southwards from the equator for two thousand miles. Cuzco was quite unlike the mental picture which Bryce had formed of it from early reading. "I had fancied a walled city visible from afar on a high plain with a solitary citadel hill towering above it. But Cuzco lies inconspicuous, with its houses huddled close in its *bolson* at a point where three narrow glens descend from the tableland above, their torrents meeting in it or just below it; and no buildings are seen except a few square towers, till you are at its gates."

Another disappointment was in store for the travellers. There was nothing in the monuments of the Incas, which could by the utmost stretch of historical courtesy be described as artistic or beautiful. "The traces of the Incas to be seen in Cuzco, and indeed anywhere in Peru, are all of one kind only. They are walls. No statue, no painting. No remains of a complete roofed building, either temple or palace; nothing but ruins and mostly fragmentary ruins. The Besom of Spanish destruction swept clean."

On the other hand the Cuzco ruins left upon the beholder the impression "of energy and will in those who planned these works, of patient and highly trained labour in those who executed them." How then had this Indian race which must have been strong and in a way gifted fallen so suddenly from its high estate? Was the whole ruling class destroyed in war? Was the Spanish conquest so thorough and terrible as to break down the spirit of the nation and the self-respect of the individuals who composed it? Such historical speculations crowded into Bryce's mind as he stood in the great Plaza of Cuzco, where in 1571 an innocent youth, the last of the Inca line, was executed in the presence of a vast Indian crowd. That there were dark sides to this ancient civilisation might be admitted. But was it worth destroying in order to erect on its ruins what the conquerors brought to Peru? Such were the final reflections inspired by the strange melancholy of this ancient, mouldering, malodorous city, with its tragic memories and suggestion of vistas stretching far back into the past.

From Cuzco the journey proceeded through wild and wonderful mountain scenery to the Lake Titicaca which has occupied Bryce's boyish dreams. Here were Inca shrines to be visited and anticipations of scenery to be confirmed or corrected. Everything was of interest, the quality of the water, found by the taste not to be saline as reported, its colour thus nicely defined:

"The blue of Titicaca is peculiar, not deep and dark, as that of the tropical ocean, nor opaque like the blue green of Lake Leman, nor like that warm purple of the Aegean which Homer compares to dark red wine, but a clear, cold crystalline blue, even as is that of the cold sky vaulted over it. Even in this blazing sunlight it had that sort of chilly glitter one sees in the crevasses of a glacier; and the wavelets sparkled like diamonds."

After a two days sail on the great Lake, which is some 12,500 feet above sea level and about 130 miles long and 40 to 50 miles across at its widest point, the Bryces took train for La Paz the capital of Bolivia, and seeing that it stands 12,470 feet above sea level, the loftiest capital city of the world. But high as is La Paz, this curious city is so tucked away at the bottom of a deep ravine as to be invisible to the traveller as the train climbs slowly towards it over the dusty and shrubless plateau.

"Where can La Paz be?" asks the traveller. Then a spot is reached where the railway itself seems to end between a few sheds. He gets out and walks a few yards to the east and then suddenly pulls up with a start on the edge of a yawning abyss. Right beneath him, fifteen hundred feet below, a grey, red-roofed city fills the bottom of a gorge, and climbs up its sides on both banks of the torrent that foams through it. Every street and square, every yard and garden, is laid out under the eye as if on a map, and one almost seems to hear the rattle of vehicles over stony pavements coming faintly up through the thin air. In this strange city, at the bottom of a deep hole and yet nearly as high as the Jungfrau, Bryce attended the sessions of the legislature, where the orators speak seated, and with Mrs. Bryce was received by the Bolivian Vice-President and driven in state round the plaza to the sounds of martial music. But there was little time to penetrate into the heart of Bolivian civilisation. On the afternoon of October 6th the travellers were again upon the coast, sailing from the Chilian port of Antofagasta in the Orita for Valparaiso, which was reached early on the morning of the 9th. A day had to suffice for the great Chilian seaport. On October 10th the Bryces were on the wing once more, making for the Transandine railway and Mendoza, a city founded in the reign of Queen Elizabeth, which lies on the Argentine side of the mountain range.

Here at last Bryce found the characteristic South American arboreal flora he had been looking forward to, "a forest where all that we saw was new, unlike the woods of Western North America and of Europe, not only because the variety of trees was far greater than it is there, but also because so many bore brilliant flowers upon their higher boughs where the sunlight reached them." But meanwhile the clock was moving on. Even an earthly Paradise could not prompt a defiance of the inexorable limits of an Ambassadorial holiday. Other things were calling, Aconcagua, loftiest of the summits of the Western Mountains, the Transandine tunnel, the great bronze statue of Christ which stands upon the level summit of the pass between Chili and Argentine, symbolising the conclusion of a long and bitter controversy between the neighbour states, Mendoza the first Spanish town on the eastern side of the Andes, Santiago, and Southern Chili and then the romantic voyage through the grim and storm-swept Straits of Magellan.

Santiago, the capital of Chile, and in population the fourth city in South America, is well known by name, but how many who have read the name have formed a distinct image of the reality? Bryce enables us to form such an image. He compares Santiago to Innsbruck.

"At Santiago as at Innsbruck, one sees the vista of a long straight street closed by towering mountains that crown it with white as the sea crowns with blue the streets of Venice. But here the mountains are nearly twice as high as those of the Tyrolean city, and they never put off their snowy vesture."

The interior of the city however did not offer very much to the traveller, and on the evening of October 18th the Bryces started off in a special car kindly placed at their disposal by the Chilean Government for a nine days tour in Southern Chile, a region little known or visited but full of lovely scenery and showing evidence of great fertility. Bryce was delighted. "Of all the parts of the new world I have seen," he wrote, "there is none that struck me as fitter to attract a young man who loves country life, is not in a hurry to be rich, and can make himself a home in a land where English is not the tongue of the people."

On the afternoon of October 26th the Bryces sailed from this land of delights on the Pacific liner Oravia, heading for the Straits of Magellan. The voyage opened with three days of cold wet weather and heavy seas, the south west wind sometimes rising to three-quarters of a gale, during which time Bryce observed his rule "to keep the deck whenever you can do so without the risk of being douched or perhaps knocked down," and occupied his mind in default of more substantial objects by observing the wheeling flight of albatrosses and gulls. As the ship neared the classic waters the emotion of the historian deepened and every moment of visibility became precious.

"In the afternoon of the 29th," writes Mrs. Bryce, "we came in sight of the four isolated rocks called the Evangelists, bare and lonely in the great swell of the Pacific and soon after we turned more to the East and began to come in sight of the entrance to the Straits of Magellan which we reached about 6 P.M. It was a very impressive scene as we passed the great headland of Cape Pillar which guards the entrance and saw the wild peaks and crags of the range (like the Cuchullin hills of Skye on a large scale) lighted up with the brilliant gleams and cloud effects of sunset." Those moments were for Bryce also charged with historic emotion. "Behind us the sun, now near his setting threw from among the scattering clouds a flood of yellow light over the white topped surges that were racing in our wake. One thought of Magellan's tears of joy when these long surges on which his little vessel rose, told him that here at last was that ocean he had set forth to find and over which lay the path of glory which for him led only to the grave."

The next morning the travellers rose at 4 A.M. and spent between four and five hours in bitter cold upon the bridge drinking in every detail and change on the landscape. "It was," wrote Mrs. Bryce in a proper spirit, "well worth it." And so they steamed on, wondering how Magellan managed to tack against the strong head wind in so narrow a channel, what use he made of the tides, where he moored for the night, and noting every feature in a prospect very different from that which they had imagined but full of the solemnity and grandeur of desolation.

On October 31st Bryce was on the bridge at dawn to see the last of the Straits and the passage into the Atlantic Ocean. Henceforward Clio, the Muse of History, ceased to be the presiding deity. They visited the Falkland Islands, little dreaming that five years later the Muse would select that distant and windswept region as the scene of one of her great battle-pieces, and then descended upon the capitals of Uruguay, Argentina, and Brazil. Forty-eight hours in Montevideo were succeeded by five strenuous days in Buenos Ayres ("on the go from 9.10 A.M. to 1 A.M." writes Mrs. Bryce) with business and political talks, visits to the Chamber and Senate, an official dinner with a speech in Spanish from the Foreign Minister, "to which James replied partly in Spanish and partly in French," a degree at the University, "where James had to make two speeches," a luncheon in the country among woods and meadows and familiar Herefords and Shorthorns, attendance at the races, a necessary, almost a religious ceremony in Argentina, two dinners with the British Minister and Lady Susan Townley, one of which was followed by a reception of British residents, and other entertainments congenial to the lavish hospitality of this opulent and brilliant capital.

A visit to South America would hardly be complete without the experience of a revolution and on their last day in Brazil fortune afforded the travellers the spectacle of a naval mutiny in the harbour of Rio. From the spirited narrative of this episode in *South America* it is clear that the Bryces used to the full every opportunity afforded them of seeing what was going on. Indeed it was an appropriate finale to an interesting tour. "To have been in a city under fire and to have boarded our steamer under a flag of truce," wrote Mrs. Bryce, "were the last things we expected but as South America is a continent where anything may happen, we went to bed feeling that we had seen one more aspect of western life."

Late at night on November 27th the Bryces left Pernambuco for Lisbon *en route* for Liverpool and New York. The Cape Verde Islands were reached towards evening on December 2nd, as the low rays of the setting sun were gilding the dark volcanic rock of St. Vincent. Early on the 5th the Oronsa was abreast of the Canaries and two days later crossed the bar of the Tagus in a tossing sea. As she steamed up towards the white and blue washed walls and red-tiled roofs of Lisbon, the travellers beheld signs of the revolution which two and a half years before had sent a shiver of horror through the civilised world. Here was the yacht which had carried King Manoel and the two Portuguese Queens into sudden exile and with them the last hopes of the great Braganza dynasty. There from the vessels in the harbour and the public buildings in the town waved the red and green colours of the new Republic. They landed, lunched with Sir Francis Villiers, an old Foreign Office acquaintance, and from him learnt many private details of the revolution. Nor did they leave unvisited the spot, in the north corner of the Square of the Black Horse by the arcades, where King Carlos and his eldest son were cruelly murdered. Now all was tranquil. Lisbon seemed as far removed from storm or tragedy as a quiet cathedral city of the eighteenth century. The Republic had apparently been accepted with unconcern and without challenge.

. . . .

No more important addition could be made to political literature than an account of the impression left by the civilisation and institutions of South America on the mind of a cultivated Englishman of the highest order of ability at a point of time when after much revolution and disorder the different states of the Continent were assuming a personality of their own and tasting the benefits of a relatively settled form of government. Such a book Bryce could undoubtedly have written had time permitted; towards such a book, after a stay of less than four months in the country, he has by a truly astonishing effort of physical and mental energy made a valuable contribution. What he says about the absence of any true principles of democracy in the South American States, and in historical explanation or extenuation of the fact, was worth saying in view of the circumstance that even so distinguished a writer as Sir Henry Maine had dipped frequently into the cauldron of South American revolutions for arguments against democracy. Again, though there may be nothing original in a demonstration that the Teutonic Americans and the Spanish Americans have nothing in common except two names, the name America and the name Republic, and that the United States is spiritually and historically far more closely bound to Britain than to any of the Latin Republics of South America, the elementary truth was well worth setting out carefully and cogently for, ever since the Pan American Congress in 1899, a good many loose clouds of untested opinion and sentiment had been obscuring the true face of reality in the United States. In his judgment of the South Americans themselves, Bryce was indulgent of set purpose, defending his optimism on the ground that we are disposed "when we deal with another country to be unduly impressed by the defects we actually see and to forget to ask what is, after all, the really important question, whether things are getting better or worse;" and consequently finding himself able to pronounce a more lenient judgment upon South American civilisation and to entertain brighter hopes as to its future, than had been common to European critics. There might yet, despite all her drawbacks and difficulties, be salvation for South America, for the historian takes long views and recalls how Europe itself, after the eclipse of the brilliant civilisation of Greece and Rome, experienced an iron age, in which all the arts which embellish life were intermitted and the very idea of liberty seemed irretrievably lost.

It is not, however, as a contribution to political philosophy that Bryce's *South America* will hold its place in the libraries. That there are observations and reflections, seemingly just and accurate, on the government of these so-called democracies and upon the society out of which they spring, is true enough, and from these the reader may obtain a preliminary notion of what political life is like in those parts of the continent which the travellers were able to visit in their four months' holiday. But it is the setting in which these political dramas are played, rather than the dramas themselves, which furnishes the subject matter of Bryce's *South America.* To portray to English readers the South American continent as it appears to the eye, to paint its mountains, rivers and lakes, its arid plateaux and fertile valleys, so that the world, which had never visited South America and was never likely to do so, might derive a distinct impression of the general features of its landscape and climate, and through these, inferentially, of the modes of life compatible with such external circumstances, that was Bryce's primary object and in that enterprise he succeeds. In a series of fresh and vigorous descriptions he brings his readers face to face with one scene after another which struck his imagination during his journey round South America selecting scenes that are typical of contrasted aspects of the country, the low rolling hills of the Isthmus of Panama, the high Bolivian desert, the snowy Andes, the flowery paradise of Southern Chile, the stern, rock-bound desolation of Patagonia, the opulent monotony of the Argentine plain, the tropical luxuriance of Brazil, and painting these without affectation or any effort at a curious felicity of phrase, but always with fidelity and with a certain broad poetical emotion which help to fix the image and to give it an abiding place in the mind.

One consequence of Bryce's South American tour is so characteristic of him that it deserves mention. In the course of his visit to the Isthmus of Panama he was specially attracted by the geological interest attaching to the great Culebra Cut. "It is," he observes, "the deepest open cutting anywhere in the world, and shows curious phenomena in the injection of igneous rocks, apparently very recent, among the loose sedimentary beds, chiefly clays and soft sandstones of the latest tertiary period." It had not, however, as yet occurred to the Government of the United States to institute an investigation into the geological aspect of this gigantic section. Bryce was resolved to remedy the omission and at once wrote to President Taft to suggest that a geological mission should be despatched to the Isthmus in order to report on the cut. The President read the letter to the Cabinet and the Cabinet at once proceeded to act on the writer's advice. "How like Mr. Bryce," they exclaimed. The geologists of Washington were delighted. "We had been pining to go," they said to him on his return, "but we had not been allowed. Your letter smoothed away all difficulties."

CHAPTER XXII

THREE DISAPPOINTMENTS

When I have applied my mind to politics so that I might examine what belongs to politics with the same precision which we use for mathematics, I have taken my best pains not to laugh at the actions of mankind, not to groan over them, not to be angry with them, but to understand them.

SPINOZA.

THREE large diplomatic issues, overshadowing in their significance even the most important negotiations of the preceding years, came into the field of practical politics under the Taft administration. The first was the question of a treaty of commercial reciprocity between Canada and the United States, the second the conclusion of a general treaty of arbitration between the United States and Britain, the third was the question of the Panama tolls. With each of these three questions, affecting in differing measures Anglo-American relations and each and all bearing upon the problem of world peace, Bryce was intimately associated.

In Home politics the British Ambassador was known to be a free trader. He believed in Free Trade for his own country and he regarded it as desirable for other countries as well. In private he did not conceal his disappointment that President Taft, coming in as he did with Tariff revision as a plank in his programme, should have given way to the normal tendency to raise rather than lower the tariff in Congressional discussion. He was therefore prepared to look with sympathy upon proposals to lower the tariff wall between Canada and the United States, believing that reciprocity would not only benefit the farmers in the Canadian West but permanently improve the relations between Canada and her Southern neighbour. Sir Wilfrid Laurier, himself a Liberal and a theoretical Free Trader, was also for lowering the wall. No one knew better than he the strength of the arguments for relieving the farming community from the burden of the tariff, and for dispelling the suspicion that agricultural interests in the West were being sacrificed to the appetites of the Eastern manufacturers.

At a meeting in Albany between the American President and Mr. Fielding, the Canadian Minister of the Interior, Mr. Taft threw out the suggestion of a treaty of reciprocity between Canada and the United States, and since the idea was welcomed it was agreed that a Conference should meet at Washington in January 1911 to consider the draft of a Treaty. To a British Ambassador who had been in the forefront of a vehement controversy at home as to the respective merits of Free Trade and Protection such a conference was not without embarrassment. The Canadian tariff was primarily a matter for Canada to settle. The merest hint of British interference, whether on one side or on the other, would be likely to give umbrage and to be generally misinterpreted, and the stronger the personal opinions of the ambassador, the more important was it that they should be strictly kept under lock and key.

The conduct of Bryce and of the British Mission was the quintessence of diplomatic discretion. While the substance of the negotiation was left entirely to the Dominion representatives whom the Mission did not try to influence either way, every effort was made to keep them informed of the state of opinion at Washington and to remind them of the British and imperial interests concerned. The view taken was that Canada must not be made to suffer by reason of the fact that she had no separate diplomatic representative at Washington. Everything which a Canadian ambassador would do for his country, the British ambassador acting for Canada should be prepared to undertake. All communications coming from the United States Government with reference to the question under discussion should be promptly communicated to the ministers negotiating on behalf of the Dominion. There should be no secrets, no reserves, nor yet the faintest suspicion of diplomatic pressure. The mission of the British Embassy was to help, not to guide and still less to dictate; and so though he held a watching brief for any Imperial interest which might be involved, the Ambassador was careful to abstain from attending the meetings of the Washington Conference.

It is the more important that these facts should be stated now, inasmuch as on the other side of the Atlantic mythology was then busy with Bryce's reputation. The prospect of a Treaty of Reciprocity between Canada and the United States was by no means welcome to the young bloods of the Tariff Reform Party in the British Parliament. Standing for Colonial Preference and Domestic Protection, they held that their ideal would be seriously, if not fatally obstructed, if, instead of entering into closer fiscal relations with the Mother Country, Canada were to sign a Reciprocity Treaty with the United States. To some minds such a Treaty seemed the first step on the road to secession, a betrayal of the Empire, a note of dissolution. Canadian trade would flow North and South, not East and West. A huge American immigration into the Western Provinces of Canada would be encouraged, republican ideas would spread, the British connection would be weakened, and much of the good work accomplished by the prophets and promoters of British Imperialism during the last generation would be thrown to the winds.

Of this calamitous project it was freely alleged that the British Ambassador in Washington was the original artificer. The statesmen of Ottawa and Washington had been enmeshed in the toils of his Free Trade convictions. It was from beginning to end Bryce's plot. In all this there was not a word of truth. With the inception of the Reciprocity negotiations Bryce had nothing whatever to do and with their conduct only so much as was absolutely required by his official position. That he was himself a Free Trader, and that he held quite strongly that the Empire had everything to gain from the adoption of a fiscal policy likely to increase the wealth of Canada made not an iota of difference to the march of events.

What happened to the Conference and its work is an illustration of the value in diplomatic negotiations of the gift of reticence and of the danger of conducting international affairs from the platform. The Conference reached an agreement and the terms of the agreement were made known to the countries concerned on January

26th, 1911. Then delays supervened. Opposition sprang up in the North-Western States of America. A new Congress had to be summoned to pass the Treaty, and in effect it was not until July that the assent of the Senate was obtained. But meanwhile some indiscreet language had been used in the United States by the advocates of reciprocity, not excluding the President himself and the Speaker of the House of Representatives. Loose phrases distorted into threats or prophecies of the absorption of Canada aroused the susceptibilities of Canadian patriotism. A gale of unreasoning panic spread over Montreal and Toronto. The loss of protection would be bad, the loss of independence would be disastrous. The whole Imperial connection seemed to be involved in a concession to the facts of geography.

At the Canadian General Election in September, reciprocity was heavily defeated, and with the fall of the Laurier government power passed into the hands of Sir Robert Borden. The rejection of a Treaty already assented to in the United States after a Canadian general election which had been largely fought on the fear that fiscal reciprocity would lead to political absorption, might have been expected to inflict a serious injury upon the relations between the two countries. This did not, as Bryce gratefully noted, prove to be the case. A tactful speech by the new Canadian Prime Minister at a dinner of the Canadian Club in New York assured the American public that there was on the Canadian side no element of ill-will, and both in its delivery and reception confirmed the idea that there were on both sides of the line sufficient reserves of commonsense and friendly feeling to stand the miscarriage of the plan. After all, the Government which passed the Aldrich tariff had no ground of complaint at a renewed victory of the Protectionist cause in Canada.

The conclusion of a general Treaty of Arbitration between Great Britain and the United States exempt from the limitations of the Treaty of 1908 and stating that any dispute between America and Britain, however grave it might be, should be settled by arbitration and not by war, would have been an achievement memorable in the annals of international relations and a powerful counterweight to those menacing forces on the Continent of Europe which were giving unceasing concern to the British Foreign Secretary. Such a treaty Bryce at one time believed himself to be within an ace of concluding with the Government of Mr. Taft. Never, indeed, were the omens more favourable. The American President, himself an eminent lawyer, was a great believer in the principle of arbitration. So, too, were the British Ambassador and his political chief Sir Edward Grey. In the midst of the gathering storms, which were so soon about to break upon the world, the conclusion of a treaty between the two great Anglo-Saxon democracies, containing in the forefront a solemn declaration of their intention to submit all future disputes, however vital, however closely affecting national honour and national sentiment, to arbitration, would be like one of those spaces of blue sky which are regarded as the harbinger of fair weather. It was, indeed, impossible to measure the advantages which might be expected to flow from so close a conjunction of the two leading democracies of the West. "The example," wrote Sir Edward Grey, "would spread, and I am not without hope that one or more great European Powers would eventually make a similar agreement with us and the United States. The effect of such agreements upon disarmament and the *morale* of international politics should be considerable." [1]

On January 1st, 1911, Bryce opened the discussion with the President. There was no hitch. The business proceeded pleasantly, with goodwill and indeed with enthusiasm on either side. At the end of February the Ambassador was discussing the preliminary draft with the Secretary of State. On May 1st the draft, agreed upon in Washington, was sent over to London for the approval of the British Cabinet. On August 3rd the Treaty was signed by Bryce and Mr. Knox. So far as the government of the United States was concerned the Arbitration Treaty was an accomplished fact. There was, however, another body whose consent was necessary before the Treaty could finally go through. The Senate of the United States, which is entrusted by the Constitution with the duty of ratifying treaties with foreign powers has broken the heart and foiled the expectations of many a foreign diplomatist. Containing some members of high intellectual eminence, but for the most part consisting of politicians unversed in world affairs, accessible to sectional influence and intensely susceptible on the point of senatorial privilege, the Senate not infrequently takes pleasure in upsetting the best laid schemes of the President or his Secretary of State. In this case there was perhaps some failure of tact on the part of the State Department. The treaty was published to the world before its terms were communi-

[1] 30th March, 1911.

cated to the Foreign Committee of the Senate. The *amour propre* of the august body was wounded and the discussion dragged on without a conclusion until Congress rose for its summer holiday. Nevertheless there was still good ground for hope. In November the President was confident that when Congress met again in January the Treaty would be carried, but the psychological moment was not seized in mid January, when the Senate was comparatively fresh and the President's speeches in favour of arbitration were telling on the country; and the chances for the Treaty, which were rosy then, had become obscure when the matter was taken up at last in the month of March.

We may here pause in our narrative briefly to describe the instrument upon which such care had been lavished and so many hopes were built. The preamble of the Treaty set out that the two nations, being equally desirous of perpetuating the peace which had happily existed between them since the Treaty of Ghent in 1814 and had never since been interrupted by an appeal to arms, had appointed two plenipotentiaries to conclude a treaty which should "provide means for the peaceful solution of all questions of difference which it shall in future be found impossible to settle by diplomacy."

Then it was laid down in Article 1 that differences between the high contracting parties, which it had not been found possible to adjust by diplomacy, "relating to matters which are justiceable in their nature by reason of being susceptible of decision by the application of the principles of equity and justice, should be referred either to the Court of Arbitration at the Hague, or to some other arbitral tribunal as may be decided in each case, by special agreement," and finally in Article 3 that a Joint High Commission of Inquiry should be set up, which at the request of either party might investigate any controversy coming under the scope of Article 1 before arbitration and also any other controversy thereafter arising between them, even if they are not agreed that it falls within the scope of Article 1.

In these sweeping provisions a party of senators at once discerned the seeds of possible danger. Surely, it was argued, there are some questions upon which the United States is not prepared to arbitrate even with the most friendly foreign power? The majority of the Senate concurred with this view and while they (March 7th, 1912) advised and consented to the ratification of the Treaty with some minor amendments they appended a provision excepting from the scope of the arrangement any question affecting the admission of aliens into the United States or to the educational institutions of the several States, any question affecting territorial integrity or the alleged indebtedness of any State of the United States, or the Monroe Doctrine or "other purely governmental policy."

A resolution so drafted made nonsense of the Treaty since it expressly excluded all the most important occasions of controversy from the scope of arbitration. Mr. Taft, whose reputation was intimately involved in the successful ratification of the instrument, urged upon the British Ambassador that negotiations should be continued despite the rebuff which had been received, and a further effort was made to save the Treaty from destruction. All was unavailing. The original resolution was set aside, but only in favour of an amendment proposed by Mr. Root (a friend of the Treaty) which in the view of Bryce and of the British Government was even more deadly to the usefulness of the instrument than the resolution.[1] So the Treaty was lost, a failure, not to be charged to any remissness on the part of the British Ambassador but bringing to him the keenest disappointment of his diplomatic career. To have carried an arbitration treaty, wider and more comprehensive than the treaty of 1908 between the Government of the United States and Great Britain, would have put the crown on his diplomatic work in America and on his labours to improve by speech, writing, and action the relations between the two peoples. Such satisfaction was denied him. The auspicious moment had been allowed to pass and the star of Mr. Taft was already paling in the horizon when the dream of a treaty to secure eternal peace between the two English-speaking democracies was fatally pierced by the arrow of the Root amendment.

Roosevelt did not like the Treaty. "Of course," he wrote, "as regards Great Britain, if we only had to consider her and the United States I should be willing to agree to any arbitration treaty; just as I should be quite willing to say that as between you and myself I would without reservation be ready to submit any possible difference to the judgment of reputable outside parties." There were other countries, however, of whom the same proposition would not hold, "and if we start discriminating between nations as to the kind of treaty

[1] Sir E. Grey to Bryce, Sept. 17th, 1912.

we make it would almost be better to make no treaty at all."

And in a later letter he returns to the point:

"I am a dreamer of dreams. I venture to hope that ultimately there may be some kind of intimate association between Great Britain and Ireland, Canada, Australia, South Africa, New Zealand, and our own country which will put us upon some such footing that we can literally have every question that may arise within our own limits settled exactly as similar difficulties within the British Empire, or within the United States, are now settled. But this does not purport to be a treaty of that kind. It purports to be a treaty which shall be followed in making treaties with other nations."[1]

Another cloud of disappointment proceeding from the same quarter of the political horizon settled upon the British Chancellery during the concluding year of Bryce's American Mission. In July 1912 a Canal Bill passed through Congress exempting American ships from payment of tolls in the recently constructed Panama Canal. The Bill, though not in itself unreasonable from the American standpoint, was in flat contradiction of the terms of the Hay-Pauncefote treaty signed between Britain and America in 1901, which provided that the canal should be "free and open to the vessels of commerce and war of all nations observing these rules, on terms of entire equality, so that there shall be no discrimination against any such nation, or its citizens or subjects, in respect of the conditions or charges of traffic or otherwise," and was for that reason assailed in the Senate by three of its most eminent members: Root, Lodge, and Burton. Nevertheless to Bryce's surprise and chagrin it passed Congress

[1] Roosevelt to Bryce, August 19th and June 2nd, 1912.

and was actually signed by the President, whose misgivings on the point of legality were not sufficiently strong to overcome the counsels of domestic and parliamentary convenience. What depressed Bryce was not so much the substance of the Bill itself, though this might be deleterious enough, as the revelation of the irresponsibility with which Congress was liable to handle a solemn treaty with a friendly Power only recently concluded. On his return from leave in September Bryce at once sought out the President in his summer retreat at Beverly and urged the alternative of repeal or arbitration; but the night was hot and the President plainly indisposed for heroic resolves. It was even wholly uncertain whether the Government would allow the matter to go to arbitration.

Nothing then was to be hoped either from Congress or the Executive. To Bryce's private enquiries Senator Burton replied that the Senate would be unlikely to reconsider the question at their December sitting or to arbitrate it under the Treaty of 1908. It can readily be imagined how sharp was the mortification with which Bryce learnt that the American Senate would be likely to reject arbitration upon the interpretation of a treaty, one of those justiceable issues which, readily lending themselves to a judicial decision, were the proper and predestined matter for an arbitral court. To press forward arbitration in such circumstances would have been folly, for nothing would have been more injurious to the cause of peace than the divulgation of the fact that the United States had declined to refer to arbitration the meaning to be attached to the words of a treaty.

In America, however, Senate and President do not

count for everything. There is also the public opinion of the country, sometimes overborne by extravagant emotion, but generally sane and prudent and in any matter of legal significance apt to take its cue from the accomplished masters of American jurisprudence. What consoled Bryce for his keen disappointment was the evidence that the feeling in favour of observing the Hay-Pauncefote treaty was spreading among thoughtful people in the States and that it was supported by four-fifths of the American Press including nearly all the best organs of public opinion. The minority of eighteen who voted against the Tolls Bill in the Senate were in fact voicing the sentiment of the majority of the nation in favour of the scrupulous observance of international good faith. "The thing is a small one in itself," he wrote to Roosevelt, "both for the United States and for us. What does signify is that it should not cause misunderstanding or ill-feeling. I am personally anxious that there should be no misconception in Europe of the attitude of the United States people; for no people seems to have shown itself through its history more generally wishful to act fairly and rightly and observe its national obligations." [1]

[1] January 14th, 1913.

CHAPTER XXIII

A GLIMPSE OF AUSTRALASIA

The Australians, like the Americans, may not have used to the best purpose all the gifts of nature, and especially the great gift of a new land in which they could make a fresh start, delivered from the evils that afflicted the old societies. They have committed some serious mistakes and tolerated some questionable methods. But they have a great recuperative power.

BRYCE.

THE South American volume had been an unexpected interlude, a task suggesting itself as the natural outcome of an interesting holiday voyage, but no part of the general plan of operations which Bryce had framed for the occupation of his leisure moments. The first item of this ambitious programme was to be a comprehensive treatise on the working of Modern Democracies, the second a life of Justinian; and so when South America had been happily disposed of, the book on Democracies, first conceived in 1904, slipped back at once into its appointed place as the magnet of disengaged thoughts and new enquiries.

In this connection a visit to New Zealand and Australia seemed desirable, if not imperative. Here Modern Democracy stalked open and unashamed in its native homespun, whereas in the South American States democracy, if indeed it could be said to exist at all, was only to be found in perverted shapes. Besides, Bryce had been much consulted by Australian statesmen over the Federation of the Commonwealth and was naturally anxious to take stock of its results. Accordingly on the evening of April 26th, 1912, the Bryces left Washington for San Francisco *en route* for the Australasian States.

The imagination of a home-staying biographer quails before the energy with which this holiday, if such it can be called, was conducted through its various and contrasted phases to a happy conclusion. Nearly twenty-three thousand miles covered by sea and land in four and a half months! Nearly all the States in the Southern Hemisphere and all the principal cities visited, the accommodation of seven separate steamers of all sorts and sizes tested, speeches, more than thirty in number, delivered on demand, degrees received from the Universities of Adelaide and Brisbane, the cold winter months of the Antipodes with their high winds and snow-storms shown to be utterly ineffectual impediments to the execution of a voyage so rigorously planned as to admit of no languors or delays!

The Labour Party was in power in Australia. For the first time in history apart from moments of revolution, the Hand-workers of a country had obtained effective control of the Executive. Here there was a new phenomenon of great and wide-reaching significance and not a little disconcerting to the Liberal statesman of orthodox Gladstonian views. What had come about in Australia in 1911 might be copied in other democracies. Europe too might experience, in less favourable circumstances, proletarian rule and state socialism. The change was too recent to enable a confident estimate to be made of its bearings. *Prima facie*, however, the Government by a class for a class, even were that class the largest in the community, was not attractive. To Bryce class government in any form or shape had always appeared to be unsound, and he was not tempted to revise his opinion of it by what he saw in Australia. Yet, deficient in elevation as he found Australian political life to be, he was compelled to acknowledge that the stream of change continued to flow in the well worn channels of Parliamentary constitutionalism; and in the virile energy and sanguine temper of the Australian people he found some compensation for the lack of inspiration in Australian politics and for the selfish materialism of Proletarian rule.

Such political impressions as Bryce derived from his voyage through the Australasian States were subsequently distilled into the pages of *Modern Democracies;* but political philosophy was not to be the only quarry of the chase. Bryce was after wild game as well — volcanoes and geysers, mountain ranges and primitive bush, the changing beauties of sky and sea and plain, the stars above and the flora and fauna beneath. It was one of his disappointments that he returned from Australia without seeing a kangaroo in its wild state. He had to be content with emus and ibises, white cranes and parrots, a wallaby and in a remote part of the Queensland Bush the surprising spectacle of an Anglican Archbishop in gaiters.

The distinguished British visitor has himself to thank if he fails to enjoy a visit to one of the Dominions. He passes from Government House to Government House, delightfully entertained by pleasant people and receiving all the delicate attentions which these well-appointed establishments know so well how to bestow. Special cars are provided for him on the railways. State visits are arranged to places notable for their beauty or interest. The hospitality of all is endless and bountiful. Flat races, steeple chases, agricultural shows, visits to typical industrial processes such as meat-freezing in New Zealand or sheep-sheering at Brisbane, are arranged almost as a matter of course. The main difficulty which such a traveller encounters is, escaping from the official circle, to establish a contact with the underworld.

For the principal purpose, however, which he had in view, that is of appreciating the political agencies and modes of life in the Australasian States, Bryce's plan of campaign would appear to have been conducted with remarkable skill. The attack upon the Continent was brisk and vivacious, the responsive regions well selected and the point of interrogation driven home fast and hard. Wherever he went, Auckland, Wellington, Sydney, Melbourne, Adelaide, Brisbane, Hobart, men of every calling were brought into contribution, lawyers, politicians, pressmen, scholars in the first place, but also industrials and farmers. The political philosopher returned across the Pacific with a rich booty from his lightning raid.

"Two things stand out in my memory," writes Lord Chelmsford, who entertained him at Sydney, "the first his masterly handling of the Press Reporters. It was late when he arrived at our house after a tiring journey and many young men were waiting eager to flush their pens upon him. I heard of this and said to him, 'You must be tired, let me get rid of them.' 'Oh! no, by no means,' he said, 'I will see them.' So arrangements were made and Bryce took in hand some half-dozen young men. After half an hour or so, it being time to dress for dinner, I went in to rescue him and found him sitting on a sofa faced by a band of gaping young fellows, enjoying himself to the full. In the space of half an hour he had cross-questioned them on every conceivable subject and they, though full of admiration, had no more spirit left in them. One of them said to me afterwards, 'The Professor never gave us a chance of putting him a question.'

"The other thing I remember was his extraordinary kindness to my children. They were all young then, the eldest not being more than sixteen. I arranged for a day's expedition to the National Park where he might botanise to the full of his bent. My wife and I were engaged, so two or three of my girls went with him and Mrs. Bryce. They came home delighted. He had known every flower and plant and told them all about them. But what pleased them, I think, most was his activity. 'You know, Dad, he skipped from rock to rock like a mountain goat and never missed his footing.'"

One of the advantages of approaching Australasia from San Francisco is that it enables a visit to be paid to the beautiful isles of the South Pacific. Bryce had visited the Hawaiian group in 1883 and climbed Mauna Loa, its highest mountain (13,675 ft.) but the Southern Polynesian Islands were as yet unknown to him. Accordingly he and Mrs. Bryce explored Tahiti "walking into the heart of the mountains for some five miles along a trail through a tropical forest, with wild oranges and limes, mangoes, coffee and bananas and the ferns around us," and visited the little-known Cook and Society Islands on the way out and on the return voyage touched at Tutuela and Honolulu. These lovely little islands, with their coral reefs and light green lagoons of an exquisite transparency, their long rows of cocoa nut palms tossing their feathery plumes in the breeze, their romantic mountains and gentle aborigines could not, indeed, be brought to contribute to the *magnum opus* on *Modern Democracies.* But for the student of life upon this planet what could be more attractive than a vision of this miniature world, so secluded and select before the last remnants of primitive belief and custom had been obliterated by Chinese immigration and the Christian missions? To feed on the native dishes, to listen to the native songs, to be present at the ceremonial brewing of the Kaba, to be entertained by the last of the Tava clan (descended on the male side from a shark), to watch the unearthly brilliance of the dawn, to brave the dancing surf in a light canoe, or to plunge under the warm Trade wind into a cool mountain stream, could any other combination of experiences be more entrancing? Even the fish in the Aquarium at Honolulu were not as other fish. "There were," writes Mrs. Bryce, "fish that looked like birds, or snakes or rocks; fish that looked like feathers or ribbons; scales that looked like velvet or silk — a perfect sea garden of colour or design."

In a paper subsequently published Bryce describes the impressions left upon his mind by the spectacle of these magical islands, where the very perfection of beauty is a source of sadness.

"The sense of melancholy which floats over the scenery

is heightened by compassion for a dying race. Everyone seems to see the ghostly figures of the native past melting into the air soon to be no more remembered. One of our last evenings in Tahiti was spent with a man, the son of an English father and a Tahitian mother who had been the head by descent of the great clan of the Tavas. At my request he gathered from the neighbourhood some thirty or forty of the native villagers at his house on the shore of Paparra, where a rushing stream from the mountains meets the ocean billows. Seated under a wide-spreading trellis work close to the house, roofed in by the boughs of a gigantic bougainvillea, they lifted up their voices and began to sing, or rather to chant, in a soft, long-drawn melody, the men's voices in a somewhat monotonous undertone, not unlike the drone of the Scottish bagpipes, while the women's voices formed a recitative in a higher key, and one single voice introduced at intervals a theme, resembling a Swiss jodel, which formed a recurring refrain. We could catch no words, for the language was unknown to us, and being composed entirely of vowels, the words seemed to slide into one another. These people sang with spirit and feeling, their voices sweet and full of a strange pathos. Our host told us that the songs were in praise of the deeds of ancient heroes handed down from generation to generation, but there was in them no note of strife or triumph."

Six days steam brought the travellers out of fairyland and as they travelled eastward across the American Continent the Mormon Temple at Salt Lake City revealed its huge deformity.

the Applied Sciences would be overwhelming, he speaks of the claims of humane learning. To the inhabitants of Vermont he preaches the need of conserving from the ravages of Philistinism the rare beauty of their scenery. When he goes to California and sees the greater part of the population aggregated in two large cities, he discusses the means of reviving rural life and the part which the University of California may play in collecting and focussing whatever science and learning can provide for any form of State service. To the New York Bar Association he delivers an appropriate address on the Conditions and Methods of Legislation, to emphasize the moral that a lawyer alive to the dignity of his profession should endeavour to make the law as perfect as it can be. We may feel pretty certain that wherever the Ambassador spoke and upon whatever topic there were many members of his audience who found in his discourse something fresh and instructive.

The thoughts which most frequently recur in these addresses are, in the political sphere, the continuity of English and American history and the value of that common heritage of free institutions which belongs to every branch of the English-speaking race. When he spoke to Universities and other learned bodies he was prone to dilate upon the services which learning might bring to an individual or a state, and especially upon the importance of real as opposed to spurious culture, as a force making for the elevation of character and mind. He was, however, equally ready to talk about the importance of Canals, the influence of Natural Science or the art of Saint Gaudens.

Before he left America, he had visited every State in

the Union, many of them several times. No British Ambassador had ever before travelled to the Pacific Coast during his term of office, but Bryce paid an official visit to California in the spring of 1909 and was able to compare his impressions of the Pacific coast with those which he had formed on the occasion of two earlier visits many years before. We write of an official visit and yet how different from the conception ordinarily attached to the ceremonial visits of official personages. The Ambassador, who was received in San Francisco with extraordinary manifestations of interest and enthusiasm, spoke to a spell-bound public in crowded halls, not on ceremonial subjects save once at a banquet when responding to the toast of Edward VII, but of California and its opportunities, of the function of a Californian University, of the relation of religion and ethics before Christ, in the apostolic ages, in the middle ages and in modern times. To audiences occupying every inch of standing room, he discoursed of Plato and Aristotle and the Stoics, of the absorption of ethics in religion under Christianity, of the forces making for the divorce of religion and ethics in mediæval times, of ethical standards as applied to modern problems, of arbitration and internationalism and the duty of the superior to the inferior races and of the means by which California might avoid the curse of urban pauperism which was so unhappily prevalent in Europe. In all this there was no startling Evangel. To well cultivated minds, versed in historical studies, there was nothing particularly new either in the Charter Day address to the Berkeley University or in the five Earl lectures on Religion and Ethics, delivered under the auspices of the Pacific Theological Seminary. But in San Francisco these addresses, so clear and eloquent, opening so many attractive vistas of knowledge and containing so much direction on public and private affairs, left a deep impression on the minds of those who heard them. Such long flights of elevated and stimulating instructiveness upon the largest subject of human interest were rare in California. They were, for this reason, the more keenly appreciated.

It is little wonder then that he was treated not as a stranger but as a distinguished American. At a Presidential Election he received a touching proof that he was regarded as a citizen of the Republic, for requests came to him from each of the great political parties to contribute to their funds. He was invited to address the New York Legislature at Albany in joint session. As he walked through the streets of any large American town strangers would come up to him, shake hands and pass on. At public luncheons and dinners large assemblies would rise cheering and waving their napkins for several minutes at his appearance. If there was to be anywhere a celebration of national importance, whether it was the centenary of Champlain or of Jefferson or the celebrations in connection with the initiation of the Panama Canal, Ambassador Bryce was expected to speak, being regarded as one of the public orators of the Union and an almost indispensable ornament to such proceedings. He could discourse, too, with the authority of a veteran who had known the States for more than a generation and had carefully noted the changes which had come over many departments of American life. How immense these had been in the economic sphere since that first visit in 1870 with Albert Dicey! The population of the Union which was then 38½ millions had swollen to 92 millions; its exports which were then 392 millions had grown to 1,744 millions; its estimated wealth which was then 3,008 millions had mounted up to 127,000 millions and its railway mileage, then 53,000 miles had increased to 244,000 miles. In those days there were few great fortunes. He could remember only three in New York. Now everyone knew how many gigantic fortunes had arisen. And the political changes consequent upon this enormous development of material wealth, if less conspicuous and requiring the trained eye of the expert to measure their true volume and direction were none the less important. There was the problem of the Trust and the expansion of the Federal Power at the expense of the States and the question of limiting the powers of the Electoral Machine. On all such questions the Ambassador could speak from a vast and long experience of the country. He was more than an official, a visitor or a friend. He had become an essential and familiar adornment of the home.

A glance at Bryce's itinerary during the period of his American mission brings one fact, which seems natural enough in him but would be singular in others, into startling prominence. He is continually travelling up and down the Union to give literary or educational addresses to Universities or other seats of learning. Sometimes he delivers a single address, but sometimes, as at New Haven and San Francisco and Amherst College, he gives a course of lectures. And at great University ceremonies such as the installation of his friend Lawrence Lowell as President of Harvard University, he is careful to be present. The question how he found time to fulfil such engagements is, in the case of a man of such elastic force and ripe attainments, less interesting than another question — why did he find time? To lecture to the Universities of the country to which he is accredited is no part of the ordinary duty of an Ambassador. Lord Pauncefote did not do it, the gifted James Russell Lowell did not do it, though nobody could have been better fitted for the task. Why then did Bryce, with so many important diplomatic transactions on his hands, spend so much of his time in the preparation and delivery of discourses to University audiences?

That he was an academic man himself and fond of the society of students is only part of the explanation. The searchings of a Presbyterian conscience were too strict to permit him to go only where he expected to find pleasant and congenial company. The Universities happened to be congenial to him, but they were not visited on that ground. What Bryce saw was that the mere improvement of the diplomatic relations between the Foreign Office, the Government of Ottawa, and the State Department at Washington, valuable as that undoubtedly would be, was not sufficient. The diplomatic work of the Chancery must be supplemented by the endeavour to create, especially among the young who might be expected from their presence in the Universities to be the future leaders of the nation, a favourable view of British character and British culture, and that not by the direct method of self-applause but by speaking simply and naturally of the things which occupy the mind or delight the leisure of a highly cultivated Englishman.

The enterprise was the more hopeful, by reason of the high place which the Universities occupy in the life of the nation. An American University is a very democratic and comprehensive institution, and supported to an extent unparalleled in Europe by the faith, the enthusiasm, and the financial strength of the community it serves. He then, who wishes to reach the agencies in America which are likely to make the most effectual contribution to public opinion in after years must speak to the Universities. To stand well with them is to take out an insurance with the future. To enlist the imagination of youth is to secure the support or at least the neutrality of middle-age. Political attachments are very much more often the result of personal sympathy than we are inclined to suppose. Important leaders of opinion in America gravitated to the pro-German side in the war on no more substantial ground than that they had received civilities from the Kaiser in Berlin. How many young Americans, sprung it may be from Scandinavian or Italian ancestry, must have formed their idea of British intellect and character from hearing one of Bryce's addresses at their University and must have been unconsciously biassed in favour of the Allied cause by that experience? How many superstitious prejudices, fostered by the Hearst Press, as to the iniquities of the British race must have melted away at the mere appearance of Ambassador Bryce upon the platform! The haughty Briton of legend was no ogre after all, but a simple friendly veteran, as mild as milk. The down-trodden serf of tyranny spoke

"We have, as you know, the prospect of a long, laborious and not over-promising session. One question in all our minds — though not so much upon our lips — is the likelihood or otherwise of the Prime Minister[1] being strong enough in health to accompany us through the year or beyond it. What is certain is that he will not desert the bridge until the doctor or Nature, who is the doctor's enemy, orders him off. The results of any change then are obscure enough, but they cannot tend to the strengthening of party unity, though they may tend to increase of cabinet efficiency and *drive*. We have one valuable asset in the weakness of the other side in personnel and their incoherence in policy. Balfour's skill and tenacity in debate, and his assiduity in daily business, have brought back to him something of his old parliamentary position. People tell me that the disorder in Ireland (grossly and villainously exaggerated in the English Press) and the refusal to use the Crimes Act in putting it down, are causing much searching of heart among our friends in the country. The session will doubtless open with that dish and if the Irishmen should for any reason prove implacable, they will bring disastrous obstruction to bear upon our bills, which expose a mighty large surface for contention in any case. Education, Licensing, Roman Catholic University, House of Lords, and above all *Old Age Pensions*. It is in the last of this list that the public mind is now most keenly interested and expectant. The danger of it to the Government and the party is pretty plain. It raises in lively concrete form, the burning abstract debates on socialism, or rather, it does not raise — it

[1] Sir Henry Campbell-Bannerman.

concentrates them. It will be injurious to us with the lower middle-class, who after all are no inconsiderable contingent of our party strength. On the other hand, we shall hardly be able to produce proposals magnificent enough to make the workmen ardently enthusiastic, or even decently satisfied. . . .

"You would follow the satisfactory external features of the German Emperor's visit. I saw a good deal of him for three or four days at Windsor, and found him very attractive — *riant*, unaffected, buoyant, good-humoured, genial, alert. The general impression, so far as I can collect it, was that he is not profound in character, nor firm in mental texture; that he is over-rapid both in forming and expressing judgments; that he is apt in his excitements to mistake surface for substance; and so on. You can fill in the type from these cursory indications. Yet I confess that, like Butler of Columbia, I was constantly reminded by his tone and ways of your illustrious neighbour at the White House. Only the German is a good deal less solid in his vehemence.

"The only political subject discussed was the Bagdad Railway, and on this, various talks of much importance took place, as you may perhaps have heard: the Emperor, Grey, Haldane, J. M., Metternich and Schön being the talkers. The Germans are very stiff; the concession is theirs and we are out of construction and control alike. But they would agree to a commercial sort of conference at Berlin, to settle rates, etc., and they would bind themselves against preferences, unfair rebates and the like. They swear that they mean nothing but what will benefit the whole universe. Meanwhile they hunger for French

a full measure of that moral and intellectual courage which is nourished by austere and secluded labour upon noble themes. On looking into the matter, the new President came to the conclusion that whatever might be said for the Tolls Act from the point of view of policy, it was, in effect, a breach of faith. With a fine disregard of consequences, he came before Congress and demanded its Repeal (March 5th, 1914) and after three months of heated discussion, Congress by a large majority gave him what he asked. Legislative bodies are not easily persuaded to retrace their steps, especially when it is to the interest of Foreign Powers that they should do so. The decision of the President and the vote of Congress are all the more honourable on this account.

Meanwhile, the last months of the American mission witnessed a continuance, without any relaxation or diminution of endeavour, of those multifarious activities which helped to make it memorable in diplomatic annals. In January 1913, two lectures were delivered to the University of Virginia, in February the Ambassador attended the County Bar dinner and the Harvard Law School Alumni dinner in New York, and the dinner of the Transatlantic Society in Philadelphia. In March he delivered an address on the Beautifying of Washington, and paid his last official visit to Canada. Then on April 24th he went to the White House, had his final audience with the President, and presented his letters of recall. He was within a fortnight of completing the seventy-fifth year of his age.

On the evening of April 25th the Pilgrims' Society gave the retiring Ambassador a great banquet, at which Mr.

Choate, who was in the chair, made a speech full of the kindly wit and warm-hearted appreciation for which he was famous. To this Bryce replied and then Mr. Walter Page, the newly appointed Ambassador to Britain, added a few cordial words and the proceedings ended, not however without overflowing manifestations of genuine friendship and affection for Bryce and the partner of his labours. Two days later, Bryce had a private meeting with his successor, Sir Cecil Spring Rice. He too, like Bryce, a gifted son of Oxford University, was destined to experience memorable things in America.

The regrets of the American people at Bryce's resignation were real and unaffected. President Wilson wrote to express his deep distress, Mr. Joseph Choate wrote: "You have been a real ambassador to the American people and they will never forget it." Not less gratifying was the tribute which was paid him by the Prime Minister of Canada: "May I be permitted," wrote Sir Robert Borden, "to express my very deep and sincere appreciation of the valuable service you have rendered Canada in respect of many important and difficult questions with which you have had to deal since we assumed office in October, 1911. Your interest in all that concerns the welfare of Canada has been unfailing." The appreciation of the British Foreign Secretary was equally generous. He wrote of "the tremendous public service," which Bryce had rendered all through these years, "in improving our relations with both Canada and the United States."

What were the final impressions of the wise and experienced friend who after forty-two years knowledge of the United States was now preparing, perhaps for ever, to quit

American soil? Gratitude for a splendid welcome, for innumerable kindnesses, for many close and precious friendships, for a spirit of hospitality, such as the old world hardly knows, for touching manifestations of friendly and enthusiastic feeling on the occasion of his public appearances in every part of the Union was certainly the emotion uppermost in his mind. Yet he could not honestly avow that the passage of time had obliterated that clear-cut distinction between the American people and the American government which he had drawn after his first visit in 1870. A close inspection of the ways of Congress had not raised his respect for that body. In the selfish power of the Machine, in the weakness of the State Judiciary, in the recklessness of the Press, he descried formidable and menacing evils. Too often the purity of city government left much to be desired. But to be set against these evils, which were quite as apparent to his chief American friends as to himself, there were encouraging features, a growing sense of public responsibility, a fervent faith in the power of education, a gradual but perceptible elevation in the standard of public virtue. He recurred to a thought which had been present to him twenty-four years before as he was concluding his survey of the American Commonwealth.

"The Americans have fortunately the power of recognising, trusting and following a strong and honest man. In this quality coupled with that instinct for order, that sense of justice, that freedom from class bitterness which belong to the native American, we may perhaps find the best ground for hope for the future of the nation."

CHAPTER XXV

THE VOYAGE HOME

Travel in the younger sort, is a part of education; in the elder a part of experience.

BACON.

THE reader who has followed the Bryces in their holiday excursions round South America and to Australia and New Zealand will not be surprised to learn that, finally released from official duties at Washington, they did nothing so commonplace as to return to England by the Atlantic. Bryce had not yet visited China, Japan, or Siberia. Here were new hills to be climbed, new mountains to be viewed, new seas and rivers and lakes to be bathed in, new flowers to be enjoyed and identified, strange types of civilisation, ancient and modern, to be tasted and appraised. Moreover an immense revolution, the character of which had to Bryce's surprise enlisted little interest among American public men, had recently transformed the ancient fabric of the Chinese State. A Republic had been proclaimed in China and a Parliament set up in Pekin. The results of so momentous a change deserved to be inspected *in situ* with as little delay as possible. So, when the last valedictions of New York had been spoken and the incoming ambassador had learnt what his predecessor had to tell him the

Bryces turned their faces westward and crossed the Continent to San Francisco.

Hence at mid-day on Saturday, May 3rd., they sailed in the "Mongolia" for Honolulu which was reached on the 9th., and after a grey and rather cold afternoon a night ashore amid the enchantments of a Pacific Island was not unwelcome. There was a lunch, followed of course by a speech at the University Club, a beautiful drive with the Governor to the north side of the island, a dinner at the Moana Hotel on the famous Waikiki beach with the moon silvering the bay in the still tropical night, and early next morning, need it be added that "James had a chance of getting a quick bathe in the surf" before the travellers had to return to the boat?

The "Mongolia" having some business to transact in Japan the Bryces were enabled to spend a few days ashore before proceeding to Shanghai, and to gain some preliminary impressions, among which was an earthquake shock, of the country and its inhabitants. They marked the wonderful care with which the land is cultivated, the ugliness of modern Japanese architecture, the disappointing prevalence of European costume even among artisans, the great similarity in externals between a Buddhist service and the Roman Mass. On May 27th the "Moldavia," having accomplished its affairs in Japan, put out from Nagasaki with the Bryces on board for Shanghai.

It is safe to assume that whatever two Europeans, ignorant of the language, can see and learn of China within the space of a short month was accomplished by the Bryces. Two observers, equally active and accurate are better than one. Moreover though Sir John Jordan, the

British Ambassador at Pekin, was absent on leave, the resources of our diplomatic mission were placed at their disposal by the kindness of Mr. Alston, the chargé d'affaires. There was Mr. Archibald Rose of the Chinese Department who was told off to be their special guide and friend in Pekin; and outside the legation Mr. Backhouse, that admirable Chinese scholar, Dr. Morison for many years *Times* Correspondent in China, and Sir Charles Eliot, then Principal of Hongkong University, who has since written a monumental work on the religions of the East, proved to be available. In the provinces the British Consuls were everywhere eager to assist. One impressive illustration of the radical character of the Chinese revolution was furnished by the spectacle of the ruined examination halls at Nanking. "We climbed," wrote Mrs. Bryce, "a rickety stair to the top of a great gateway, that led to the inner courts and from that we looked down on these rows and rows of little alleys alongside of which opened tiny cells (suggesting criminals rather than scholars) in which these unfortunates were confined for eight or ten days, shut up with their pens and papers and the necessary food. These Halls were used until about thirteen years ago and could accommodate some twenty thousand students. They are now desolate, falling into ruin and the stones are being taken for other buildings."

Another sign of the times was the new Republican Parliament, the Speaker in a frock coat, and top hat, but many of the members in pigtails and Chinese dress. Bryce visited both chambers and had in addition an interview with Yuan Shi Kai, the President of the Chinese Republic.

"Yuan Shi Kai," writes Mrs. Bryce, "is a man of about

fifty-five years of age, of medium height and inclined to be stout. He met us with an affable smile and shook hands — a rather soft pulpy hand; physically he does not look very tough. The face is keen, wary, and shrewd, for he is a man of many experiences as well as of much experience."

What Bryce thought of the situation and prospects of the Chinese Republic he put in a letter to Theodore Roosevelt:

Mukden,
June 28th, 1913.

Your interests are so universal that I fancy you will like to hear something about the present situation in China, as I should like to tell you something. It is however very difficult to reach any conclusions or venture on any predictions. The Europeans most friendly to the Chinese themselves say they see no daylight. Everyone agrees that China is as unfit for republican institutions as any country can be, but the chances of any restoration of a monarchy are slender and the Manchu dynasty had become so feeble and effete that nobody regrets it. The Legislature consists of men nearly all inexperienced and most of them young. Among those I saw there seemed to be a good many of talent, and animated by a patriotic spirit but so far they have done nothing but talk and intrigue and have not secured the confidence of the nation. Europeans generally desire to see Yuan Shi Kai establish his power as a strong executive and think that the more he is left to run the country the better. But he does not look likely to live many years, and is exposed, as every prominent man is, to the attack of assassins. There is a great deal of bomb throwing and bomb sending here. No man has yet appeared fit to take his place, and when he goes, power will probably fall to the person who has money to pay the troops, especially if he is himself a good soldier. This seems a dark prospect, yet the Chinese have such an instinct for organization and such an interest in preserving the order necessary for industry and trade that one must not be despondent. The only Republicans among them are the few who have received their education abroad, and they will readily be swayed more by facts than by theories. One must wish that they be left alone; the less foreign intervention the better.

The great sights of the country, the gorges of the Yangtse, the Wall of China, the tombs of the Ming, the temples of Pekin were visited with sustained energy and an exceptional measure of interest and enjoyment. Here is a characteristic incident:

"On our way back (from the Ming tombs) we stopped to try and see the tomb and temple of the last of the Ming Emperors who committed suicide when he realised that the Manchus had conquered the Mings, and was in consequence not permitted to be buried in a permanent place with the rest of the dynasty. We found the place — a forlorn, neglected spot — but the enclosure was locked and no key was to be found. James climbed the wall at the back and looked into the courts."

From China the route lay through Manchuria and Korea back to Japan. Mukden, Port Arthur, and then Seoul, the first the ancient seat of the Manchu dynasty, the second famous for its siege by the Japanese forces during the Russo-Japanese war and the third the seat of the Japanese Government of Korea were in turn visited under competent guidance.

So passed the month of June. July was pleasantly spent among the dainty lakes and hills of Japan with short downward flights to the cities of the plain, Tokyo, Yokohama, Osaka. The travellers were seldom stationary, but nine days were spent in delightful excursions in and about Kyoto, the ancient capital, a grey brown city standing in a spacious valley then emerald under rice and cereals and ringed by a coronal of graceful hills. Afterwards the famous temples of Nikko, shining in gold red and black lacquer amid a boscage of cryptomerias attracted a pilgrimage; as did the volcano Asarna, then active and in eruption, but veiling to the disappointment of the visitors its fiery crest in the clouds. A voyage is never complete without vicissitudes. Dining in Tokyo with their friends Baron and Baroness Kato the Bryces were sumptuously entertained in the European rooms with a European dinner, though the table decoration — a pool of water with pebbles and a group of tall rushes in flower at one end of it — was thoroughly Japanese. A few days later among the hills they were sitting cross-legged on the floor of a village inn, eating out of lacquer bowls with chop-sticks. To court such abrupt changes of condition is part of the æsthetics of travel.

Before leaving Japan one last rite was accomplished. At 11 A.M. on August 4th the travellers reached Tsuruga on the western coast of the island and duly boarded the Russian steamer Simbirsk which was bound for Vladivostock. It appeared however that the boat was not to leave before sunset. There was then time to go ashore and to climb the rocky wooded heights which overlook the bay. This was done; but there was occasion for a yet more important part of Bryce's travelling ritual. The Sea of Japan lay helpless at his feet. He rushed down, laved himself in its waters, and counted among the seas and oceans of the world his fifteenth victim.

The passage through Siberia on the International Express could then be accomplished in relative comfort.

Though baths were not to be obtained, the travellers, being accommodated with two comfortable compartments in which to live and sleep and a well-furnished restaurant car in which to take their meals, had not much to complain of save the inevitable monotony of a train journey of seven thousand miles. For the Bryces, however, there were many means of mitigating the ennui of the Trans-siberian voyage. At that season of the year the wild flowers of Siberia are enchanting and at every stop of the train's progress through a brilliant profusion of willow herb, asters, golden rod, aconite, gentian, pinks, columbine, campanula, and campion, Bryce rushed out into the fields to botanise. But a more important diversion had been carefully planned some time in advance. Bryce had made up his mind that he must view the great snow range of the Altai Mountains, more than four hundred miles south of the railway, and tread the historic trade road which binds Russia with Western Mongolia. Such an enterprise involved no little contrivance and a good deal of hard travel. The comfortable international express had to be abandoned for a local train at Tauga, in order that they might reach Tomsk, the principal seat of government, to obtain the necessary permits. Here they attended a service in the Cathedral for the birthday of the Czarewich, at which all the officials and dignitaries in their uniforms and orders were present, and derived from the spectacle an impression of the curious vitality of the Imperial cult in Russia. Here too they obtained an interpreter for their southern voyage and the necessary official permits.

From Tomsk a day of train brought them to Novo-

Nicolaiewski; then followed two days pleasant sail up the broad and winding waters of the Obi to Barnaoul, another day on a smaller steamer to Birsk (a centre of the butter trade, and an emporium for the hides and wool which come over the mountains from Western Mongolia), and then "eight of the hardest days of travelling we have ever gone through." The skies were grey, cold, and forbidding, the roads abominable, the villages at which they slept or changed their horses, seas of mud almost to the knees. Rising early and getting in late, they drove forward in a jolting tarantass, with little to eat but eggs, black bread and tea and with many a risk of an unpleasant overturn in slippery or precipitous places. Late in the afternoon of August 22nd they reached the summit of the Semensky Pass (about 3,000 feet) and beheld unrolled before their eyes the great panorama of the Altai mountains with the high snows gleaming in the distance. This was the southernmost point of their excursion. Here everything spoke of central Asia and its wild primitive ways — the great flat uplands, the wandering Kalmuks in fur coats and caps, the round conical tents of the inhabitants, the herds of horses and cattle and dromedaries. They felt themselves back in the savage life of that early world against which, in the brilliant narrative of Herodotus, the fabric of Hellenic civilisation shines in such noble and effectual contrast. To buy such experience twelve hundred miles of rough travel by boat and tarantass is no excessive price.

The remaining stages of the journey were accomplished with relative expedition. In September the Russian cities are empty of notabilities and save for M. Rokovstoff the Prime Minister with whom Bryce had a conversation at St. Petersburg, no important people were drawn into contribution. At Königsberg the travellers stopped to salute the tombs of two very different incarnations of the Prussian spirit — Albrecht of Brandenburg, the last knight of the Teutonic Order, and Immanuel Kant. Prussians of a more modern type, such as Von Jägow the Foreign Minister, and Dr. Adolph Harnack the theologian and Herr von Gwinner the Chairman of the Deutsche Bank were interviewed in Berlin. All appeared to be peaceful, but what they had seen of Russia in a brief week aroused dark forebodings of impending evil. In the inhabitants of Russia proper they beheld a people presenting a melancholy contrast, whether as a result of serfdom or from some other cause, to "the cheerful and confident air" of the Siberians. They saw a Government, as reactionary as it dared to be, backed by the tyranny of the Orthodox Church. On the one hand they were sensible of an all-pervading system of police repression; on the other of vague and secret forces of discontent. What was, could not last. "When the revolution does come," wrote Mrs. Bryce in her diary (Sept. 6th, 1913) "one feels that it will be a wild torrent that will sweep away more than things evil."

CHAPTER XXVI

PALESTINE AND SYRIA

So Joshua took all that land, the hills, and all the south country, and all the land of Goschen, and the valley, and the plain, and the mountains of Israel, and the valley of the same.

JOSHUA xi, 16.

HARDLY had the Bryces returned to England, when they were again on their travels. This time the quest was Palestine and Syria, provinces still languishing under Turkish misrule, but offering to the student of Biblical and mediæval antiquities an incomparable wealth of historical interest. Bryce prepared himself for what he was to see by reading upon the voyage George Adam Smith's *Geography of Palestine* and the books of Numbers, Joshua, and Judges. The following letters will give to the reader an idea of his experience and impressions: —

Grand New Hotel,
Jerusalem.
April 4th, 1914.

Our passage from Port Said to Jaffa was fairly smooth and we landed there on April 2nd, and spent the forenoon rambling about the old seaport, on the beach on which Perseus rescued Andromeda from the sea monster, and where St. George, who was a native of Lydda hard by, killed the dragon, and where St. Peter had his vision; we saw the house but not the street of the vision, and where he raised Dorcas or Tabitha — we saw her grave. And from the tower of a church beside it we looked over the sites of the ruined cities of the Philistines, Ekron, Ashdod, Askelon. We have spent two days sightseeing in Jerusalem, the chief things being the Church of the Holy Sepulchre and the place where was the Temple of Solomon, and afterwards the temples of Nehemiah, and of Herod's building; and we have traversed many of the streets, narrow, irregular, dirty, crowded, of the city.

What is one to say of Jerusalem? Never have I been in an ancient city, whose history was so familiar, where I have found it so hard to call up and create as a reality the scenes of former times. Because the surroundings are unlike those of modern England or modern America, one thought that they might suggest the days of the Israelite kings or those of the New Testament. But the sight doesn't help at all. Samuel and David and Hezekiah, Christ and the Apostles, are clearer to one's imagination through the mind alone than they are when one tries to people these streets and hillsides with them. I can fancy the Crusaders attacking the walls of Jerusalem, I can even imagine the Empress Helena looking for the Cross, and Procopius coming up here from his native Caesarea, but I can't summon up a vision of Jesus and the disciples walking hither from Bethany; still less of the trial and the Crucifixion. This can hardly be because the City has been lately so modernised, and ugly suburbs stuck down all round it, incongruous even with the city. It must rather be because all these events and persons, from Abraham down to St. Paul, belong to an ideal world which cannot be fitted on to these actual hill slopes and ruined walls. To see them here would seem as strange as to meet an angel walking on the Bayswater Road.

Regarded as a real city, there is only one thing beautiful or striking about Jerusalem — the view across the Dead Sea valley to the mountains of Moab. That is splendid, solemn, mysterious, especially at sundown, when their bare slopes glow with purple and violet light. The nearer hills are featureless, except for the

The next letter is addressed to Bryce's Italian friend Professor Ugo Balzani, the historian.

Dampfer "Prinzregent Luitpold,"
Alexandria,
May 6th, 1914.

The moment of leisure on our homeward journey from Palestine gives me a long-desired chance of writing to you. We had always meant to make the pilgrimage, but were many times hindered by the difficulty of leaving England in April, so when at last delivered from the obligations of the House of Commons, we took the first opportunity. Better had it been to see Jerusalem long ago, before it had pushed out suburbs and covered the Mt. of Olives with obtrusive modern buildings, German and Russian and Franciscan. There is nothing ideal, little even that is poetical, in the aspect of the Holy City as it is now. Buildings so crowded on one another that they can hardly be seen, narrow and dirty streets, heaps of shapeless ruin and rubbish encumbering the open spaces, the brook Kedron dried up, the Valley of the Son of Hinnom defaced, a rude Muslim population making the environs dangerous for solitary walks, the place is not attractive for a long stay. Nor is it beautiful; save for the wonderful background of the purple mountains of Moab thirty-five miles away beyond the Dead Sea. They are the most solemn and mysterious curtain hung in front of the Arabian Desert to the East one can imagine; and in the evening it was hardly possible to turn one's eyes away from them.

The rest of the country is more enjoyable than Jerusalem. Very strange and grand is the Wilderness of Judæa, with the ancient Monastery of Mar Saba nestling in the rocky gorge where the lion shared the saint's cave in the days of Anastasius and Justinian. Very grand in its ruins is Samaria, looking forth from its hill top on ruined Caesarea by the sea, where Paul defended himself before Festus and whence Procopius went to be Secretary to Belisarius, with the heights of Carmel beyond on which Elijah strove against the prophets of Baal and prevailed. From the top of Mount Tabor we looked down on six famous battlefields, that where Barak overcame Sisera, that where Saul fell before the Philistines under Gilboa, that where Josiah succumbed to Pharaoh Necko at Megiddo, that where the Muslims wrested Syria from Heraclius, that where the Crusading kingdom of Jerusalem was destroyed by Saladin, that where Bonaparte smote the Turks in 1799.

Not even Italy seemed to me so full of history as Palestine. One treads on it at every step. Nazareth has suffered like Jerusalem, but the Lake of Galilee is unspoiled. We penetrated to Petra among its lovely rocks, and wondered at a city whose records have all perished, and where for fourteen centuries, except for a short occupation by the Crusaders, there have been no inhabitants but a few wretched Bedouin, huddled together with their goats and in the caves.

Often did we think of you and how much you would have enjoyed these historic sites.

All one's impressions as to the barbarism of the Turks and their government were confirmed. It seems no better now than it was under Selim I, or for the matter of that, than was the government of the Ommiyar Khalif or the Egyptian Sultans. Will they ever be better, and is it Islam or their racial defects that make them so hopelessly corrupt and incompetent?

Some ideas regarding the Roman Empire in the Sixth Century have come to me in studying the country and its ruins which may be helpful when, if ever, I get back to Justinian, taking up the long dropped threads. Alas, that our friends, Hodgkin and Creighton and Freeman are no longer here to write for us. You are now the only one of all our historical group on whose encouragement and criticism I can lean.

What are you now occupied on? How long it seems since we have looked on one another! May we hope that you and Nora will come to England this summer? Are you tempted to be a witness of that Civil War in County Antrim with which we are

camp, in the now nearly dry bed of a pool which the Crusaders made, is the spot where Jacob dreamed his dream, and where afterwards the golden calves were set up by Jeroboam, the son of Nebat, who made Israel to sin. From a hill just above this camp, we have seen at sunset the Mount of Olives and part of Jerusalem away to the South of us.

Camp life is pleasant in one way, that you feel deliciously free and that the air is sweet and fresh, and the breeze shaking the tent walls, if not too strong, is soothing. The drawback is the trouble of unpacking everything one needs every night and repacking next morning, all in the half light and with things strewn all about on beds and the small iron chairs provided. And in wet weather there would be little comfort at all.

Nazareth, April 14th. We have seen many more interesting spots these three days —among others the Well where Our Lord talked with the Woman of Samaria; Mts. Ebal, and Gerizim, Shiloh (where the child Samuel lived with Eli, serving the Tabernacle); Samaria, the palace of Ahab, and afterwards the stronghold of Herod; Jezreel, where Jehu killed Jezebel; En Dor, where Saul consulted the Witch; Gilboa, where Saul and Jonathan fell fighting against the Philistines, and other famous battle-fields nearby. But Nazareth is the one that most interested me, for there, at any rate, there are the hills on which the eyes of the Child rested, and over which He must many a time, as I did last night, have watched the evening star set. Unluckily, Nazareth has grown into a centre of pilgrims, for whom all sorts of fancied sites are provided — the room where Gabriel appeared to Mary; the workshop of Joseph; the synagogue where Our Lord taught. Even the Well where Mary may have gone to draw water, has, like those other spots, been covered by a church.

Damascus, April 26th.

Petra,
April 23rd, 1914.

You have often read of this strange city, with temples, tombs, and dwellings all hewn in the rock, and now all deserted for more than a thousand years. Nobody knows who first dwelt there; probably the Edomites, who refused leave to the Children of Israel to pass through as they were on their way to Canaan. The excavations to be seen now — or at least the more highly finished of the tombs and the temples — are attributed to the Nabotheans, an Arab people who ruled here from B.C. 250 to A.D. 100, and to the Romans, who thereafter held the place as the border fortress against the wild tribes of the Desert.

'Tis an extraordinary place, lying among savage rocks, and approached by a gorge a mile long and only eight yards wide, between tremendous precipices. The only inhabitants are a few wretched Bedouin huddled together in some of the caves.

We have spent three nights here in our tents, and are now leaving for Damascus. Having beds and food enough, we are quite comfortable, except for the cold. It has been chilly ever since we reached Palestine, except one day at the Dead Sea and Jericho, but the severest cold has been here, far South, where one expected to be scorched and have been frozen. However, we have both kept well so far, and yesterday we rode over the most unspeakable track I have ever seen — sheets of steep rock much of the way — up to near the top of Mount Hor, where Moses buried Aaron (see the Book of Numbers or Deuteronomy, I forget which) and saw his tomb on the top, venerated by Muslims, who call him Nebi Harun — the Prophet Aaron. The last few hundred feet were impossible even for these Desert horses, and we had to climb up a rock staircase.

Damascus, April 25th. We arrived in this ancient city, which was a city in Abraham's time, this afternoon, from Petra, through the Hauran, the great plateau East of the Jordan. Our Hotel is just over the rapid stream of the Abana, that river of Damascus "which Naaman, the Syrian, said was 'better than all the waters of Israel.' " It stands on the edge of the great Desert that stretches Eastward from here to the Persian Gulf, but round it are luxuriant gardens and orchards and cornfields, for the rivers that descend from the sunny ranges of Hermon and Anti Lebanon irrigate the soil, and make the spot an oasis

snowed, is the centre of every landscape, a glorious object, over 9,000 feet in height. See Psalm LXXXIX, 12.

Who was to replace the Turk in Palestine and Syria and to give to these unlucky regions a better chance? This question which was asked by Bryce in 1914 was answered after a surprising fashion five years later. The "dead lands," "*les terres mortes*," as they were termed by a gifted French writer, were to change masters and the Near East was on the brink of a revolution more far-reaching than any which had passed over its patient and poverty-stricken populations since the dazzling conquest of Alexander the Great.

CHAPTER XXVII

WAR AND PEACE

For nothing is so conducive to greatness of mind as the ability to examine systematically and honestly everything that meets us in life, and to regard these things always in such a way as to form a conception of the kind of universe they belong to, and of the use which the thing in question subserves in it; what value it has for the whole universe and what for man, citizen as he is of the highest state, of which all other states are but as households.

MARCUS AURELIUS.

IT is not strange that returning to England after an absence of more than six years in the United States, Bryce should have felt himself in an unfamiliar atmosphere. Outwardly things looked very much the same under George V as they appeared in the closing years of Edward VII. The Liberals were still in power, jaded, indeed, and harassed by years of close and anxious contention, but led with consummate skill by Mr. Asquith and commanding a majority adequate to all Parliamentary needs. Irish Home Rule remained the question of the day. The House of Lords, though recently deprived of its absolute veto in legislation, was still unreformed in composition and consequently open as before to the contention that it could be no efficient Second Chamber in a Democratic country. But beneath this show of continuity there were disconcerting changes, the force of which it was difficult to measure after so long an absence abroad, a new and unparalleled fierceness and violence of party feeling, threats of civil war in Ireland, a movement for woman suffrage supported by acts of lawless violence, an increase in the power of the Independent Labour party coupled with concessions to Socialistic doctrine (such as old age pensions and workman's insurance) by the Liberals, and, finally, a vague, uneasy feeling that all was not safe on the continent. New policies and new men were coming to the front. More ominous, an implacability of temper, common enough in Irish, but rare in English politics and alien to the English tradition, was evident among those who concerned themselves with public affairs.

"Our situation in England," Bryce writes to Lawrence Lowell, 17th June, 1914, "is not only interesting, but extraordinary, and I must add deplorable. Five years ago no one would have dreamed that such things were possible as the open advocacy of civil war and the toleration by Government of two armed and drilled bodies of men threatening one another. The situation is darker at this moment than it has yet been because the leaders on both sides are not in command of the position. Carson is believed to be uneasy at the point to which he has led his men and willing to enter into an arrangement but he dare not do it except upon terms which the Nationalists cannot be expected to accept. Redmond himself would, I believe, be willing to go a long way to meet Carson, and he would be right in doing so, because, from his point of view, the vital thing is to get the Home Rule Parliament established in Ireland, even if it only includes three-fourths of Ireland. The exclusion of Ulster could hardly be permanent. If the Home Rule Parliament works well, Ulster will come in. If it does not work well, the situation will somehow change, and the Imperial Parliament will again intervene. The sentiment of the Ulster volunteers is quite genuine, although their apprehensions of the increase of the power of the Roman Catholic Church or of any kind of religious persecution are absolutely groundless."

These disquieting symptoms in the public life of the country Bryce was now to view from the red benches of the House of Lords. He had been selected to head the New Year Honours for 1914.

For the title of Viscount he cared nothing, but a seat in the House of Lords, since it gave him an opportunity of expressing his mind on public affairs and kept him within the arena of politics, was now welcome. One letter of congratulation on the event and one only was characteristically preserved. "I made a pilgrimage," writes Sir J. B. Doherty, "in Ulster with Mr. Birrell about six weeks ago, and on our journey to my own native village about five miles to the south we passed Killaig. Mr. Birrell was greatly interested to see the Irish cradle of the race. In all that country the name of Bryce is still a household word, and the latest honour conferred on one of that name will give general pleasure to gentle and simple alike."[1]

Nobody who has lived through those days is ever likely to forget the terrible political anxieties of the spring and early summer of 1914. It seemed as if the fierce feud

[1] January 15th, 1914.

between Protestant Ulster and the Catholic South might involve the whole country in the unspeakable misery and humiliation of a civil war. Never had party feeling run so high. Ireland over-shadowed everything, even Mr. Lloyd George's Budget and Mr. Asquith's Parliament Act and the menacing perplexities of the European situation. "We have been passing through strange times," Bryce wrote to Elihu Root, "men (including ex-ministers of the Crown) talking of civil war as if it was a natural thing to look for in a constitutional country and as I write, the crisis is on us and no one knows to-night[1] whether the Amending Bill which we have been debating in the House of Lords may not fail and Tyrone and Fermanagh see collisions between two armies that ought never to have been allowed to be formed and drilled and armed."

The Bill to which Bryce makes allusion was one for the provisional exclusion of Ulster from the operation of the Home Rule Act. This measure Bryce supported as perhaps offering the only way out of a very difficult and dangerous situation. He did not profess to like the exclusion of Ulster, and his view was that the opposition between the North and the South of Ireland was not more fierce than had been the antagonism between Highlander and Lowlander in Scotland in earlier days, and that as the discords in Scotland had been happily appeased under the Union, so there was no reason to believe that Protestant and Catholic Irishmen would not, if once faced with the necessity of working together in an Irish Parliament, contrive to adjust their differences and to find much com-

[1] July 12th, 1914.

mon ground. That the fears of the North were honestly entertained, he had never questioned. He believed them, however, to be groundless, and that the power of the Roman Church so far from being strengthened would be likely to diminish under a system of Irish Home Rule. "As far back as 1886," he said to the House of Lords,[1] "I represented very strongly to Mr. Gladstone as I did again when the Bill of 1893 was brought in that Ulster constituted by far the gravest part of the Irish problem and that when all the other difficulties had been dealt with, the problem of dealing with Ulster would still remain. On that occasion Mr. Gladstone made an offer to the Protestants of Ulster to declare what provisions they would like in order to safeguard their interests and remove their apprehensions. That offer was not accepted." He felt, however, that the time had now come when a measure of exclusion, objectionable in many respects, might have to be accepted as a relief from imminent danger. He did not, however, contemplate a permanent partition of Ireland. The exclusion of Ulster should be provisional only.

A month after this speech was delivered the Irish question then so formidable and dominating had sunk into almost universal neglect. There burst upon Europe in Bryce's words, "the most tremendous and horrible calamity that has ever befallen mankind by mankind's own fault,"[2] and Ireland slipped into the dim background of the national consciousness or was remembered only as an incubus, happily removed, as the one bright spot in a dark horizon. Yet the Irish problem still remained. "Remember," said John Morley one evening in that first

[1] July 1st, 1914.

[2] Bryce to James Ford Rhodes, 1st July, 1914.

winter of the Great War at the conclusion of a discussion with Sir Edward Grey, "that there is a little island across St. George's Channel, her wounds unstaunched, her wrongs unremedied. She is waiting for you, and after the War you will hear of her."[1]

The outbreak of hostilities between Britain and Germany came to Bryce as a great shock. From early youth he had drunk deeply from the wells of German literature and German historical science, counting as one of the happiest recollections of his life those student days in Heidelberg, in that delightful, old, idealistic Germany, which had been so easy and hospitable and so intent upon the things which minister to the higher needs of man. Then as a young man he had made his literary reputation by a treatise on German history, which won for him a widening circle of friendships among German students, which he was careful and glad to preserve. Having been brought up in the strong anti-Louis-Napoleonic atmosphere of his generation, and being somewhat defective on the side of the French humanities, he was perhaps inclined to over-rate the specific contributions of the German genius to the literary culture of Europe. Moreover, though he was alive to the dangers of Prussian militarism he had always hoped and believed that the forces of moderation and good sense which he knew to be widely spread among the German people would prevail against the mania for violence. He was never, therefore, in the company of the alarmists. On the contrary, he believed that despite many conflicting interests, peace between Britain

[1] The reader may perhaps here forgive me for repeating words spoken in my hearing at a private party.

and Germany might be kept and should be kept. The rapid growth of the German Fleet which alarmed so many of his Liberal colleagues seemed to him to be not disproportionate to the vast expansion of the German commercial navy.

The invasion of Belgium brought Bryce into the War. Before, his judgment, always inclined to peaceful solutions, had hung in suspense, but the violation of a small and innocent country by a great Power expressly pledged to defend it, was so flagrant a transgression of elementary morality, that he saw no alternative but to fight and to fight to the end. With his immense experience of human history Bryce knew well enough how complicated is the web of international affairs and how difficult the task of justly appraising the moral claims of contending nations; but if ever there were a situation in which all the right appeared to be on one side and all the wrong on the other, here it was. Germany had signed a treaty and had broken it. Britain had signed the same treaty and must keep it. All his sentiment in favour of the rule of law and the rights of small nations was aroused by this manifest defiance of international right and morality. German militarism disclosed itself to him as the enemy of all that he valued most in European civilisation. His mind was clear that the war should continue until the Prussian system was decisively broken.

By a happy departure from precedent the task of moving and seconding the Address to the Crown in the House of Lords when Parliament met in November was entrusted not to a pair of young and inexperienced noblemen but to Lord Methuen, a distinguished Field Marshal, and to the Ambassador who had recently returned from Washington. Bryce's speech, in its breadth of outlook, strength and moral power was worthy of the solemn occasion. He began by commenting on the unprecedented unity of the nation, only to be explained by the fact that the war was a conflict of principles of universal application. We were fighting against the doctrine that Treaties might be broken whenever it was to the interest of the stronger Power to break them, against the doctrine that whatever is necessary becomes thereby permissible, against that terrible application of the doctrine which seizes innocent citizens and treats them (perhaps shoots them) as hostages for the good behaviour of others, whom they cannot control. Our quarrel was not so much with a people as with a system and with the military caste which had invented and was applying that system. Thence he passed on to pay an eloquent tribute to the courage of the forces of the Crown, to the loyalty of the Dominions and India and to the sympathy of the neutral countries. "Doubtless," he observed, "Your Lordships have received as I have done a stream of letters from eminent men of that nation which is nearest to us in blood and speech telling us how deep and wide is the sympathy which is felt for our cause there. The United States is not only a nation which is able from its high intelligence to judge wisely and well of questions such as this, but it is also sufficiently detached to be impartial, and it is upon moral grounds and large considerations affecting all mankind that those to whom I refer are giving us that moral support which we so highly prize." As for the Turk he was being hurled to his destruction and here Bryce drew upon the impressions which he had gathered from his recent visit to Palestine and Syria. "The fame of British Administration in Egypt has gone out over all neighbouring countries. There is many a Syrian peasant who envies the security and justice which the peasantry of Egypt receive under British rule." The speech closed upon two notes, the dangers of a patched up peace and the hope that after the war some machinery might be set up for the peaceful adjustment of international differences.

What was to be the attitude of the United States Government towards the war? Bryce realised that it could not be otherwise than one of neutrality, but was disappointed that no protest was made "against such a flagrant breach of public law as the invasion of Belgium." [1] He admitted that a Government of a neutral state could "not go entirely by its personal feelings" nor say all that it might think right, but neutral powers were, in his opinion, entitled to express opinions on "any backward step towards savagery," such as the violation of neutral territory or the destruction of non-combatant ships; and he was disturbed to think that no such pronouncement had been made by the Government of President Wilson.

He was eager, however, to assure his American friends of the general spirit of cordiality which prevailed in England towards the American nation. "I hope," he writes, "that the foolish utterances of a few organs in the English Press do not mislead your people into supposing that there is any general impatience here with your government's raising questions of contraband or the use of the flag; for that is not the case at all. Our people continue

[1] Bryce to Seth Low, February 5th, 1915.

to find great cheer and encouragement in the sympathy of the vast majority of your people and are grateful for the splendid liberality with which you have come to the help of Belgium."[1] It was however important that American opinion should be under no illusions as to the determination of Great Britain to persevere in the war. On this subject he wrote in the most explicit terms to President Wilson.

Sept. 24th, 1914.
Hindleap,
Forest Row,
Sussex.

My dear President,

May I say to you that so far as I have been able to collect their opinion, the wisest friends of peace on this side the Ocean think you were altogether right in not renewing at this moment your offer of mediation in this war? There would have been little or no chance that any of the contending parties would accept it; and the prospects of a successful issue to your intervention at a later moment might have been prejudiced.

The general feeling is — and though one of those who worked hard for peace up to the last I share it, — that any attempt to patch up a peace now could only lead to a sort of truce rather than peace, an uneasy respite during which preparations for renewing the struggle would go on, armaments growing larger and engines of destruction still more deadly. In this country the great desire is to get rid once for all of these huge fleets and armies.

We do continue to hope that a time may arrive, though it may be months distant — how many no one can conjecture — when an offer of mediation from you as the greatest and most respected neutral may be helpful.

[1] Bryce to Seth Low, February 10th, 1915.

In time of war it is easy to catch the contagion of the war spirit and not difficult entirely to repel it. What is less easy, and the sign of superiority, is to participate in the national sentiment and within the full measure of one's power to work for the success of the national cause during a war, and yet at one and the same time to be able to rise above the dust and din of the conflict and to view war in its universal relations. Bryce was capable of both attitudes. He accepted gladly such public tasks as were devolved upon him and lent his pen readily to the development of the British case before the tribunal of the neutral countries. At the same time he was able, as for instance in his two Presidential Addresses to the British Academy and in his Huxley address to the University of Birmingham in 1916 to direct his mind to the largest questions raised by the War. What is the relation of war to progress? What novel aspects of war are disclosed by the present struggle? How will population be affected in quality and quantity by the war? What influence does war exert on the behaviour of nations? Are the forces which work for peace likely to grow? Upon all these questions Bryce employed his large discursive intelligence, drawing instruction from the most unexpected sources, as for instance from the dispossession in Haiti of certain plants by plants whose seeds or seedlings have been brought from another country, and keeping his utterance clear of the passionate prepossession of the moment.

What he has said on the fundamental ethical issue will be disputed by the disciples of Treitschke and Bernhardi; but those, whose predilections incline them to the view that neither on biological nor on historical grounds is war proved to be a salutary tonic for humanity, will find the argument for their faith set forth with much balancing of evidence drawn from many quarters of knowledge and experience and great sobriety in the best of Bryce's war pieces,[1] the Birmingham Address on War and Human Progress.

Not long after the opening of hostilities a task was devolved upon him than which none could have been more repugnant to a man of his sensitive nature and political antecedents. He was invited by the Prime Minister to preside over a small committee of historians and jurists [2] "to consider and advise on the evidence collected on behalf of His Majesty's Government as to outrages alleged to have been committed by German troops during the present war, cases of alleged maltreatment of civilians in the invaded territories and breaches of the laws and established usages of war." The evidence to which allusion is made in the terms of reference to the Committee consisted of a large number of depositions (over twelve hundred) which had been taken down in England by men of legal knowledge and experience who had been directed to treat the evidence critically and as far as possible to satisfy themselves, by putting questions which arose out of the evidence, that the witnesses were speaking the truth. In addition to these depositions and to

[1] *War and Human Progress.* Essays and Addresses in Wartime.

[2] Other members of the Committee were Sir Frederick Pollock, K.C., Sir Edward Clarke, K.C., Sir Alfred Hopkinson, K.C., Mr. H. A. L. Fisher, and Mr. Harold Cox. Sir Kenelm E. Digby was appointed an additional member on the 22nd January 1915. The Committee was set up in September, 1914.

numerous statements collected in France from British soldiers by Professor J. H. Morgan, the Committee had before it a number of diaries (nearly a hundred) taken from the German dead as well as a collection of German proclamations.

It is my impression that Bryce approached this great body of evidence with a real hope and expectation that the Committee would be able if not to return a verdict of acquittal,[1] at any rate to reduce within a small compass the burden of the charge, but as it became clear that the lawyers who had taken the depositions had done their work well and carefully, that the depositions, though taken at different places and at different dates and by different lawyers often corroborated each other in a striking manner and were in many cases supported by the diaries taken from the dead, this hope vanished and he was confronted with the sad conviction that the cheerful estimate of human nature which had accompanied him through life was altogether too high, and that despite all the optimism of historical writing, with its laws of progress and advance of civilization, and tale of busy legislative improvement, there was still persistent in the European family the hateful appetite of the savage.

To some minds the Bryce Report gave pleasure, as supplying evidence of barbarities which might serve to steel the resolve of the Allied nations and to impress the uncertain and wavering conscience of the Neutrals.

[1] He had suggested to his American friends that it was desirable that a small Committee of U. S. A. citizens should investigate the alleged barbarities of the German troops. 'Only neutrals could investigate and report in a way to inspire confidence.' Bryce to Seth Low, September 25th, 1914 and November 4th, 1914.

himself during the ensuing years. He joined in the Autumn of 1914, a small group formed to promote a scheme for a League of Nations and entered into an active correspondence with a circle of eminent men in America, including Mr. Taft and Mr. Lawrence Lowell, who were occupied on a similar project.[1] Such activities were clearly to be distinguished from those of the Pacifists who were clamouring for an immediate cessation of the war without reckoning the political cost. With these Bryce had no sympathy. He saw that there could be no true peace in Europe until Germany had been thoroughly beaten and compelled to make restitution to France and Belgium. He set himself therefore to discourage the well-meaning efforts to promote mediation which during the early years of the war were so popular in the United States. His American friends were clearly and repeatedly told that mediation was out of the question, that the Allied Powers would not for a moment consider a patched up peace and that the war must proceed until they had accomplished their object. But such an attitude was quite consistent with the quiet and unadvertised prosecution of a scheme for the creation of a better international order when the last shot had been fired. Such a scheme was not lightly to be improvised. It involved large problems and raised a cloud of formidable difficulties. Preparatory labour

[1] The American League to enforce Peace was inaugurated at Philadelphia on June 17th 1915; at Mr. Taft's request Bryce wrote a letter to be read at a League dinner in New York 24th November, 1916. Bryce's group published in 1917 "Proposals for the Prevention of Future Wars." Their treatise was, together with other schemes considered by the Phillimore Committee (appointed Jan. 2, 1918) whose report furnished the basis for the Covenant of the League.

was, therefore, required. On August 8th, 1917, Bryce forwarded to the Government an influentially signed memorandum, with a covering letter to the Prime Minister from himself in which the suggestion was thrown out that the Government might set up a Committee upon which certain specially qualified persons from the United States of America might be invited to sit, with a view to a thorough examination of the project.

Lord Bryce to the Prime Minister:

"I feel sure you are in sympathy with the sentiment this letter expresses, and cannot but feel, speaking for myself, that a declaration by His Majesty's Government that it looked hopefully forward to the creation after the war of some machinery for the preservation of a permanent peace — a combination of free peace-loving nations — and was prepared to take practical steps in that direction, would have an excellent effect not only here and in America but also upon the mind of the Russian people. It might also do something to lead better sections of the German people to understand that we are carrying on this war in no selfish or vindictive spirit but for the sake of preventing aggression and strife in the future. I greatly hope that it may be found possible to say something in this sense.

"If it were previously ascertained by unofficial communications that the Unit d States Government would receive favourably a proposal officially made to them that a small committee consisting of competent persons be set up to examine the idea and the best means of giving effect to it, an invitation publicly addressed to that Government and favourably responded to by them to create such a committee would be accepted as a pledge that the matter would be taken out of the region of theory and with a desire to deal with it in a serious and practical way."

Though nothing came, by reason of President Wilson's opposition,[1] of the scheme for a joint Committee, Bryce's project did not fall upon deaf ears. "Your paper," wrote General Smuts, 27th October, 1917, "has been circulated in the Cabinet and the only delay in dealing with it is due to the feeling that the matter should be informally discussed with Colonel House on his arrival here before it is formally raised with the American Government. I need not say how strongly I personally approve your idea. The League of Nations may well prove the most beneficent and far-reaching result of this war; and the foundations of the idea and its practical application should be carefully explored in advance."

A new idea in proportion as it is fruitful and luciferous at once suggests to the mind a variety of modes in which it may be embodied. The men who were working on the project for a League of Nations in England and in the United States differed among themselves as to the particular form which the institution was to receive. The American League to enforce Peace of which Mr. Taft was President was all for strong military and economic sanctions to be applied automatically in cases of aggression and for that reason it failed to secure the concurrence of influential citizens like Mr. Root and President Nicholas Murray Butler.[2] There were again in England divergencies of view as to the extent and character of the sanctions

[1] Woodrow Wilson to T. Marburg, 6th May, 1918.

[2] Art. 3 of the platform of the American League to enforce Peace runs as follows: — The signatory Powers shall jointly use forthwith both their economic and military forces against any one of their members that goes to war, or commits acts of hostility against another of the signatories before any question arising shall be submitted as provided in the foregoing.

to be applied, the methods for securing disarmament, and the relation of the Council of Conciliation to the Government of the League.

The minute historian will compare with interest the conclusions published by Bryce as the result of these preliminary and informal discussions in England and America with the text of the Covenant which was ultimately embodied in the Treaties of Peace. It will be seen that the whole ground was thoroughly explored by Bryce and his friends, that the difficulties were examined, the alternative plans weighed and tested and that in its main features the structure of the League of Nations corresponds to the outline traced by Bryce in the last year of the War. The chief difference is one of important detail rather than of principle. Bryce thought that the League would require four organs for its action (*a*) a tribunal to arbitrate on justiceable matters, (*b*) a Council of Conciliation to enquire into and apply mediation on non-justiceable controversies, (*c*) a representative Conference or Congress to amend, develop and codify International law, and (*d*) an Executive authority to decide on the time and method of applying (and to supervise the application of) measures for compelling disputant States to submit to arbitration and to allow time for conciliation before resorting to hostilities. In the Covenant the Council of Conciliation and the Executive are fused. Otherwise, the structures are identical.[1]

There is much to be said for the plan favoured by

[1] Lord Phillimore compares Lord Bryce's "Proposals for the Prevention of Future Wars" revised up to 1917 with those of five other bodies which were engaged on a similar task. Phillimore, *Schemes for Maintaining General Peace*, 1920.

Bryce of a Council of Conciliation composed of representatives of the member States appointed for a term of years, and deliberating and voting freely, as members of a court of arbitral justice would do, upon the issues submitted to them. The members of such a Council, though alive to the views prevailing in their respective countries, would not be acting under instructions from home nor be regarded in any way as committing their Governments. It was to be expected, therefore, that they would act with a greater sense of freedom, and that their suggestions for compromise would be less likely to be affected by a consideration of the manner in which they would be viewed by the Foreign Office at home, and more likely to be acceptable to the contending parties, as coming from a body independent of any Government or group of Governments. The plan followed by the Covenant has the advantage of economy, but recent history raises the question whether a Council of Government delegates is ideally fitted to act as a Council of Conciliation.[1]

Meanwhile Bryce was clear in his own mind that the war must proceed. When on September 18th, 1917, M. Loudon, the Dutch Foreign Minister, a friend of old Washington days, approached him with the view of securing an unofficial and secret meeting between representative men of the leading belligerent countries, he thought it

[1] See Bryce, *Essays and Addresses in War-Time*, c. 8., and *International Relations*, lecture vii. Bryce drew attention to the work of the American League in a letter to the *Times*, October 27th, 1916. For a speech urging the Government to prepare plans for a League, cf. House of Lords Debates, 26th June, 1918. Bryce was also in communication with the League of The Nations Association, presided over by Mr. H. G. Wells, whose views were published in the *Atlantic Monthly*, January–February 1919.

right to communicate the overture to the British Foreign Secretary but told his correspondent that he concurred personally with Mr. Balfour's opinion that, in view of the unsatisfactory declarations of the German Government, no good could come of such a *démarche*.

In February of the succeeding year a similar approach was made from the same quarter. It was suggested on behalf of a Peace Society in Holland (Nederlandische Anti-Oorlog Raad) that a basis for negotiation might be found in a recent declaration of the German Reichstag and that the matter should be pursued in a private meeting to which certain members of the German Reichstag should be invited. To this overture Bryce sent a carefully reasoned refusal.

March 1918.

"I am not in a position to judge of the amount of authority over their respective parties in the Reichstag which the three leaders in that body, mentioned above, could exert; nor can I tell what power the Reichstag might be able to exercise over the action of the German Government in the direction of peace. But I must observe that the Reichstag Resolution of July 19th does not appear to have, so far, influenced the conduct of the German Government in the least degree. Its recent action in Russia is in the plainest contradiction to that policy of 'no annexations' and of the respect for the rights of other peoples which the Reichstag wished to proclaim. The German Government is now dismembering Russia, and endeavouring to carve out of what have been parts of Russian territory new small States, which will obviously be mere vassals or subjects of Germany, and Austria; and its last act has been to annex to Turkey, by the treaty which it has extorted from the Russian Bolsheviks, a large part of Transcaucasia, inhabited by Christians, who are to be handed over to those who have recently perpetrated the Armenian massacres.

After such action, what weight can be attached to the Reichstag Resolution of July, or to any professions made by the German Government?

Both I, and the distinguished friend whom I consulted,[1] desire to see an end of this war, and the terrible sufferings it has brought, as earnestly as any German or Englishman can do. But we feel, with everyone else in England, that the necessary preliminary to any negotiations must be an unreserved declaration by the German Government that it not only withdraws from Belgium, but abandons all claims to any sort of control over Belgium and undertakes to compensate her people for what they have been made to suffer. Without such a declaration it is useless to begin to think of discussing terms of peace. We are still awaiting it, but it does not come."

Ever since the Turks entered the war, the fate of the Christian populations under the Crescent and more particularly in Asiatic Turkey had been for Bryce a matter of most profound concern. At first little was known. The cloud of war came down upon Asia Minor and obscured from Western eyes the happenings in the Anatolian highlands and beyond. Then in the summer of 1915, accounts began to come through, scanty at first but increasing in volume later, which seemed to indicate that a massacre of Christians on a scale unprecedented even in the blood-stained annals of the East was in progress or had been already brought to its premeditated conclusion by the extermination, without distinction of age or sex, of the whole Armenian population.[2]

By the beginning of 1916 it became possible to form a

[1] Lord Lansdowne.

[2] House of Lords Debates, 28th July, 1915.

fairly accurate idea of what had happened. It then struck Bryce, who, as we have seen, had been ever since he voyaged in Transcaucasia in 1876, unremitting in his exertions for the relief and protection of the Armenian race, that in the interests of historic truth as well as with an eye to the questions which might arise when the war came to an end, it would be well to complete and test the evidence with a view to the compilation of a general narrative which might stand critical examination. "As materials were wanting or scanty in respect of some localities," he says, "I wrote to all the persons I could think of likely to possess or to be able to procure trustworthy data, begging them to favour me with such data. I addressed myself in particular to friends in the United States, a country which has long had intimate relations with the Eastern Christians and to which many of those Christians have in recent years emigrated. Similar requests were made to Switzerland, also a neutral country, many of whose people have taken a lively interest in the welfare of the Armenians."[1] When the responses had been received, the material was handed over for examination, arrangement, and comment to a distinguished young historian, Mr. Arnold Toynbee. The result was a bulky volume[2] published in the autumn of 1916 to which Bryce contributed a brief preface dealing with the credibility of the evidence collected.

The story of the attempted deportation of the Armenian race from their historic homelands to Mesopotamia

[1] Viscount Bryce to Viscount Grey of Fallodon, July 1st, 1916.

[2] *The Treatment of the Armenians in the Ottoman Empire, 1915–16.* Documents presented to Viscount Grey of Fallodon by Viscount Bryce. Misc. No. 31 (1916).

and of the massacres and cruelties by which it was accompanied constitutes one of the most terrible chapters in recorded history. Bryce was concerned to establish the facts: but he was still more interested in the moral to be drawn from them.

"European travellers," he writes, "have often commended the honesty and kindliness of the Turkish peasantry and our soldiers have said that they are fair fighters. Against them I have nothing to say, and will even add that I have known individual Turkish officials who impressed me as men of honesty and good will. But the record of the rulers of Turkey for the last two or three centuries, from the Sultan on his throne to the district Mutessarif, is, taken as a whole, an almost unbroken record of corruption, of injustice, of an oppression which often rises into hideous cruelty. The young Turks, when they deposed Abdul-el-Hamid, came forward as the apostles of freedom, promising equal rights and equal treatment to all Ottoman subjects. The facts here recorded show how that promise was kept. Can anyone still continue to hope that the evils of such a government are curable? Or does the evidence contained in this volume furnish the most terrible and convincing proof that it can no longer be permitted to rule over subjects of a different faith?"

The hopes which Bryce conceived were destined to be disappointed. Had the great alliance held together until the peace of the Near East had been secured, something might have been done for the miserable remnant of the Christian populations of Asia Minor: but one by one the Great Powers, who had brought about the defeat of the

German Armies, wearied of the dragging contest in the East. First the United States held aloof, then Italy, then France, and with the demoralization of the Greek army and the recapture of Smyrna by the Turks, Britain was left alone threatening the enemy and in a position to beat him to his knees. The British nation, however, was also weary of war. There was a sudden change of Government, and at the Treaty of Lausanne, concluded in 1922, the cause of Armenia, despite the dreadful history of the massacres and all the eloquence of Lord Curzon, was finally abandoned to the wolves.

Bryce did not live to see the Treaty, but he lived long enough to realise that nothing effectual could be done for the establishment of an independent Armenian State. To the numerous speeches in which with unremitting and devoted persistency he raised the question of Armenia and of the Nestorian and Assyrian Christians in the House of Lords there was always the reply that the British army was already fully employed elsewhere and that no troops could be spared for the policing of the Armenian districts. In point of fact Great Britain was in 1919 shielding a hundred and fifty thousand Armenian refugees from utter starvation and employing nearly a million men in the task of pacifying various portions of the Ottoman Empire.[1] More could hardly be expected. It was a sufficiently onerous task to police and to organise the liberated regions of Iraq and Palestine. Failing help from the United States or from France, it was almost inevitable that the remote homelands of Armenia should be left to their fate.

[1] House of Lords Debates, 20th February, 1919.

On laying down his office in Washington, Bryce had been appointed to succeed Sir Edward Fry as British representative on the International Court of the Hague. After the events of 1914 the profession of international lawyer was not particularly encouraging. Almost every canon which had been established in his sacred texts was now held in open scorn. A solemn treaty had been broken, a neutral territory had been invaded, the white flag had been fired on, poison gas had been used, the civilian population of an invaded territory had been terrorised and oppressed. What, it might be asked, is the use of international law, if under the temptation of war it is openly and persistently flouted? Bryce's American friends were anxious to obtain a new codification of International Law. It was more important to secure its observance.

One of the conclusions which Bryce drew from the responsibilities which he had recently assumed at the Hague was the desirability of a visit to the Front. The British representative on an International court who might hereafter be concerned with the codification of international law and might be required to form an opinion as to what old rules should be rejected as impracticable and what new rules accepted as beneficial, should clearly know something of modern war. He must see the fleet at its war station and he must visit the armies in the field. Nor would such experience be indifferent to the historian who intended to devote some part of his declining years to a study of the age of Belisarius and Narses.

Of the many pilgrims who crossed the Channel to visit the trenches in France, few surely were more remarkable than this veteran of seventy-eight years, who had preserved into extreme old age the brilliant curiosity and active bodily habits of early manhood. And though the visit had in itself small importance, his behaviour under the strange conditions and searching tests of actual war is so characteristic as to justify a brief description.

He crossed to Boulogne on 28th July, 1916 and motored to Amiens, where he spent the night with Colonel Wilson, the head of the Press Branch of the Intelligence Department. There he met a number of Press men and censors and learnt much of the methods by which censorship of news is exercised in modern war. The next morning he set off with Colonel John Buchan and Mr. C. E. Montague for the front by way of Albert, Pozières and "Windmill Hill," which enabled him to visit the German trenches and the "dug-outs" which had been evacuated about a week previously. Stopping for tea with Sir Henry Rawlinson at the headquarters of the Fourth Army, he expressed a desire to see Ypres. The general discouraged the visit and described the place as "very unhealthy." Nevertheless, once clear of Headquarters he proceeded with Mr. Montague to Ypres and though the German aeroplanes were circling overhead and the town was deserted save for a few British troops he had the great satisfaction of seeing on the spot the concentrated results of German artillery fire. The night was spent at General Headquarters as the guest of Sir Douglas Haig. The central machine of the British army was here inspected at close range and much interesting information collected from members of the Staff.

On the 30th of July he left for Calais, where he was shown the great repair shops and the vast organisation for clothing and feeding the Armies. The order and efficiency which everywhere prevailed made a deep impression on his mind.

"I remember," writes Col. Buchan,[1] "that during the Battle of the Somme I took him into the ruins of Contalmaison the day after it had been occupied by the British troops. The place was being shelled with fair regularity by the enemy, and we ate our luncheon with crumps falling unpleasantly near. I am certain that he had never in all his adventures been mixed up in a battle before, and the situation might have produced in him a more emotional temper than it did. For all he said, as he calmly watched the adjacent shell bursts was that, as soon as I thought it safe, he would like to measure the holes they made. It was characteristic of the man for his first interest was in concrete facts."

The two letters which follow give his impressions of the war zone.

Amiens,
July 28th, 1916.

"You will have got a Post Card from Boulogne written this morning. Thereafter at 2.25 P.M., I started in a motor, General Delmar Radcliffe whom I had met long ago and who introduced himself to me on the boat, Mr. Beck (the American lawyer) and his son and Harry Brittain following in another car. The day was lovely — brilliant sun with white clouds, fresh easterly breeze, the country beautifully green, undulating, mostly cornfields, wheat and oats, ripening to harvest, with woods interspersed, soft meadows along the clear swift streams in the valleys — a church tower or a château rising here and there among the trees. All silent, scarcely a human creature on the roads or at work in the fields: only a few women and children in the villages whose shops were mostly closed. It was as if one were in a land bewitched whence the inhabitants had been all spirited away.

[1] Oxford Magazine, March 1st, 1923.

At Boulogne no sound of guns, but a distant booming when we got within about fourteen miles of the front at a place called Beauquesne, where we halted and had tea with General Charteris, head of the Intelligence Department, a big, cheery Scotchman. Lots of troops round here, filling all the peasants' houses. The whole country seems English: it is the spoken tongue, the road directions 'Dead slow,' 'No passage for lorries' etc., all in English. Hence at 7 p.m. we dashed along at a tearing pace to Amiens where I was received by Colonel Wilson, head of the Press Branch of the Intelligence Dept., and have been dining with him and some of the press men and censors under his direction, including a representative of the 'Morning Post' named Irvine, whose father was a constituent of ours in Aberdeen, and a *Times* man named Robinson who came to see us in Washington, and Frederick Palmer, a well-known American correspondent. From all these I have been picking up many facts. Our losses very heavy during last three weeks, as you know: but spirit excellent and hopeful. The bright weather now is in our favour as it enables air-scouting. Our air control distinctly superior. Strange to see sweet peaceful landscapes, and warm sunshine over the wheat, with terrific scenes of death so near. Surely the world has gone mad."

General Headquarters,
British Army in the Feld.
July 29th, 1916.

"Impossible to tell you half of what I have seen to-day and how what is seen explains what one has been reading of. You know how much more one learns through the eyes.

"After breakfast and a look into the Cathedral at Amiens I started at 9.50, with the ubiquitous John Buchan and Mr. Montague, (C. P. Scott's son-in-law) for the front. Day fine, hot, hazy, but clear blue sky. Eighteen kilometres to Albert, a small town half knocked to pieces by German shells. A mile beyond it we got out of the car and walked across fields ploughed up —

or rather, deeply pitted by German high explosive shells to the top of a long swell of the ground whence we saw all the field of recent fighting. On the left, four miles off, Pozières which we recently stormed, and the Windmill height, just beyond which a fierce and unsuccessful fight went on last night. Machine guns too much for the Australians. It is the nearest point still held by the Germans. From their batteries further back, shells were flying towards us with a singing rush — the high explosives striking the ground and sending up a thick cloud of black smoke, while the shrapnel shells burst in the air, sometimes with a white cloud like steam, sometimes with darker smoke. The nearest fell about half a mile or so from us, some perhaps less. We were easily within their range, but they were not aiming at where we were, so we walked on further till we reached the first line of German trenches from which they were driven out a week or two ago, and entered some of their deep 'dug-outs' and saw one prodigious hollow, a Crater, 400 yards round and 70 ft. deep — bigger than some of the extinct craters of Auckland or Auvergne. Hard by, one of our own batteries was firing heavy shells at German batteries invisible on the distant slopes. The guns on each side, it seems, scarcely ever see one another. All are located by aeroplane, and now we have complete mastery in the air. All to-day I have spent partly walking, partly in covered motor, for the sun is very strong, but I don't feel a bit tired to-night. When at the General Headquarters I am the guest of Sir Douglas Haig, with whom are several Generals and other officers, besides that still more ubiquitous Esher, who seems to be located in Paris on some mysterious mission and comes running up and down here. I had tea at the headquarters of the Fourth Army with Sir Henry Rawlinson, a very agreeable man, in a charming park and château. There is general hopefulness — he and the Commander-in-Chief both seeming to believe that the Germans are now getting to their last legs, with few reserves, and doubting — even their officer prisoners — whether they can escape defeat. Our men are in very good heart, and not, it seems, really ferocious to the individual German. On Sunday, the

30th, I start for Calais, via Ypres, and hope to cross by Monday's boat."

During the first three years of the War the British Government, in addition to all the patent dangers which assailed the Empire was besieged by an anxiety, the full nature of which was carefully concealed from the public eye. Our relations with the State Department at Washington were far from easy, for the enforcement of the Naval Blockade against Germany necessarily interfered with the commerce of neutral countries and raised in a new, and indeed in an aggravated form, most of the questions which had contributed to bring about a War between Britain and the United States in 1812. Among the "trade advisers" of the Department at Washington a conviction had sprung up that Britain was aiming through the blockade at the destruction of American commerce, and this feeling of suspicion was fanned into a white heat of indignation when it was known in America that under the "black list" of our Ministry of Blockade vessels accepting the cargoes of more than a thousand exporting houses in the United States would be denied bunker coal in British ports. The isolation of President Wilson, the strength of German influence in Washington, the defective appreciation of the European issue by Mr. Bryan and Mr. Lansing, who in turn occupied the post of Secretary of State, the clamorous activity of the firms on the black list, contributed to make a situation full of dangerous possibilities.

Readers of the *Life and Letters of Walter H. Page* will not need to be reminded of the valiant efforts of the American Ambassador in London to procure a better understanding between London and Washington or of the assistance which he received from Sir Edward Grey. They will recall the feeling almost akin to despair which came over Mr. Page as proof after proof accumulated that the lawyers who were controlling the State Department at Washington had not only lost sight of the great moral perspective of the quarrel but were wholly out of touch with the sentiments and sympathies of the leading men in their own country. For Bryce too these were times of great sadness and anxiety. He was constantly at the American Embassy and endeavoured by correspondence with his American friends to present the situation as he saw it and to smooth away the difficulties which arose out of the enforcement of the blockade. When more than a year and a half after the sinking of the Lusitania the President (December 18th, 1916) issued a peace note to the Warring Powers, in which he appeared to draw no distinction between the aims of the combatants, saying that "each side desires to make the rights and privileges of weak peoples and small States as secure against aggression and denial in the future as the rights and privileges of the great and powerful states now at war," Bryce was moved to write a personal letter of protest to Mr. Wilson. On another occasion in a mood of depression he said to Mr. Page that he almost despaired of the possibility of two nations ever understanding one another.

From the first he had faintly hoped that America might enter the war, but that hope soon vanished. A well-informed correspondent writing from Washington warned him that Britain must rely on her own right arm and that alone.

Trust not for freedom to the Franks
They have a king who buys and sells
In native swords and native ranks
'Tis there alone that Freedom dwells.

That there was a strong feeling in favour of intervention, especially after the sinking of the Lusitania, Bryce did not doubt, but under the American system that feeling had no means of effecting a change in the Administration until the Presidential term had run its course, and meanwhile much mischief might ensue. "Has not" he asks, 8th August, 1915, "the time now come when your Government ought to take a very firm stand against Germany's war methods, which are nothing less than a challenge to civilization? Wilson's Notes have been clear and good. But you can't sit down and see yourselves flouted. It is not a question of dignity, but of duty to humanity. The Turks have for the last few months been deliberately exterminating the Christian population of Armenia, massacring the men of full age, driving the elders, the women and the children from their homes into the deserts to perish from want. The Germans are, according to the accounts we receive, encouraging this policy. We in Western Europe can do nothing. It is just possible that a strong remonstrance from you — the greatest of the neutrals, with no interest except that of humanity, you who have done so much by men like Washburn, Bliss and Hamlin for the Turkish East — might have some effect in checking this horrible annihilation of an ancient people suffering for having cherished its nationality and preserved its religion."

The letters which Bryce addressed to his American

friends during the early years of the War were naturally inspired by the desire to communicate to them something of the sentiments and ideals of his own people and to smooth away possible sources of misunderstanding and friction. He enlarges upon the magnificent response to the call for Volunteers, upon the courage and patriotism of the young, upon the national resolution to persevere in a struggle involving such deep moral issues, upon the futility of premature peace talk, upon the indifference of the British population to air-raids, upon cotton and contraband and the freedom of the seas, upon a possible League of Nations, and a possible reform of International Law. Could not the President advance further and faster? Was not resentment expressed at the numerous outrages to which the American people were subjected? "As to W. W.'s European War policy," he writes "my conception has been that he is really pro-Ally but afraid to move any faster or farther than he feels sure that the country is prepared to go. That is prudent but could not the country follow further, if he led with more vigour? Surely the outrageous conduct of the Germans in blowing up manufactories and placing explosive bombs in vessels, with other defiances of the laws of the United States will move the Administration to deal more firmly than they have done with German agents up to the German embassy!" To this sentiment he recurs again and again. "We are beginning — his (Wilson's) friends included — to be surprised at the extreme leniency extended to outrages by German sympathisers."

To an old Academic friend like Charles Eliot he can communicate his sentiments on fundamental questions of national ethics.

3, Buckingham Gate, S. W.
June 25, 1915.

The question of the moral effects of war occupies one very much at this moment. There is doubtless an ennobling of the individual who from high motives offers his life for his country. What more can a man do? There is a stimulation of national consciousness, perhaps of highstrung sentiment, among some of the civil population at home. Both these we see. But how far the bulk of the civil population are really raised morally, and how long the moral elevation of those who fight continues are more difficult questions. It used to seem to me that the best of your young men who went through your Civil War were the better for it through their lives, but they were not a majority of those who fought, and it seemed doubtful whether the momentary moral elevation given to the nation as a whole lasted long. Certainly politics in the United States generally were at a lower moral level, and business methods also, in 1870 than they are now after fifty years of peace. These impressions, of course, are only the reflection of what I have gathered from you and others in America. I should like to know if you agree.

One point of similarity your Civil War has to this one. Had the curse of Slavery prevailed, all moral ideas would have been sadly set back, not to speak of political ideals. So now if Germany were to succeed, the sense of right and the sentiments of common humanity would receive a terrible blow from the success of her inhuman methods. This is what makes some of us here feel that we must fight till Germany is beaten. It is not revenge we want, it is to save the principles of justice and humanity. You have given now, as before, a clear note on this. Let us hope that the President will not recede from his position. Would that we could talk over these and much else, with the waves, murmuring on the rocks below your house to us, as in 1911. Our love to you both.

We have just lost a nephew in the Dardanelles, a bright and promising young fellow. There is not a household that is not so suffering.

CHAPTER XXVIII

AMERICA GOES TO WAR

Hark I hear the tramp of thousands
And of armed men the hum
Lo! a nation's host have gathered
Round the quick alarming drum
Saying come
Freemen come
'Ere your heritage be wasted' said the quick alarming drum.
WALT WHITMAN.

A FEW words may fitly here be said about Bryce's relation to President Wilson. They were old acquaintances rather than close friends. From time to time they had corresponded on academic questions (Bryce for instance had been consulted as to the choice of a professor in Political Science at Princeton in 1899), and Wilson had entertained him on the occasion of his visit to the University in 1907. But it was natural that, with a Republican Government in power during almost the whole period of his ambassadorial career, Bryce should have seen little of the Democratic academician. Any apprehensions, however, which he may have entertained with regard to the incoming President were swept away by his courageous handling of the Panama Tolls question. 'I cannot,' Bryce wrote, 'deny myself the pleasure of saying to you how much I admire your speech on the Panama Tolls question. Whatever happens, that stands as the experience of the finest kind of American feeling. It is just as John Bright would have put any similar question here, and he was, of all our statesmen, the one in whom the sense of moral obligation always found expression in the simplest and noblest words.'[1] And when the Canal Tolls Exemption Repeal Bill was formally passed, against the combined forces of monopolists and mischief-makers, Bryce wrote a hearty letter of congratulation to the President. 'Such a victory has a moral value reaching far beyond this particular case, and is the more valuable because the worst elements in the press seem to have excited themselves more virulently than ever before. Eighteen months ago, I told my Government at home that I believed you would carry this because the best sentiment of the nation would respond to an appeal issuing from you as its head. It is a satisfaction to me, who love your people, to see that this has happened.'[2]

Equally, or perhaps even more satisfactory, was the President's declaration in favour of a League of Nations in which America should participate. 'The lead you have given,' he wrote in a letter congratulating the President on his re-election,[3] 'is invaluable, and we are most grateful. Here we cannot yet start a public movement in that direction, for the conduct of this war absorbs all thoughts, but we are walking quietly in the direction you indicate.' Nor was Bryce disposed to pass a severe verdict upon the President's handling of the International situation. He was disappointed, as we have seen, that the President did not protest against the invasion of Belgium, that he

[1] March 6th, 1914. [2] June 19th, 1914. [3] Nov. 16th, 1916.

did not move more swiftly, that he showed so little signs of actively resenting the insults and injuries put upon his country by the German method of conducting the war. But knowing America well, he appreciated the President's difficulties, greater, as he thought, than any which had confronted an American President since the days of Lincoln, and was not disposed to be censorious.

It may readily, then, be imagined that, when the United States finally decided to come into the war on the side of the Allies, there was no happier man in Britain than Bryce. That the two branches of the English-speaking world should be thus auspiciously reunited in a great campaign for international justice was a compensation for many of the sorrows and hardships of the time. Moreover, in Bryce's view, the action now taken by President Wilson in bringing his country into the war expressed the real America. "There are," he said, "three things which are especially dear to the American heart. One of these is freedom; the second is International Law and practice; the third is tenderness and compassion for innocence and suffering." [1] A way was now cleared for the satisfaction of all three congenial impulses.

Two letters to American friends, the first written in anticipation of America's entry into the war and the second on the receipt of the news, may here be printed.

To Mr. Theodore Roosevelt

March 21st 1917.
3, Buckingham Gate, S. W.

From what I can gather it is all but certain that within the next three weeks and probably before this reaches you there

[1] House of Lords Debates, April 18, 1917.

will be a state of war between the United States and Germany. Needless to tell you this has long seemed to me practically unavoidable, and desirable in the interests of mankind, desirable for reasons reaching far above the interests of the present Allied belligerents.

The moral effect of the appearance in the War Line of an American force would be immense not merely as showing the German people that their cause is hopeless but by emphasizing the fact that their detestable inhuman methods have arrayed against them the conscience of the world.

I have been trying by letter and pamphlets to make neutrals in Switzerland and in your western States realise these supreme moral issues. Needless to say how grateful we all are to you for your incessant activity in this direction. May success crown them! If America is to fight she will, we trust, fight 'not only with hands but with hatchets also.' (It was an ancient Greek saying.)

To Mr. Bayard Henry

Ap. 5. 1917.

I was just writing to you to congratulate you both on this grateful decision when your cablegram reached me. Thank you for it. We have thought much of you and of the suspense in which you have been kept. If this long patience has had the effect of giving the German Government more rope to hang itself with and making your people more unanimous, and united in the resolve to prosecute this war with all possible energy, it will not have been in vain. At present we rejoice to believe that it is not going to be a war of half-measures and limited liability. War is one of those things that if done at all ought to be done with all one's might. Your action will, we trust, shorten by many months the world's sufferings. Personally I hope you will send an expeditionary force to Europe. Small it may have to be, at least at first, but it will help to make the German Government feel it can't win and the German people hate a Government which has aroused the whole world against them. Moreover it will keep the spirit of your people higher and stronger if they know their own flag is seen on the battlefields of Europe in a *righteous* cause. That is the thing to be constantly impressed on your people now. A Righteous Cause, in which the interests not only of freedom but of humanity itself are involved. For nothing less would it be right for you to fight here.

Our naval authorities still regard the submarine peril as serious, but we expect to pull through. Send us, however, all the food ships you can, and that quickly. We have some hopes that the entrance of the U. S. A. and the fall of the Russian autocracy will weaken the resistance of Germany, because the people will more and more withdraw support from the Government, recognizing that it has brought universal condemnation on them. I have tried to express this in several answers to newspaper enquiries. These you may have seen in your press.

A wider range of political topics is disclosed in the ensuing batch of letters to American friends.

To President Lowell

Hindleap,
Forest Row,
Sussex.
8th, April 1917.

Much has indeed happened since I last wrote, much even since you wrote yours of March 13th, though once Bernstorff had been dismissed it was pretty clear that war would follow. It seems to me that it was quite as well there should not have been during Febuary and March any Englishmen in the United States who could be accused of propagandizing. But I also feel that though now everything seems to be going as well as we could wish, for your people are throwing themselves with characteristic spirit into the war, moments may arrive when an exchange of ideas as to the settlement after the war, and as to the nature of a scheme of permanent peace, could be facilitated by visits from some of you here or by similar visits to you from some of us here.

Meantime, as to the League of Peace propaganda. I agree with your views (1) that the entrance of the United States into the war is a great step forward, for your people, associated with the Allies in defeating the common enemy of peace and in effecting a settlement of the war issues, will find it natural to join in measures to prevent the recurrence of wars. (2) That the principal thing now is to impress upon your people now the general principle of a permanent machinery for enforcing peace, and the necessity of America's co-operation therein. (3) That the settlement of the details of such machinery must be left to practical statesmen.

This I have always felt, and have told our British fellow-workers that the use of our schemes is not to provide the machinery that will ultimately be adopted, but to shew that the idea is capable of being put into a practical shape, and also to fix public attention on the difficulties that will arise, so that there may be profitable discussions of these difficulties, and the best means of overcoming them, to this your scheme and ours may usefully contribute.

As soon as your coming into the war was announced, it seemed that the moment for publishing our scheme had arrived, so it is being sent to the leading Liberal newspaper, and I will send you a copy of it (with Preface and introduction) as soon as it appears in a separate form. Paper is scarce and printing slow in these days, but I hope it will be very soon in type.

I entirely agree also with what you say as to the obligation to declare war. It is really no more a difficulty with Congress than with a European Government. Neither a Cabinet nor a Parliament can be compelled by a Treaty to declare war. All that can be undertaken is a moral obligation which an honest Government will try to fulfil when the time comes. It would be in the power of any Government to withdraw from an offensive and defensive alliance if the circumstances had so changed as to justify it in honour for doing so, and to announce that withdrawal beforehand. The real difficulty rather is — How far does the moral obligation go? *i.e.* Suppose two of the Powers refuse to fulfill the joint obligation, does it subsist in full force for the rest? All these are difficulties which need not at this stage prevent us from advocating the principle.

The permanent executive body seems to me of less importance than the Council of Conciliation, which is, of course an experiment.

Mr. Elihu Root

House of Lords
May 12, 1917.

Uncertainty as to where to find you has kept me from writing sooner to tell you how great an impression was made here by your speech urging a complete suspension of all political differences for the sake of a vigorous prosecution of the War. I wish we had done so here more completely — for despite Coalition Governments there has been an eye too frequently on other aims.

I am sorry to have troubled you about your letter in reference to Ireland, but the occasion seemed to justify it. The 'Times' newspaper had heard from its correspondent that you had replied to its request for a message by saying you had written to me — and thereupon it asked me if I would not let it publish your letter. I told it that your letter as a whole was clearly not meant for publication, but that if they got your leave for me to publish the few lines relating to Ireland there would be no objection on my part to complying with their request, for those lines were true and weighty. They did make an impression here, but our Administration, though admitting the extreme urgency of the problem seem unable to find a means of reconciling the adverse pretensions of the two parties in Ireland. The situation there is still bad, and (I fear) not improving. Every sensible Englishman is prepared to do almost anything to bring about peace and goodwill there. The trouble is that there are three hostile parties in Ireland itself — and the Government hesitates to compel submission to its own plan.

As today's paper states again positively that you are going to

Russia, I will say a word about the persons whom you will see there that are personally known to me.

Baron Rosen you will remember from Washington as an open-minded and honest man. He was recently removed from the Council of the Empire (by the Czar's advisers) as too liberal. Miliukoff impressed me when he was here a year ago as a sensible, firm, and clear-headed man.

Our English working men who are now starting for Petrograd are good fellows, not remarkable personally, but straight. Our Ambassador is not brilliant, but has lots of good sense and knew how to stand well with the Liberals while not offending the Government. We all respect and trust him. I wish you a safe and pleasant journey and trust to see you here on your way back.

To Dr. Charles W. Eliot

Hindleap,
Forest Row,
Sussex.
July 16, 1917.

Your letters are never too long; all they contain is of interest to me and sets me thinking. Would that I could answer you by a typewriter, but here, in this remote clearing in an ancient forest, that luxury is unattainable. I come here as often as possible, to escape the incessant interruptions of London, which make progress with my book impossible. Longer would I write and oftener had I learnt in my youth to typewrite, but when it was discovered, I was already too old.

Talking of age, think of Albert Dicey writing a book about Wordsworth! To be sure it is about Wordsworth as a political thinker, but it is full of quotations from the poems. It is a good reading, and I hope you will read it.

Your view that Germany will not yield to the United States until she has been quite defeated seems to me correct. Her argument was that before you could do anything effective the submarines would have finished us. Whether her rulers ever believed this, who can say? They thought it good enough for their people. They have set their backs to the wall and will fight like wild cats, for they know that if they are beaten, the military caste rule, and perhaps the dynasty, are done for. Since that is the only thing that will give the world a chance of tranquillity, we must fight till we win it, as you admirably pointed out to the Baptists. But the loss of Russia, for some months at least, is such a blow that it is only your coming into the war that will save us. France is at a very low ebb. There have been perilous moments of which I may speak more freely to you later. Italy has kept two hundred thousand Austrians employed — that is all. The brunt would have been sustained practically by England were you not now our Allies. Your people seem to have risen splendidly to emergency. It is a pity that ten thousand of your troops had not marched through London. What a welcome they would have had. Every means ought to be taken of cementing the Alliance for the future by the exchange of sympathy.

What you say about Duncan who has gone to Russia greatly interests me. From what we hear of the wildness of those who dominate Petrograd, men intoxicated with new ideas, living in an atmosphere of dreams and vague phrases, one fears that the wisdom of Root and the childlike geniality of Charles Crane would be thrown away upon them. But a practical sturdy labour leader may have a chance.

Nothing so remarkable as the Russian revolution has happened in our time. Never before has Socialism and Anarchism — opposites mixed together — had its chance of governing. Never have the educated and responsible persons been left so completely out, for in France 1791–94 the leaders were nearly all men of education and some experience of affairs, at least as lawyers, like Robespierre and Fouquier-Tinville.

I do not substantially differ from what you say as to an army upon the Swiss model in the United States; but I feel as if one can hardly decide whether such an army will be needed either by you or by us till we see whether this war may not end in a destruction of the military and aggressive spirit in Germany as well as of her military power. Should such a happy result follow, would it not be difficult to get your people and ours to consent to the maintenance of such a national army when the need for it had apparently vanished? The Swiss have had to maintain theirs because they live between three powerful military States. Many of us have always cherished among our dreams of a future the beating of swords into pruning hooks.

As respects the British Labour Unions, there has been a good deal of trouble with them, and (July 31) on one occasion lately a sudden strike cost us two hundred aeroplanes that were badly wanted. But it is alleged, and perhaps with truth, that the government departments, while putting the workers under almost military rule, have allowed the employers to make undue profits, and not to put up the wages to correspond with the rise in prices. I don't quite know how to judge between the opposing views; and most people here seem to judge according to their preconceived ideas. But you are right in saying that what has happened tells against limitation of production and the "closed shop." Most of us always pressed that, but the unions stuck to it, in Australia even more than in England. We expect a pretty bad time between Labour and Capital after the War, and have no confidence in the capacity of this — or perhaps any — Government to deal with the question.

You in the United States seem to me in a sounder state politically than you were when Dicey and I spent soft sweet October days with you in Cambridge forty-seven years ago. But we in England have not improved our Parliaments and our statesmanship, though the people are better fed and housed; and Government is worse in France than it was forty years ago. Progress is not uniform. The moral decadence of Germany has disclosed depths of wickedness in human nature we did not believe in. I rejoice to hear that you think your press improving. Ours which was the best in Europe has been sinking rapidly, and has done more harm in this war than ever before. It is a public danger, as yours would be if Hearst and his methods ruled.

Our troops have been enlisted "for the term of the war." What will happen afterwards no one knows. We don't talk about it. Everything will depend on how the war ends. If we disband, it will be slowly; and the Swiss system is quite a possibility. What weighs upon those who allow themselves to think — they are but few — is how we are ever to bear the load of a debt which is already £5,000,000,000. The interest upon it alone will far exceed our whole revenue before the war. But the habit of extravagance has demoralized us, and there is no attempt to check the universal waste. I trust you, though so much richer, will escape this evil.

How I should like to have a few quiet days with you like those we used to have to talk over what these three years have taught us in our old age, while the fresh sea breeze stirs among your trees and the water laps upon the rocks below. Shall we ever have refreshing talks together again there or here?

House of Lords,
July 20th, 1917.

President Lowell

Your people are more than justifying all that the lovers of America have ever said of what she could achieve, and of the spirit she would shew when she entered the war. It is splendid.

The meeting which we held here on May 14th to commend to our people the idea of your League to enforce Peace had an unexpected success. The way it was received, with hardly a note of censure even from Jingo quarters marks a change in British opinion. We are now considering what further steps can be taken to get the government to take up the matter practically. All this we owe to you. But for our being able to appeal to America's sentiment, she being now our ally, the movement would have been discredited as "pacifist."

I gather that at present your League is resting on its oars, pending the preparations you are making to join in the offensive in France.

Dicey has written a striking book called "The Statesmanship of Wordsworth." Read it for its application of W's teachings to the present war.

The phenomena of Russia are without precedent in history, for in France from 1791 till 1799 there was always an authority with a fair legal title, however much power may have been really exercised by irresponsible hands. No large country ever seems to have gone so far and for so long in pure anarchy. It is to be hoped that Root will give us a perspicuous and philosophical view of such an amazing situation. Apparently the Russians have adopted the silly saying: "The way to cure democratic evils is by more democracy."

President Lowell

Hindleap,
Forest Row,
Sussex.
13th, Sept. 1917.

Very divergent accounts reach us as to the sentiment among your people about the war. Some say there is heartiness and vigour, others that the average citizen is still cold. On the whole Wilson would seem to be doing well. His despatches and speeches have been sound in principle and often forcibly expressed. The growth of "Labour" and socialism both here and in France is one of the chief, and least expected, results of the war. As to Russia, its phenomena are even stranger than those of 1789–99.

President Lowell

3 Buckingham Gate, S.W.,
14th, December, 1917.

I hear you are having a new Constitution with Referendum and Initiative. Does it make other great changes — the Initiative in Mass. amazes me — and how far is the influence of the Irish felt in it? What is the explanation of the grant of Woman's

Suffrage in New York, and the refusal in Ohio? A United States correspondent suggests that there may have been a deal with Tammany, an idea which had not occurred to me. From many quarters I hear the warmest commendations of what Harvard has been doing and an ascription to you of most of what it has done.

You will have to come here as soon as the war is over for a new edition of your book. The whirl of change here requires another letter to itself — nothing like it since 1688. Indeed the upsetting of old ideas and habits has gone farther than in that unrevolutionary Revolution.

The last letter touches upon a topic of more than passing interest.

Among the many currents of thought and action which were quickened in Britain by the impetus of the war not the least notable was the movement for constitutional reform. An ambitious measure for widening the Parliamentary Franchise and extending it to women was passed with little opposition through both Houses in 1917 and in the following year the Reform of the House of Lords was taken in hand. Here was a question which a few years before excited fiery passions and still seemed to be a matter of urgency. How, in a democratic country, could an hereditary Chamber, albeit distinguished for personal eminence, pretend to possess the necessary measure of authority wherewith to arrest rash proposals pressed upon it by the popular House? The majority of the House of Lords, the "Backwoodsmen" as they were called, notoriously took little interest in the current business. Pheasants, foxes, and partridges, ploughlands and grasslands, Quarter Sessions and Petty Sessions were more their affair. On great occasions they would be whipped up to vote against popular measures and to secure to the aristocratic Chamber its permanent and overwhelming majority of Conservatives. If they did not watch the business, they could be relied on to vote upon it provided that the occasion was sufficiently important. Moreover under the operation of the Parliament Act, passed by Mr. Asquith's Government, the Lords' veto on legislation, formerly absolute, was now only suspensory, so that the Second Chamber, already weakened by the faulty principle on which it was based, was definitely placed in a situation of statutory inferiority to the House of Commons. Most Conservatives and many Liberals thought that this state of things should not continue, and that the abeyance of party strife during the war offered a happy opportunity for the solution of the problem.

A Joint Conference was accordingly set up, consisting of Peers and Commoners of every shade of political opinion to report on the reform of the Second Chamber. Of this Bryce, as the leading constitutional authority in the country, was not unnaturally appointed to be Chairman. The work involved was considerable, "as heavy," he writes, "as that of a department." The selection and assessment of evidence, the examination of witnesses, the adjustment of differences between members of the Conference and the discovery of lines of agreement where so many varying plans were both possible and plausible, finally the drafting of the Report, all these tasks called for tact, agility, and experience. But though onerous the work was thoroughly congenial. Bryce had long meditated over the Second Chamber problem and was fully conversant with the practice in other lands. Moreover he was of opinion that Second Chambers should be strong and not weak, and that the only source of real strength in modern times was to be derived from election. That the British Second Chamber should be elected in part if not in entirety and that it should, when reconstituted on this more popular basis, be delivered from the shackles of the Parliament Act was part of his creed. But how and in what proportion was it to be elected? And what were to be its relations to the Lower House? These were delicate questions which had to be explored.

That a Report should have been issued from the Conference at all was a surprise to many of its members, who during the opening stages of its deliberations were principally impressed by the wide, and, as they feared, hopeless divergence of their opinions; and the result may fitly be regarded a tribute to the skill of Bryce's Chairmanship. It is also an indication of the difficulties of the subject that the Report took the unusual form of a personal letter from the Chairman to the Prime Minister indicating the arguments used for and against those of the proposals which were most controversial. The essential features of the plan were that the Second Chamber should be reduced in size and recruited as to 246 members by persons elected by members of the House of Commons grouped in territorial areas and as to 81 members by a joint standing committee of both Houses, that the members of the Second Chamber should be elected for twelve years, one-third to retire every four years, that differences between the two Houses should be settled by the method of joint conference and that the question as to whether a

Bill was or was not a money Bill should be determined by a small Committee of both Houses with the Speaker in the Chair and voting instead of as now by the Speaker alone.[1]

The plan was ingenious, the letter in which it was recommended was skilful and instructive but there was very little steam behind the movement. In the Conference itself almost everyone believed that in one respect or another he could have improved the draft. "We had fifty sittings,"[2] said Lord Burnham, "and we presented a Report. In regard to the main body of the Report we were mostly agreed, but I think that all who subscribed to it were conscious in the end that they did so with many questionings and not a few reservations." In the House of Lords itself the appetite for suicide was very feeble. Lord Burnham could find only five or six Peers who professed that they even wanted the plan discussed in the House. Bryce, however, continued to urge, and all in vain, that action should be taken on the Report. He wished a Second Chamber as strong as the French Senate of which he said that he never found any French statesman or publicist who did not think it a valuable and indeed an indispensable part of their machinery, and he believed that such a body could be procured on the lines of his Report.

These hopes were frustrated. Seven years have passed since the issue of the Bryce letter; the House of Lords is still unreformed; the Parliament Act remains on the

[1] Conference on the Reform of the Second Chamber. Letter of Viscount Bryce to the Prime Minister, Cd. 9038, 1918.

[2] Really 48.

Statute Book, divested by the mere efflux of time of many of its pristine terrors, and in the judgment of many wise Tories providing a substantial and adequate bulwark against popular unwisdom. But for one circumstance the problem of remodelling the Second Chamber and of readjusting its relations to the Lower House, which seemed so urgent especially to Conservatives a few years ago, would appear to admit of indefinite postponement. That circumstance is the certainty that the Labour Party will at no distant date again be called upon to govern the country. A Second Chamber in which there are no genuine representatives of the Party supporting the Government of the day would be a real menace to Constitutional stability. Something, then, must be done soon to transform our picturesque, weak, aristocratic, anomalous Second Chamber, and when the moment comes, the Bryce letter, with its clear analysis of the problem to be solved, and of alternative methods of solution, will be disinterred from its pigeon-hole and serve, if not as a basis for action, as a magazine of the knowledge and reasoning appropriate to the case.

When that time comes, it may be worth recalling that the scheme of the Second Chamber Conference did not have Bryce's complete personal agreement. "Along with several of the most experienced members I preferred the plan of having the Second Chamber filled by the choice of a carefully composed Committee of both Houses, to the plan of having the large majority chosen by members of the House of Commons. But it appeared in the course of our discussions that the former plan could not have been carried in the Conference, and members of the House of Commons declared that it would never have been accepted by that House."[1]

The autumn of 1917 was darkened by many anxieties, by successive manifestations of the revolutionary spirit in Russia, each fiercer and more sinister than the last, by huge losses at sea through the submarine warfare, and by the increasing strain upon the Allied armies on the Western Front. Bryce's letters to his American friends during this period show that he maintained a sanguine temper and the old insatiable curiosity as to events and tendencies.

Mr. Elihu Root

Hindleap,
Forest Row,
Sussex.
Sept, 15, 1917.

We were heartily glad to hear you had got back safely from Russia, though disappointed not to have a glimpse of you here on your way. No account of your mission and hardly anything about what you said in the United States on your return has appeared in our press, so I will ask you to be kind enough to direct a copy of the Report when it appears to be sent to me. Apart altogether from the importance to our cause of the concentration of Russian effort on the prosecution of the war, the phenomena of the Russian revolution are of the highest possible interest. Has anarchy, the want of all legitimate, legally grounded authority, and of any means of empowering any commands, save by the casual exercise of force on the part of someone who can get men with rifles to obey him, ever before lasted for seven months, and that with, apparently, comparatively little bloodshed or robbery? Did not the Duma make a mistake when it allowed power and the semblance of

[1] Bryce to Lawrence Lowell, 5th Sept. 1918.

authority to slip into the hands of a self-constituted body like the Council of Workmen and Soldiers, or the Soviet? Or was the Duma powerless because coerced by the revolted soldiers? We have had no connected and intelligible account presented to us either of the revolutionary movement in its origin, or of the men who direct it, or of the means by which they prevail.

I should be glad to know what you think, now that you are back, of the progress in America of the idea embodied in the League to Enforce Peace, and whether your own view regarding America's participation has been altered by your entrance into the War.

I may say, *in confidence*, that recently sixteen of us, including some very leading figures in the political and ecclesiastical world, suggested to this Government that it might be well for them to approach the United States Administration with a proposal that it and we should appoint a small Joint Commission to examine the idea, in case there was reason to believe that the President would be disposed to accept such a proposal. We think that if he were, such joint action by the United States and England would have a good effect not only at home but abroad possibly even on the more reasonable spirits in Germany.

Mr. Theodore Roosevelt

October 25, 1917.

We hear that your sons are going to the Front in France. If they pass through England, or come across on leave to England, I trust they will let us know, that we may see them again and put them in touch with some people in England they would like to know and who would like to know them.

It is so long since I have heard from you and so much has happened in the meantime that all the things we used to exchange ideas about a year ago seem like the snow of 1916. I wish you were in the war in France, for I know what your presence there would mean to your troops and how it would be welcomed by ours. I wish also that the American troops were alongside ours instead of divided by a piece of French front. Far more would be accomplished for the common cause by an onrush side by side making a big hole in the German lines which would compel them to fall back in the N. W. and deliver most of Belgium. It is said that the French are jealous. I don't know; there may be other reasons.

Things seem rather better in Russia, according to what people just returned thence tell us: we must (it is feared) write them off for the next eight months: and the issue will have been decided by then. Our people keep well together and stick to their job. Every air murder would stiffen them if they needed stiffening. We have had moments of anxiety about some of our Allies, but their recent success will cheer the French, as America coming in did when they were so deeply depressed last spring. Politics in France are a sorry business, but how finely the people have risen to their duty! Shifty and intriguing politicians don't represent what is best in a nation, nor do much to pervert or enfeeble it. That is some comfort in days when the world needs comfort, after the hideous spectacle of German degeneracy, moral degeneracy. Otherwise what wonderful force! *Now* what is most needed is to exert every effort to shorten the war by convincing the German Government that it must be ultimately defeated. Two steps seem specially useful. One, which I think you have already urged, and which certainly you will favour, is the dispatch of an American force to the theatre of war. The Front in France is perhaps the most obvious region, but if active operations continue in Palestine, there are political reasons which you can easily divine, why an American corps d'armée operating in Syria would have much to commend it.

The other step is to help us and France to meet the submarine danger both by setting more destroyers to hunt out these German pests, and by utilizing German ships, well armed, in United States ports to bring cargoes of food to French and English ports. Nothing would do more to convince the German Government that this last hope of theirs will fail. We believe it is failing; still, the danger is a serious one. Once it is overcome, nothing remains for them.

To my great regret I missed seeing Leonard Wood when he passed through. It seems odd that he is not permanently employed in France, after all his experience. We are much touched by Pershing's action in brigading your troops with ours and the French; and hope that your men and ours will get to know one another in a way helpful not only for the present but for the future also.

Sunday March 23rd was an anxious day here. One could *feel* the unspoken anxiety — I felt it, invisible, so to speak, in the Temple Church. But our people kept perfectly calm: no note of alarm.

Here in Europe, both in France and in Britain, great political changes are expected to follow the war. Socialism in France, 'Labourism,' which is mostly Socialism, in England, have gained strength such as to give them a possible majority in each legislature if not immediately, yet very soon. At the same moment we have the spectacle of the hideous breakdown of an attempted democracy in Russia, where, according to the evidence of those who have recently returned hither thence, anarchy is at last producing its natural fruit in crimes, disorder, and complete demoralization. Of course anarchy never lasts long, but the "Saviour of Society," whoever he may be, is not yet visible over the horizon. There is now nobody in Russia with any legal right whatever to authority, these Councils and Soviets are practically all self-appointed. Half of them are said to be pro-Germans, mostly rogues — the rest crack-brained enthusiasts intoxicated with high-sounding phrases.

I gather that in the United States labour troubles are feared after the war. Otherwise your sky seems much less cloudy than that of Europe. Indeed America is the only country in which political conditions seem to have slowly but steadily improved during the last fifty years — a comforting thought for those of us who feel that their time for observing the ebbs and flows of human society is drawing to a close.

Our warmest regards to your wife. I trust you and she are both well, and get good news of the boys who are in the thick of it.

Mr. Henry Holt

3, Buckingham Gate, S.W.,

14th December, 1917.

There are so many things that I should like to say to you and ask you that I must confine myself to a very brief statement or two. The first is, what is the meaning of the carrying of Woman's Suffrage in New York? Is there any foundation for the story that it identified itself with a deal with Tammany; and to what do you ascribe the success of Tammany itself? Is there a back-sliding on the part of the less earnest citizens, or is it due to the split of the good citizens by the running of a Republican candidate against Mayor Mitchel? Here it is impossible to learn the truth about any of these matters.

The other thing I want to say is, that you are not to suppose that there is any serious pacifist movement in England. All classes, with a few exceptions, chiefly among the extreme socialists, are still united and steady in the resolution to prosecute the war.

As regards the question about human nature to which you advert in your last letter, I do not venture to say more than this, that five years ago nobody supposed that civilised modern human nature was capable of the series of hellish crimes which Germany has perpetrated in the conduct of the war. I do not make this an impeachment of human nature in general, any more than I should think that the physical condition of mankind at large had deteriorated, because a violent epidemic had broken out in one country and carried off a great many people there. Germany seems to have been the victim of a disease, and we hope it will pass away and perfect health be restored; only it shows that terrible diseases may occasionally affect a great and civilised nation, or, at least, its ruling class, because I do not attribute these crimes to the German people as a whole.

and at one moment it seemed as if the French and British armies might be cut apart and Paris fall to the invaders. Then in July came a counterblow, prepared by three events of great importance, the unification of the military command under Marshal Foch, a remarkable development of tank warfare, and the successful transportation of a young and fresh American army across the Atlantic largely by British ships. A steady succession of shattering blows, beginning on July 18th and delivered with admirable constancy and force by the British, French, and American armies, drove the Germans across the Hindenburg line and completely reversed the fortunes of war. On November 11th the German Government, conscious of unquestionable military defeat and besieged by the spectre of want and revolution at home signed an armistice which in fact placed them at the mercy of their enemies. The completeness of the victory was staggering and such as few observers, however skilled, could have predicted from the situation in the early summer.

All through this year Bryce was closely engaged upon a book on Modern Democracies of which more will be said hereafter, working sometimes at his pleasant flat in Buckingham Gate which was so convenient a station for the House of Lords, but more often, and with greater satisfaction, among the quiet delights of his Sussex home. As the War seemed to be nearing its conclusion he began to revolve possible terms of peace. It seemed to him that there were some objects essential to be secured and others fit for adjustment by give and take bargaining. His list of indispensable conditions was short and characteristic — absolute independence and adequate compensation

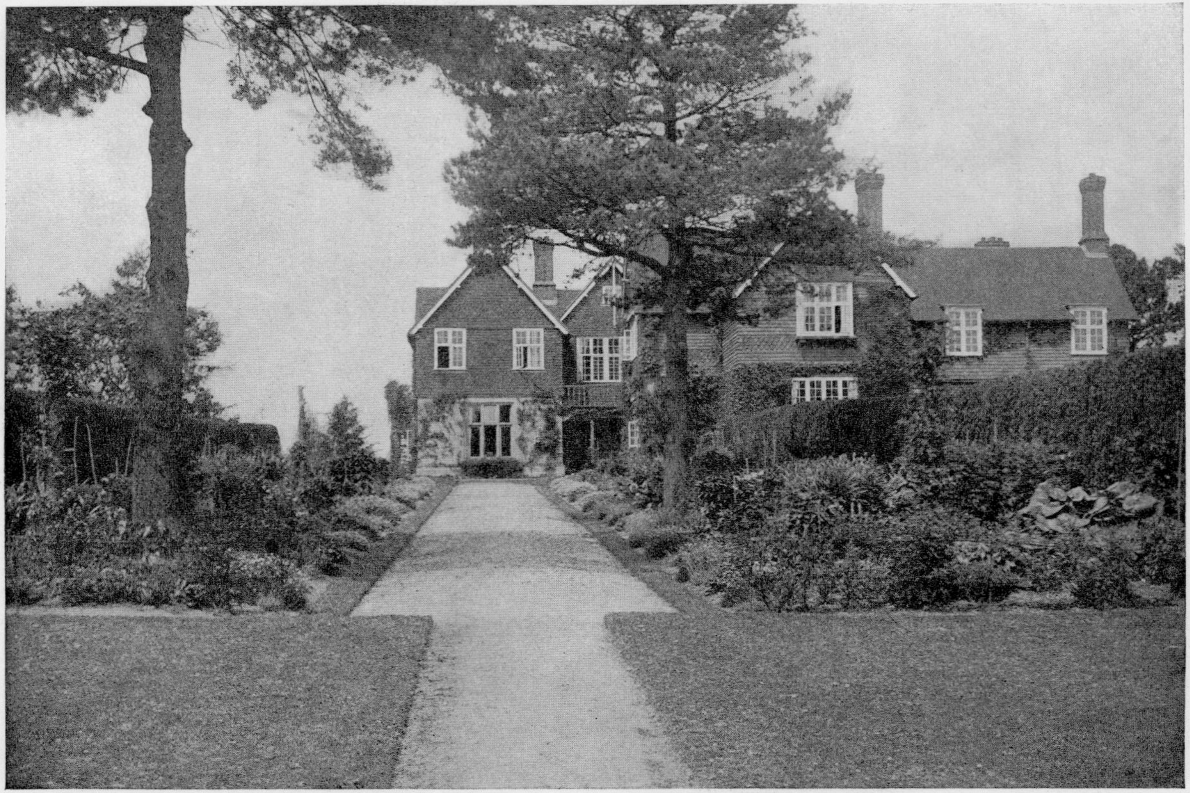

"Hindleap", Lord Bryce's Home in Sussex

for Belgium, the Trentino for Italy, and the liberation of the Caucasus, Armenia, and Syria from the Turk. Matters so important as Alsace-Lorraine, Poland, Bohemia, the German Colonies, Jugo-Slavia, and Constantinople, he was willing to leave to negotiation.[1] These at least were impressions formed before the fortunes of war had declared themselves and while it was yet thought improbable in many well-informed quarters that Germany would cede on the point of Alsace-Lorraine. To Bryce and to many other observers the completeness of the Allied victory in November came as an entire surprise.

That the tremendous anxieties of this fateful year should have weighed heavily on the mind of an old English Liberal is not surprising. There are in Bryce's correspondence during this period many signs of melancholy and disappointment, but these feelings are relieved by the irrepressible thirst for new knowledge and the desire to help forward a sounder and better international order which was part of his invincible optimism. Whence, he asks, springs the delay and confusion in American military preparations? Why has Massachusetts, of all places, adopted the Referendum? What is Mr. Root's position in the Peace League? And there is the great question of the Peace Settlement which must do "full justice to Freedom and the claims of nationalities," and thereafter the formation of a League of Nations, problems upon which Bryce abounds in writing to his American friends. Above all is the United States exhorted "to take a very strong line against the Turk and to insist that whatever else happens, he shall no longer have any power over any 'Christians.'"

[1] Bryce to Lord Lansdowne, August 3rd, 1918.

To Mr. M. Storey

3 Buckingham Gate, S.W.,
18th, January 1918.

Thank you for yours of December 26th. Our regular Government has been, practically, suspended. There is no Cabinet Government in the old sense of the word. There are a number of Departments, each going its own way, and a so-called War Cabinet, which is too much occupied with the war and the emergencies of the moment to think problems out, and lay down consistent lines of action. When there has been so much confusion in a small country like this, no wonder that there was chaos on a larger scale in an immense country like yours, confronted constantly by absolutely new problems. When in Washington, I was struck by the rarity of men of first-rate administrative capacity, or even of much scientific administration, perhaps in part due to the old Spoils System and all that it involved. It is not true that emergencies always bring able men to the top. That depends, partly, upon the proper schemes for promotion, and partly upon the capacity of judging men possessed by those with whom the power of promotion lies; and yet nothing makes so much difference to the efficiency of a country as the thinking power and energy of the twenty men at the top. One Bonaparte is, for administrative purposes, more than equal to one hundred fairly capable heads of departments.

To Dr. Charles W. Eliot

3 Buckingham Gate, S.W.,
8th February 1918.

Our winter has been the most melancholy since the war began. The collapse of Russia has seemed to throw back the day of victory into an unpredictable distance, making military success doubtful or, at any rate, long delayed. In fact the best chance seems to lie in the growing discontent of the German people, against which, if it should increase, even the iron hand of the military caste may not for ever prevail. We are constantly here threatened with fresh strikes and other labour troubles, and seem to live from hand to mouth in pacifying one burst of unrest after another. Nevertheless, there is very little of overt pacifism. Our people have come to feel that a peace without victory would offer no security for the future.

To Mr. M. Storey

3 Buckingham Gate, S.W.,
8th, Feb. 1918.

You will like to hear something as to how things are going with us. There has been, of course, and still is, great discouragement owing to the total collapse of Russia, which has had the further effect of relieving the blockade upon Germany, from which so much had been hoped. But against this we set the prospect of the action to be taken by American troops within the next six or eight months. The moral effect of that action ought to be very great in convincing the German people that they never can win when the Allies have been reinforced by a new country of your illimitable resources. Everything, therefore, will depend upon the spirit of our three nations, and at present the French seem likely to stand firm, as we feel quite sure your people will do. I should like to know how far you think the delay and confusion which is said to have shown itself in the preparations for war in the United States is due to the unsatisfactory condition which the "Spoils System" must have produced in the rank and file of the Administrative Departments? One had hoped that owing to the reforms of the last thirty years, the efficiency of that rank and file had been greatly raised, but it may be that it was, nevertheless, quite unequal to the strain which the outbreak of war has put upon it.

To Mr. Theodore Roosevelt

Hindleap,
Forest Row,
Sussex.
April 6th, 1918.

We were delighted to receive, two days ago, a letter from your wife — pray give her my best thanks for it — telling us that you had quite recovered from the attack which had caused some anxiety to your friends here. You have a splendid constitution to have triumphed over both bullets and tropical fevers.

Is it you whom I have to thank for a copy of the Metropolitan Magazine containing an article by you on social relations, and the honourable character of service? It seemed to me to put the thing on exactly the right line and I wish it were published here in Europe, where it is probably more needed than in America. Your army ways are excellent. So in France equality does not hamper discipline in the army, nor in Switzerland. We are in this respect better now than formerly.

How you must be now wishing, those of you who foresaw that the United States could not avoid coming into the war, that preparations had begun in 1915, when the Lusitania was sunk! What would it have meant to have had a million of American soldiers now in the field in France! However, already the moral support is enormous, and the material support will grow from week to week.

I need not tell you how well the shock is being borne; before this reaches you something decisive may have happened. Edward Grey was with me a week ago; his eyes are no worse, but he has not been well, though happily better now; he lives among his birds and squirrels in Northumberland and has not appeared in Parliament for months.

Here we are deeply grieved at the death of Cecil Spring Rice, just when an evening of peace seemed to be before him after the sultry day of his time at Washington. A hard time it must have been, though when he occasionally wrote to me he never complained. He seemed to me to have shown great dignity and self-restraint. I wonder if it is true that the Administration wished to have Rufus Isaacs as his successor. Of course the post is far easier now, and public speeches are in order.

To Mr. Theodore Roosevelt

April 17th, 1918.

Best thanks for your very interesting letter which has crossed one I wrote to you some ten days ago. We are much concerned to hear that Archie has been wounded, and trust that he is making a good recovery. I congratulate you and his Mother heartily on the Croix de Guerre conferred on him.

The anxiety over the battle in Flanders continues acute as the villages and ridges in the line are lost and retaken from day to day. Two years ago I was all over this bit of ground between Bethune and Ypres; and have been able to realise the danger if our advanced position at Ypres became untenable; but doubtless arrangements have been made for withdrawal should it become necessary. Our men seem to have maintained the old British valour and tenacity. As you may suppose the situation in Ireland has harried us. The successive governments have not dealt wisely with it ever since the war began: but indulgence must be extended to those who have had so many difficulties to handle at once.

Your Maine address is most interesting. All you say about the need for the melting pot to melt, and the efforts to be made for the economic reconstruction and better feeling between classes after the war is most true and reasonable. There may be some Bolshevism even in England, possibly, though less so, even in America.

It rejoices me to know that the Republican party has done its duty so heartily and in so non-partisan a spirit. This ought to be responded to by non-partisanship in all appointments made by the Administration.

You will have been pleased to see how completely Lichnowski exonerates Edward Grey. His absence is a great loss to our politics; but he still needs rest. Not all of us have your constitution and energy.

You refer in your address to the end of the war. I wish you would indicate what you think can be done then to avert the recurrence of such another calamity. Britain, France, and Italy can't go on supporting gigantic armaments; we are almost beggared already. Something must be done for common safety.

To President Lowell

3 Buckingham Gate, S.W.,
1st, March 1918.

Thank you for your letter of Feb. 11th. It is a real disappointment to me to be unable to accept the invitation to come to the United States, the finest part of which would have been to have stayed with you, as you invite me to do, and radiate out from Cambridge on visits for League of Peace purposes, but I am bound to stay here to do whatever can be done for carrying out, if possible, the Second Chamber proposals of our Conference. That is the first and directest duty.

What you tell me about the volunteering of the Harvard students is one of the most remarkable things I have heard, and shows more strongly than anything else the whole hearted entrance of America's best into the world movements of Europe and the East.

Of the Referendum I may say, in strict confidence, that our Conference appears to be hopelessly divided. On the whole I am with you in thinking it undesirable for England, and a weapon which might become dangerous in the hands of such a democracy as ours is coming to be, but there seems to be little or no chance that the House of Commons would accept it in any case. The principle of the League to Enforce Peace is now generally accepted by thinking people here, and by Labour people also. Their statement of War Aims, published a week ago here, is about the best that has yet been formulated by the Allies, much better than that which the Allied Governments pronounced fifteen months ago, which was ill-conceived, and has proved injurious. The difficulty is to get our Government to take up the question in a practical way. They are, of course, much hindered by recurrent urgent work, but still they ought to approach your Government and try to get them both together to appoint some Commission which would work the thing out in a practical spirit, and have a scheme, or alternative schemes, ready before the war comes to an end, which, unluckily, is an event which seems to recede constantly into the distance. In fact, things are darker here now than they have been for a good while past. Everything depends upon our finding an adequate remedy against the submarines, as to which we are hopeful, and on the time when your people can come in large numbers into the war. We realise the energy which is now being put into the matter, but ship-building cannot be extemporised. So far as I can make out your President is not very keen on coming forward with the matter at present. If so, why? Of course we cannot call it into being immediately, but the difficulties of framing a scheme are so great that they ought to be approached at once, and the world ought to be publicly assured that it is the one great and good result which we hope the war will bring about. We are grateful for the scheme you have sent me, which has many excellent points. (I hope before mailing this to you to get a careful criticism of it from some people who have studied the subject, which I will enclose.) It is a more thorough examination of the difficulties than we have yet had.

To Mr. M. Storey

3 Buckingham Gate, S.W.,
26th April 1918.

Thank you very much for the extremely valuable letter just received from you. It gives me more light upon the United States Administration and the head of it than I have had from any other quarter. He has been to me rather a puzzle and, of course, he is much more so to those in this country who know neither him nor the United States. But his public deliverances by the force of their language and the spirit of earnestness that seems to pervade them have made a great impression here, and are looked to as better indicating the war aims which the Allies and America ought to follow than perhaps any utterances from British or French statesmen. I note particularly your view that his chief deficiency lies in the power of selecting men. At critical times, when the pressure of work is great, it is a serious fault, but I am sorry to say that the same thing is happening here.

The impression you have got that there was a larger number of capable people in the front ranks of our public life between 1860 and 1890 seems to be true. At present such men are few. The supply in these things bears no relation to the demand, when the critical moment comes it has often happened that the man was wanting. There was nobody, for instance, to replace Oliver Cromwell; there was no one to replace Pitt and Fox, but fortunately there was at any rate a great general.

The causes you state for the deficiency in both Republican and Democratic parties of powerful and impressive figures, showing both high capacity and the power of inspiring confidence, are doubtless true ones. But I had supposed that within the last twenty years the power of the party machine had been so much shaken that it was becoming easier for able and public-spirited men to enter Congress, to become Mayors of great cities and Governors of States, than it had been fifty years ago, and that as the result more of such men were coming forward in public life. Am I wrong in this impression? It was one of the points in which there had seemed to me considerable improvement in the United States, and I had intended to dwell upon it, and to associate with it the distinct improvement which there surely has been in municipal Government. Are not your cities generally, with the possible exception of Philadelphia and Chicago, at a higher plane of honesty and efficiency than they were in 1885?

To Dr. Charles W. Eliot

London,
May 8th, 1918.

We have suffered a good deal from strikes from time to time, but under the pressure of the present war crisis they have dwindled away. On the whole I should think your working men have behaved better than the British. There has been a good deal of socialistic activity here, and a revolt of the younger men against the more conservative, older Trade Union leaders. Everyone expects that when the war ends all these troubles will become more serious. The wages have been extremely high; the working class have suffered less from the war than any other, but this, as usually happens, has not tended to produce any more contentment.

As respects the two points you raise, a National Army on the Swiss model, and a permanent alliance of Britain, United States and France, the latter would commend itself to the great majority of our people, because it would be understood to be a defensive alliance. As to the former I am more doubtful. We have not yet faced up to the question. Everything will depend upon how the war ends. If Germany is really beaten, people will say there is no need for a National Army, and all the expense it must involve in the way of providing it with artillery and other appliances. If, on the other hand, the war is not won against Germany, we might have to keep a big army, as well as a big navy, on foot. But how can we support the prodigious cost which would be incurred? Our Debt has reached proportions undreamt of before, and very heavy taxation is draining Capital at a rapid rate, while, at the same time, some few people, who have made profits out of the war, are growing so rich as still to excite jealousy and suspicion among the masses. It is hardly worth while in such conditions to venture on any predictions.

I am struck by the fact that in conditions such as those we have that people become reckless. They think only of the moment. They cannot exercise foresight, and though they know when they stop to think what the consequences must be, they go on blindly much as people did, according to Thucydides, when the plague was raging in Athens, and nobody knew whether he might not be dead next week.

To your three groups, if Anarchies can be called groups, I should add Oligarchies. Russia was really more an Oligarchy than an Autocracy, and Germany is an Oligarchy which acts through a monarch, the monarch being tossed about from one group of advisers to another. He is a man of no great force of character, but of intense vanity, and without the high quality of mind which would enable him to hold his own course between the different influences that play upon him. Anarchy cannot last. If we knew the inside of Russia should we not find, as in the parallel case with that of France from 1791 to 1799, that comparatively small groups of men held power? There never was a really popular government, and in Revolutions there never is, and it may be doubted whether there ever will be, except in countries like Switzerland, where everybody has been long familiarised with truly popular government in very small communities. You have in America a rule of public opinion, which is nearer to a true democracy than anything else, and yet public opinion is still imperfectly organised, even in the United States.

Do you think there is any likelihood that your Government will continue to hold the railroads? To give any government control of such an enormous number of voters, or, to put it at the other end, to give an immense class of voters power to control the Government through its votes would surely be a dangerous experiment. In Australia the railway men at one time practically did control the Government, with the worst results in one important state.

Is it true, as some critics say, that the business men who were put in by the President to run some important branches of war service, have failed when confronted with the problem of war organisation? One would have thought that if the right kind of men had been selected, they would have done better than the army and navy officers.

You are quite right in thinking that Socialism has made far more progress here than in the United States. It is our great misfortune that the bulk of our working population, four-fifths or more, are dwellers in large centres of industry, and that so little of the land of the country is in the hands of small cultivators.

You will, I suppose, soon be going to North East Harbor. How often do I wish to be cruising in the pair-oar boat through the channels between your islands, or sitting opposite you on the piazza looking across to Bear Island and hearing the cheerful plash of the waves on the rocks below! In our Sussex home, where the noise of the guns in Flanders makes doors and windows rattle, it would be impossible to forget the calamities that are destroying mankind even if the thought of them did not come back to us each morning with the songs of our woodland birds.

To Mr. Theodore Roosevelt

3 Buckingham Gate, S. W.
5th, June, 1918.

Thank you for your two letters. We are greatly concerned to hear that your two sons have been wounded, but I trust that those lightly wounded have already recovered, and that this will soon be the case with Archie also. You have good reason to be proud of your boys, as you have of your country. It is perfectly splendid to see the spirit which your people are throwing into their efforts. Here in Europe very few understand what it means to America to have foregone the old traditional ideas of complete abstinence from Old World affairs, and what a moral passion must have swept over your country to make it throw itself into this struggle with such enthusiasm and energy. Our hopes are now fixed on the arrival here of your men. All that I hear from the Front shows that they are fighting strongly, but, of course, these are not the days when men can be thrown into the fighting line without much more careful preparation than was needed fifty years ago. So the great question to us is, Will the British and French lines hold out successfully till your full fighting strength begins to develop itself, in two, three, or four months from now? It is useless to conjecture the future when something decisive may have occurred before this reaches you.

I have just heard that your nephew, young Sheffield Cowles, is entering the navy. I remember him as a bright boy. What you tell me about the turning down of so admirable an officer as Leonard Wood is distressing. But the minds of men do not always rise and expand when great occasions call them so to do. We have melancholy instances of that here all the time, and the confusion one hears of in Washington can't be worse than the Governmental atmosphere. What cheers us as it does you, is the spirit of the people, the men volunteering for the most dangerous enterprises, and the willingness of our civilians of forty-five to face all the hardships as well as the perils of the Front. I hear that the French are more bent on sparing their men and look to you and to us to save them. No doubt they suffered terribly in the first two years. Their soldiers from the South are far inferior to the Northern and Western men, and the latter have probably borne the brunt. There is a cry, not unnaturally, to help Russia, but where are we to try it? It is a most hazardous thing to try to reach Tiflis from Bagdad with our small force, and it would be still more perilous to land at Archangel and march South on Petrograd. Nothing remains but to try to help the well-disposed Russians to save Eastern Siberia, and it is said that your Administration is unwilling to encourage Japan to do this. It is regrettable that there should be no strong man in the State Department.

One begins to see what it meant to France from 1799 to 1811 that one mind directed both diplomacy and strategy. So Julius Cæsar also. But I must refrain from pursuing.

To President Lowell

3 Buckingham Gate, S.W.,
5th June 1918.

The Archbishop of York, who has just returned, tells me of his interesting conversations with you and Root and Taft, and of the attitude which the President has taken up, and has mentioned to me the memoranda which your small Committee has prepared and is preparing. If you are at liberty to show me them I should greatly like to see them. The President's views seem to be that the idea of a Permanent League to Enforce Peace ought to be kept quite distinct from that of a possible Defensive Alliance of the present belligerents to protect themselves from Germany after the War. In this you and I would probably agree. The two things are quite distinct. Till the end of the war we cannot tell whether the Defensive Alliance will be necessary, and also we cannot tell whether the Permanent League to Enforce Peace can have Germany for a member. There would be no use in having Germany as a member under her present Government. If she entered it, she would enter it to wreck it, but a regenerated Germany which had delivered itself from the military caste which rules it, would be quite a different thing, and might enter it. What I endeavoured through Marburg, and otherwise, to convey was that now, despite the uncertainty of how the war will end, it would be worth while for a joint American and British Committee, with official sanction but confidential, to work out the practical outline of the Permanent Peace League and arrive, if possible, at a solution of the numerous practical difficulties which it presents. To this W. W. seems to be averse, apparently because fearing it will be fancied to be an Alliance. I understand your Committee is at work, with an, at least, quasi official sanction. So far so good. I suppose we must not ask more at present, but the fullest possible interchange of ideas of your Committee with those of British helpers, will be profitable. As you know there has been an official secret Committee here, which has prepared a Report, but this Report is still confidential. I shall ascertain whether it is possible for me to send you a copy of it. Meantime I shall be very glad to hear your views of the situation, and thus complete what I have learned from the Archbishop. When your Committee has got further I will, if you like, convoke a gathering of our best men here who know something of the subject and in case you can send us your Report, will see if their deliberations can be of any use to your Committee.

To Mr. T. A. Chambliss

3 Buckingham Gate, S.W.,
20th, June, 1918.

Thank you for your most interesting letter. It is the most illuminative thing upon the way in which the South is taking the

power of the German Government for evil. Nothing less will do. It must be so thoroughly discredited in the eyes of the German people as to be put out of commission for ever and ever. The defection of Bulgaria took the keystone out of the arch, and thereafter it was clear that it would collapse. Austria has now gone to pieces, and Ludendorf's resignation is the final proof of utter failure. Now we have got to see that the peace to be made does full justice to Freedom, and to the claims of nationalities.

I am publishing a small volume of Essays, in one of which you will see a brief summary of the various questions relating to Nationalities, which have to be dealt with. Among those the most difficult seems to be that of Poland, where the nation is, as it always was, greatly divided, and that of the Western parts of what was the Russian Empire. On the whole the best plan seems to be to make Finland completely independent, to allow the Finns, the Esthonians, the Letts, and the Lithuanians to choose and determine their own fates. Probably they would be the strongest if they agreed to federate. The Ukraine is more difficult. I rather doubt whether the bulk of the people wish to be separated from Great Russia, and though we might wish that no power so large as the old Great Russia was before 1917 should hereafter arise, still we are not entitled to disregard the wishes of the Ukrainians, Little Russians or Ruthenians, by which ever name you call them. As respects Asia, the thing that must be absolutely and finally done, as I believe you have already stated, is to get rid of the Unspeakable Turk. Let him never again have power to massacre Christians. I earnestly hope that the voice of America will speak out very clearly upon this subject. Nowhere have the Armenians and Syrians received warmer sympathy, nowhere so much charitable help, as in the U. S. A., and your people will surely make it clear that these populations should be completely liberated from the Turk. Enver and Talaat, the two chief villains, ought to be hanged if they can be caught. There is a story that Enver has escaped to the Caucasus, and is trying to make himself head of a kind of Principality there. It is of the greatest importance to be sure that the wills of the peoples are plainly expressed in all these matters, because I am sure the peoples, yours and ours, and doubtless the French and Italians also, though they are much less instructed, will desire that Freedom and Nationality should be vindicated; and at all diplomatic conferences heretofore there has been a dangerous tendency to huddle things up by compromises. Never were there so many difficulties to be solved as now.

An interesting feature of the situation, little known in England or America, is that there is now on foot a movement among the Arab-speaking peoples of Arabia, Mesopotamia, and Syria, which has a promise of bringing about a better understanding and goodwill between Christians and Moslems in these countries, irrespective of creed. Fanaticism, not so strong as it has been among Turks and Moors, may decline, and better prospects for peaceful co-operation in the East than have existed since the fall of the Abbassid Khalifs may appear. There must of course be some protectorates over these countries till they can stand alone. Even the Zionists, who hope for a Jewish State to arise in the future in Palestine, recognise that there will be a large Jewish immigration into Palestine, now four-fifths Muslim: but there is not room in the country for more than a hundred and twelve millions, as far as I could judge when I travelled there in 1914, and to feed even one million there must be large irrigation works.

Your American soldiers have been fighting quite splendidly, almost too reckless in their bravery. They have not yet learnt how to spare themselves, nor the technicalities of the new phase of warfare. It took our officers three years to learn these things.

There will be great trouble in settling the conflicting claims of the Balkan nationalities. Bulgaria is entitled on grounds of race to Southern Macedonia, and the Greeks to the coast of Western Asia Minor. Albania, as you observe, should be left to her tribes.

war has become so immensely larger than ever before. When a League of Nations for Peace, with appropriate machinery, should be formed, seems again to depend upon the way in which the war ends. Beaten as Germany is, she may go on fighting for some weeks more, perhaps months. Would not the best plan be to have two separate Treaties, a Treaty of Peace and a series of Treaties, establishing a permanent League for the maintenance of Peace by means of a Court of Arbitration, a Council of Conciliation, and a body to rebuild and codify International Law. I have sketched this out in the last chapter of a book to be published in a few days, a copy of which will be sent you, and shall value your criticisms upon it when you can find time to give them.

Your President's intentions are rather dark to me and to most of us. Sometimes one thinks that he changes them from time to time, tenacious as he usually is of his own opinions. Are you in personal touch with him? I hope you are, for I know he respects your opinion.

There seem to me two risks attending the League of Peace movement in the Nations. The one is that the impulse now strong towards the formation of a League may die down when Germany has been completely beaten. People will say — "Oh, there is no danger now, we can consider the Peace League at our leisure." The other danger is that the Party in your Senate which dislikes the idea of committing the United States Government in advance, both the idea of taking action by force at the bidding of the authority of the League, and the idea of allowing any League to interfere in any matter which it considers within the competence of the President or the Senate (*e.g.* maintenance of Monroe Doctrine), will raise opposition to the entrance of America into a League imposing these obligations upon it. T. R.[1] has certainly shown himself to be of that view, and I suspect there are some in the Senate, among the Republicans especially, who share it. But as to this you know better than I.

[1] Theodore Roosevelt.

To Mr. Henry Holt

3 Buckingham Gate, S.W.,
4th December, 1918.

The German people, even their educated class, do not seem to realize the atrocious behaviour of their Government, and the horror and indignation which it has excited in other countries. Now this is a subject also which your knowledge of the Germans in the United States might enable American writers to elucidate better than we can do. To me the German "mentality" (as you call it in the United States) is one of the strangest phenomena of our time; and I am particularly curious to know whether it has shewed the same forms in America as in Germany.

To Mr. M. Storey

3 Buckingham Gate, S.W.,
20th December, 1918.

I have to thank you for several letters, all most interesting. And now I must also thank you most heartily for your congratulations on the issue of the war. It is an unspeakable blessing that the slaughter should cease, and our gratitude goes out to your people for the immeasurable help they have rendered. As for the President's journey, I note what you say as to the criticism it has aroused; and am not surprised, but, of course, there was something also to be said for it. What I most fear at present is that the irritation which has been aroused in the Senate may cause difficulty in the acceptance of whatever he agrees to in Paris. It would be awkward if the Senate rejected any essential points which would have to be reopened in consequence with the Allies. Some little feeling has been aroused here by what has been said, partly by newspaper correspondents, purporting to represent his views, and partly by indiscreet utterances on the part of Daniels and an Admiral. British opinion is naturally sensitive on the subject of the Navy. There is no reason why the relative strength of the United States Navy and ours should be dragged into this question at present. We have no sort of suspicion of the American navy, nor need

America have any suspicion of ours, so that the question ought to be settled without any friction. The subject of capture at sea is difficult. We cannot renounce an engine of war which has contributed materially to the smashing of German power. On the other hand, if the right of capture could be safely renounced, a gain for the world would have been secured. This matter also admits of adjustment.

As to the Armenians, they seem to have proclaimed a Republic in the country; and the Armenians in Paris have, also, issued notes to the Powers announcing that they claim independence on behalf of their nation, and trust that it will be recognised. They were driven into a corner in order to obtain a right to be heard at the Conference, so their action may be justified, which might, otherwise, seem premature. The only solution for Armenia seems to be recognition for the country as completely relieved from Turkish rule, and assigned as a permanent national home for the Armenian people. But the inhabitants are, at present, too much reduced by massacre to be able to defend themselves against the Kurds and surmount the other difficulties of their situation, so we earnestly hope that the United States may consent to help in reconstruction by sending administrators to establish and maintain order and security, and the development of the resources of the country. This, of course, could only be temporary, but even as a temporary measure it is a task which American public opinion may not be willing to undertake. If you can exercise influence on public opinion to secure its adoption, the friends of Armenia would be grateful.

The question of the navies, and that of the right of capture at sea are also troublesome, but into these I need not enter.

At this moment the centre of interest is in Germany. Much may depend upon what emerges from the chaos which prevails there now. We may hope that the good sense of the intelligent classes may prevail. It is regrettable that there should be no signs of penitence for the crimes committed by the German Government, and little realisation of the just indignation they have provoked in other countries.

CHAPTER XXX

THE PEACE, THE LEAGUE, AND THE UNITED STATES

La justice est le droit du plus faible.

JOUBERT.

ζῆσον ὡς ἐν ὄρει. οὐδὲν γὰρ διαφέρει, ἐκεῖ
ἢ ὧδε, ἐάν τις πανταχοῦ ὡς ἐν πόλει τῷ κόσμῳ.

Live as on a mountain; for whether it be here or there, matters not, provided that, wherever a man lives, he lives as a citizen of the World-City.

MARCUS AURELIUS.

In his speeches in the House of Lords but still more clearly in his private correspondence with American friends, Bryce gave vent to many misgivings as to the policy of the British Government during the later stages of the War and the earlier years of the Peace. As a staunch Liberal of the old school he thought the first Coalition unnecessary and the second deleterious. He did not like the large concessions made to Indian nationalism in the Government of India Act, nor the political enfranchisement of women, nor the delay of the Government in giving effect to the recommendations of the Irish Convention in 1917, (recommendations, it may be observed, which were vitiated in their authority by the triple fact that they were not unanimous, that the Sinn Fein party had declined to take any part in the Convention and that Protestant Ulster had refused to advance an inch in the direction of Home Rule), and still less did he approve of the revolver war with the party of secession which preceded the Irish treaty. The whole course of British Administration in Ireland seemed to him to be unsteady and unfortunate.

What however grieved him most was the character of the Peace Treaties. He thought them marred by a spirit of vindictiveness, too severe on Germany, Austria, and Hungary, and not sufficiently severe on the greatest delinquent in the all-seeing eye of History, the Ottoman Porte. The points which specially moved him to indignation were the transference to the Italian flag of two hundred thousand hardy Tyrolese mountaineers of German stock and speech, and the wholesale disruption of Hungary by the Treaty of Trianon. That the Tyrolese for whom Andreas Hofer fought and suffered in 1809 should now pass under an alien rule was a great shock to his historic sentiment, and though he approved of the formation of the Republic of Czecho-Slovakia, he was disposed to think that too much had been given it and that an arrangement under which the Sczecklers and Saxons of Transylvania were handed over to the tender mercies of the Roumans was clearly unjust.

For Hungary and the Hungarians, a high spirited and liberty-loving people, he cherished a warm feeling of personal appreciation which had been deepened by the good treatment which Hungarians consistently accorded to British prisoners of war. The history of the Hungarian Kingdom, the development of constitutional government in Hungary presenting so many features of resemblance with our own parliamentary story, the great struggle for liberty under Kossuth, one of the heroes of his youth, the consistent friendship of Hungarians towards Englishmen, the fact that Count Tisza, the Hungarian Prime Minister in 1914, had been opposed to the war, were considerations which pleaded with him for a more liberal treatment. 'The Treaty,' he said in the House of Lords, 'will subject three and a half millions of Magyars, speaking the Magyar language and inheriting the glorious traditions of the Magyar Speech, to alien rule to which they have the strongest possible objection. It will ruin the economic cohesion of Hungary, deprive her of all her forests, her mines, and her industries and it will leave her with a mere fraction of her former population in a purely agricultural area, without that variety of industries and sources of wealth which a great people ought to enjoy.' To the argument that the Magyars, in their hour of strength had displayed racial intolerance, he replied that there had been no racial tolerance east of the Rhine. Why then should the Magyars alone suffer?

In common with many of his Liberal friends, Bryce was disposed to blame the British Government for many of the shortcomings of the peace. He did not give full weight to the fact that France, Italy, and the United States also exercised a powerful influence in the settlement, nor realise how often it was that the British Plenipotentiaries threw their weight on the side of moderation. The statesmen in Paris were not so powerful as public opinion supposed them to be. They were limited on every side by the passions and appetites of Europe and in the collapse of the three military monarchies much had to be conceded to the urgency of the suppressed races, who had

the liberation of this ancient Christian community from Moslem despotism. To the student of this tragical period of Armenian history, Bryce's letters to such men as Nubar Pasha and C. H. Hagopian will be documents of capital importance. They show him to have been constant, chivalrous, and devoted and to have been acknowledged throughout the world as the protagonist of the Armenian cause. Effort so disinterested and so sustained deserved a better reward.

If the Treaties of Peace fell far short of Bryce's hopes, their imperfections strengthened the case for an international order inspired by the spirit of conciliation and justice. The worse the treaties, the more necessary the League, but then as he candidly admits the worse the treaties, the more difficult the task of the League, and the greater the risk of its failure. If, however, the League was to succeed, one essential condition must be satisfied. The League could not live without the co-operation of the United States. If the United States refused to join, he contended, doubtless with an excessive measure of pessimism, that the League could serve no useful purpose. What mattered more than anything else for the future peace and contentment of the world was the co-operation of the two great peoples of English speaking. Writing to his American friends he expressed distrust both of France and Italy; of France because her policy was too often influenced by financial groups and was not divested of the tincture of imperialism, of Italy as the annexer of the Austrian Tyrol. By the degree to which the Latin Powers fell short of his ideal of a humane and disinterested foreign policy he was disposed to measure the opportunity offering itself to the Anglo-Saxon democracies.

Bryce then had made up his mind that if the world was to be saved from future wars, the United States must enter the League of Nations. She could do so, he thought, without contracting serious obligations on the Continent of Europe. These he regarded with disfavour. Thus he did not approve of Mr. Wilson's Treaty of 1919 guaranteeing France against aggression. Nor yet did he welcome Article X of the Covenant which appeared to bind the members of the League to resist any violent disturbance of existing frontiers.

Yet while he was anxious to have the commitments of the United States strictly limited on the Continent of Europe he vehemently favoured the acceptance by Congress of the Armenian mandate. Here was a seeming inconsistency. Bryce, however, felt strongly that the Allies had incurred a solemn obligation to the Armenians by encouraging their resistance to the Turks, and that to leave them now to the uncovenanted mercies of their enemy was a callous dereliction of positive duty.

The letters which follow, while mainly concerned with the future rôle of the United States as a World Power and with its relations to the League, are liberally interspersed with comments, almost wholly despondent and unfavourable, upon the course of public policy in Britain and Ireland. In appraising the weight of these criticisms it must be remembered that Bryce was at this time chiefly thrown into the society of opposition statesmen. He saw the shadows, he felt the disappointments of a period crowded with hasty decisions taken under the stress of unprecedented circumstances. That the problems were too great for the men who were called on to handle them, is true enough, but there is no reason to think that the men fell below the normal stature. The transition from war to peace in a highly industrialised country must always be painful. In Britain it was accomplished with a minimum of actual distress. No citizen perished of want. Not a shot was fired in an English street.

To President Lowell

3, Buckingham Gate, S.W.,
15th January, 1919.

Thank you very much for your illuminative account of the situation in America as regards a League of Nations. You seem to me to have done quite right in not pressing any detailed plan upon your people. All that we here have ever wanted is that there should be a detailed plan with alternative solutions of the more perplexing problems, not for immediate publication but which the President could have taken with him and used, because my impression is that he has not got a detailed plan, and has never really faced the difficulties, having been content to dwell in the region of abstract propositions and elevated phrases. Let us hope that he has worked out a scheme which he has now ready, but I wish he had had someone with him, between ourselves, of a more constructive mind and more favourable to the idea than our excellent friend J. B. Scott. Probably the most that can be done now will be to lay the foundation for the scheme and appoint a Committee to work it out in detail. That ought to be an international committee, with two or three of the best men available from the four European Allies and from the United States. It could report to an adjourned meeting of the Conference later in the year. I do not believe that the men now assembled in Paris will have time or patience or knowledge to plan out a working scheme. Meantime, we are disquieted by the attitude taken up by the Senate, which seems highly critical.

To Mr. M. Storey

3, Buckingham Gate, S.W.,
20th February, 1919.

While I entirely agree that it would be unwise for the United States either to intermeddle in European politics, or to accept any African Protectorate for native races, the case of what I will call not a Protectorate, but certain responsibilities for a limited period in guiding the Christian races of Western Asia into the paths of peace and self-government, seems to be quite different. You would not make any permanent commitment, and you would have the immense advantage, if you took such a responsibility for Armenia, of being entirely disinterested, and standing apart from the jealousies of European Powers, and of knowing much more about the interior of the Near East, particularly Armenia, than any of the European nations. The Armenian people are intelligent, industrious, already largely educated, and capable of running an independent Government when the difficulties of the first few years have been overcome. The United States is the only Power which could be trusted. I put Britain out of the question because our hands are already full, and we do not want to take any additional responsibilities, but France could not be trusted; she would be followed by a swarm of greedy financial adventurers. Italy would be little better and has less strength for the work. Nothing remains except the United States and if you refuse to take it one does not see what is to happen to those unfortunate countries. However, I admit that your people may probably be unwilling. The task would not be heavy, it would amount to little more than sending out some capable men to organise and direct a police to keep the robber tribes in check, and to open up proper lines of commercial intercourse, which is the most pacific influence that can be brought to bear. The Armenians themselves earnestly desire that you should undertake this task. Is it not a duty which seems naturally to follow from what you have done in helping us to get rid of the menace of a cruel and rapacious Germany, using the Turks as her tools?

As respects the Monroe Doctrine, has it not two sides? — The negative side is that of preventing any European Power from establishing itself in the Western Hemisphere. To that we subscribe. It is in the interest of the world as well as yours, that no forts or stations should be so established by any naval power, but the positive side of the Monroe Doctrine, namely: that the United States should have a predominance over the Western Republics is another affair, and it is that which has created suspicion and jealousy among the Central and South American Republics. Would not your legitimate influence be exercised more usefully if you were a member of a League of Nations than if you yourselves were presented to the mind of the Spanish Republics as menacing them? The real difficulty of the League of Nations seems to me to lie in the obligation imposed upon the members of the League to take action in a particular case which their own judgment does not approve but would not this difficulty disappear in practice, because the League would not, in its own interests, think of forcing upon such a country as the United States or Great Britain, any course to which either was opposed? To continue the present Alliance of the Entente Powers as a means to keeping peace would look to the Germans, and probably to the smaller European States also, as a combination permanently directed against them, whereas what we want to do is to bring them into the League as soon as it is clear that Germany has repented or renounced the aggressive designs that have animated her during the last fifty years. I fear that if we lose the present chance of establishing a permanent world-embracing combination for the preservation of peace, the chance may never recur. Now that the scheme has been launched at Paris I should be grateful for your opinion on it. It is vague in parts. It is perhaps more a scaffolding than a building, but it seems capable of being worked out so as to be stable and useful, so we are hopeful that it will be carried even through the Senate by the general public opinion of your country, of course with any modifications you may think needed.

To Mr. James Ford Rhodes

3, Buckingham Gate, S.W.,
20th February, 1919.

As respects the German Emperor, I have often been surprised at the fascination he exercised over some of your visitors to him, — he did not encourage English visitors nearly as much as American, — Were it not for the kind of spell which persons in high places do seem to have for the rest of the world; c.f. Lord Chatham in his relations to George III as described by Macaulay and Brougham. (Do you know Brougham's sketches of statesmen of the time of George III? They are quite worth reading, and are among the best things that Brougham ever wrote. His elaborate treatises are fatiguing.) But the German Emperor never imposed upon Theodore Roosevelt. He used to talk to me about him in a disparaging vein, thinking him visionary, vain, and essentially not strong. There was a vein of frivolity and super-heated self-consciousness in his vanity, as the fuss about the uniforms shows. Napoleon played with that sort of thing for the sake of imposing upon other people, but William enjoyed it as adding to his self-importance. I am the more surprised that Carl Schurz should ever have believed in the Emperor, but of course, he had not seen him personally, and high-minded man as he was, his patriotism forced him to admire the head of a strong and united German people.

It is curious to see that the terror of Germany still remains strong with the French, and pretty strong here in England also, though, of course, it is increased by being exploited by our military people and by our protectionists who for their several reasons wish us to believe that the new Germany will continue

touch the questions such as those relating to immigration, which seem to me to be equally within the sole jurisdiction of each nation, and I, therefore, do not quite understand why our friend, Mr. Pepper, for whose opinion I have the greatest respect, should think it necessary to take steps to defend American Independence. We British are at least as likely, with our widely scattered dominions, to be affected by any part of the scheme which could bear upon National sovereignty, and some of our Dominions, such as Canada and Australia, are at least as sensitive about immigration of coloured races as California can be. But we are not afraid and I am, therefore, sorry that any of our friends who have at heart a project calculated to do so much benefit to the world as this League of Nations might do should take action that seems calculated to reduce the chance of its being adopted by America. Without the co-operation of America the whole thing will fail. I understand that it is agreed at Paris that the amendments to be effected should contain safeguards on the points I have mentioned, and I should have thought that it was better to wait until those amendments are published before taking any steps likely to discourage the adoption of the League. The Senate has long seemed to me quite unduly sensitive with regard to its privileges. Your Constitution, like many other good things, was made for man, and not man (in the United States) for the Constitution, and its provisions ought to be read in a large and liberal sense, such as would have influenced the minds of the great men who prepared it. The amount of personal confidence that any of you may or may not feel in the President ought surely not to prevent the adoption of any scheme which commends itself upon its merits. No country had ever a greater opportunity of serving the world, and the prospects of mankind for the future, in a high minded and Christian spirit than the United States has at this moment.

The Peace, League, and United States

To President Lowell

Hindleap,
Forest Row,
Sussex.
15th April, 1919.

A copy of your debate with Lodge has reached me. Thank you heartily for it. I have read it with the greatest admiration for the clearness and force with which you put your points, bringing the important features of the Covenant into their due prominence, and making the document much more intelligible than as it came from its framers. The only explanation of its clumsiness and obscurity is that it had to be finished in a hurry without proper revision. No one, I hear, had a complete scheme, this was cobbled up out of several. The best testimony to your presentation of our case for the League is that Lodge did not attempt to answer it. Had you possessed the right of reply, there was needed no more from you than to call attention to that fact. All you said about the Monroe Doctrine seemed to me perfectly true, so much so that I am a little surprised that Root seemed to think, if I understand aright, that an amendment was needed to safeguard it. Even as regards Magdalena Bay or any similar case, would not the presence of America on the Council be enough to protect her against any danger arising from the establishment of a Naval Base in the Western hemisphere? Would not that, moreover, be a case fit to be brought before the Council under the provision authorising representations regarding any action calculated to disturb peace? The danger alleged to be threatened seems to me a fantastic imagination, perhaps conceivable but too improbable to be worth regarding. However, it was doubtless right for the Conference to adopt an Amendment which will enable the Republican Senators to save their faces. As regards immigration and Tariffs, the same remark applies. They seem to us here to be quite outside the scope of interference by the League, but there is no harm in saying so. Canada and Australia are quite as sensitive about Oriental immigration as California can be.

James Bryce

To Dr. Charles W. Eliot.

Hindleap,
Forest Row,
Sussex.
July 20, 1919.

It is curious how little the German educated class realise the horror and anger which their war methods have excited among us. A distinguished Dutch astronomer wrote to me lately enclosing a copy of an address drafted by the Amsterdam Academy of Sciences and intended to be presented by the scientific Academies of neutral countries to the Allies and the United States scientific Academies, urging the immediate resumption of personal relations and co-operation in work between our Academies and those of Germany and Austria. This draft, while admitting that the German invasion of Belgium was indefensible, compared it to, and tried to palliate it by, the British Naval Blockade of Germany. This Dutch Academy, largely no doubt composed of men who are friends of the German professors, seems to see very little difference between the Germans and ourselves, and does not realise the anger which such a comparison would raise in the allied countries. We, of the British Academy, are much exercised as to our future relations with the German "Gelehrten." We do not want, as the French do, to go on treating them as enemies, but it is not easy "to kiss and be friends" — especially as they have shown no sign of repentance. Perhaps admission to the League of Nations may solve the problem. We are entirely without light as to what Germany will become in the next few years, save that most of us believe the Hohenzollerns to be gone for ever.

What you say of Wilson is perfectly true. He makes no real friends. At Princeton he had bitter enemies and some steady supporters, but the latter showed no personal attachment. There seems to be a vein of bitterness or what the Scotch call "thrawn-ness" in his nature.

The two worst things that Wilson has done were to acquiesce in the surrender of Shantung to Japan — a deadly blow to China, — and in the surrender of Central Tyrol, with its purely Germanic population, to the rapacity of Italy. But, of course, we say as little as possible here about his connection with these things for fear of injuring the prospects of his obtaining the ratification of the League of Nations Covenant. Faulty in some respects as that document is we must do everything possible to get it ratified. Wilson probably acquiesced in both these wrongs in order to save the League of Nations.

With all my heart do I wish that I could come out to Mount Desert. All that we enjoyed there, Nature and the society of the best friends — you and yours most of all — come up to our minds. But it is really impossible. I have been engaged for years, interrupted latterly by war duties, on a big book. I am now so tired of it that if it is not finished now, it never will be; and the next five months must be given to an effort to finish it and be rid of the incubus. This duty forbids me to attempt to write the articles you suggest, or to think of a holiday. I must use every moment of time available.

July 22.

P.S.

Perhaps I did not tell you that the book I am labouring at is a study of Democratic Government in France, Australia, Canada, New Zealand, Spanish America, and the United States. It has been a most fatiguing task and you probably know how sick one may get of a book when you have been so long over it that the ideas which pleased you at first have come to seem commonplace, and you have even begun to doubt whether they are worth putting in print.

It is a pleasure to be able, while unable to say much good of Democratic Government in England and France, in Australia and New Zealand, to find that there has been a distinct improvement in the United States since I first saw and studied them in 1870 when you and I first knew one another, and Dicey and I had a happy week with you in Cambridge. The positive evils have been reduced, and there seems to be altogether a better atmosphere. Even Labour quarrels are less dangerous than in Europe. At least I hope I am right in thinking this about America. Perhaps the sort of lunacy that now afflicts a large part of Europe will pass; but your conditions are more stable and more rational than ours.

To Dr. Charles W. Eliot

London,
August 7, 1919.

In reply to your enquiry as to what the British Universities have done in the war that is now ended, let me begin by saying that this war has been unlike any which England has ever seen before. Not only have all previous wars been small compared to this, but in them for centuries past, the brunt of the fighting had fallen upon the two classes at the opposite ends of the social scale, the private soldiers having been drawn from the poorest class and the officers from the richer, and largely from what used to be the landed aristocracy; this war, however, drew to the colours every class alike, the business men and the professional men having enlisted, quite as largely in proportion to their numbers, as any other part of the community. Thus the Universities have contributed their full share. Though this is true of all, I can speak with more direct knowledge regarding Oxford and Cambridge. From them practically every man between eighteen and forty-five who was physically fit offered himself for military service. In all the colleges only about one-tenth or even less of the undergraduates and of the younger teachers were left to learn and teach. The rest either fought in the army or navy, or were assigned to some kind of war work, at home or abroad, for which knowledge and talents qualified them. At both Universities Officers' Training Corps were formed; and when sufficient training had been given, the young men were sent to the front, where many of them displayed gifts by which they rose rapidly to high posts. Very many have fallen, and their loss, the loss especially of those who gave promise of splendid achievement in the fields of learning and of science, has been a national calamity that it will take many years to repair. We find some compensation in the fact that those who have returned to Oxford and Cambridge to complete their courses are hungering for books, and throw themselves with ardour into their studies, strengthened and inspired by the sense of their duty to help the country in peace as they helped it in war. Of those who had other functions allotted to them, some showed remarkable powers of administration in the new public departments created for war purposes, and some whose mastery of foreign languages gave them special qualifications were sent abroad, particularly to the Near East, where they were able to do work of exceptional importance. There has never been a time when the Universities — each and all of them — were so fully identified with a great national effort and bore a nobler part in it.

What I have ventured to say of them is, I am sure, no less true of the Universities of America. All that we have heard here about their activities shews that they too have been foremost in all the endeavours your people have been making during the two years of America's participation in the world struggle for justice and freedom. Indeed, not a few of your best University men had begun to work for the good cause even before 1917. I remember that some time previously I met in London a fully equipped detachment of surgeons and physicians mainly drawn from the Harvard Medical school, on their way to France to set up hospitals for the wounded and render voluntary surgical help. It was one of the Harvard Overseers, my dear friend Robert Bacon, now, alas, lost to us, who organized one of the first large military hospitals in France, which from its completeness and efficiency became a model. We rejoiced to welcome from time to time in London, during the last eighteen months, hosts of your Americans, graduates and undergraduates from your Universities, all the way from Maine to California, who impressed us as admirable specimens of American manhood. To those of us especially who had personal knowledge of your Universities, it was a real pleasure to talk to these young men and learn from each of them how his university was thriving, and note how deep was his attachment to it, and what a patriotic spirit it had fostered.

The Universities of the United States have in some ways been more prominent in the public life of your country than ours have generally been in the public life of England, as a whole, while your Universities have been, owing to the size of the country, more closely associated with particular cities or sections, as Harvard was with the Bay State and with New England till it began, shortly before the Civil War, and still more largely, I think, just about the time when I first knew it and you, in the early days of your Presidency, to draw students from all parts of the Union. I have more than once ventured to express here, and can repeat with a growing conviction, my belief that there has been no factor more powerful for good in the United States during the last half century than have been your universities.

And now what of the Future? What are the Universities of Britain and those of America called upon to do for these two countries in this period of what is called Reconstruction? Here in Europe the revolutionary changes we see in the world of politics have been accompanied by changes almost revolutionary in the world of thought. In the sphere of social and economic doctrine propositions once deemed axiomatic are now challenged. Men's minds seem to be drifting from the old moorings, a prey to uncertain currents. In this general unsettlement and flux of opinion there is an urgent need for careful and exact thinking on the problems we have to face. Everything has to be reconsidered, such of the old principles as are found to hold good, need be explained and proved afresh. For such as may be found wanting new principles have to be substituted. This work of hard thinking ought to be done by the most capable intellects, which can bring to it all that the world's experience, recorded in history, or contained in the writings of our wisest predecessors, can place at our disposal. Highly trained intellects are needed to give the clear cut, penetrating scientific kind of thinking that will help us through these days of confusion in which so many admirable aspirations are vague or dreamy, and so many proposals for destruction are made by those who have nothing definite and workable to suggest for replacing what it is desired, rightly or wrongly, to destroy. Similar changes appear to be passing on thought in America, though, as I gather, to a less extent, for things are at present more stable in the New World than in the Old.

Now it is the Universities that seem specially called upon to meet this emergency by giving us the trained thinkers we desire. An University is Organized Thought, organised for practical as well as for theoretic aims, as in many an American city one finds that the University graduates best represent the organized public spirit and civic zeal of the Community. Universities exist largely for the purpose of clarifying and testing not only ideas but schemes looking to the moral and social welfare of mankind. Whatever strengthens them and extends their influence, benefits a nation. They are its intellectual life-blood. This is nowhere better understood than in America. I cannot doubt that a generous response will be made to the appeal which, as you tell me, it is contemplated to make on their behalf.

To Mr. James Ford Rhodes

August 22nd, 1919.

Time failed me before leaving England ten days ago to answer your most interesting letter. We have now come to Switzerland for three quiet weeks in mountain air, and the renewal of acquaintances with some Swiss friends. Now that England is completely cut off from Germany it seems important to maintain relations with the men of learning and science in some other countries than France.

What do you think the attitude of American men of science and learning would be? I feel strongly that the sooner relations can be resumed the better; but there is no use hurrying things if feeling is not ripe. Professor Lammasch, the distinguished

Austrian International lawyer whom I have just seen here, tells me that many of the 93 German professors who signed in 1914 that outrageous declaration, had not seen its terms and were annoyed when they found out what the terms were.

I hope you continue sanguine about America's acceptance of the League of Nations? It is the only chance of saving what remains of the Eastern Christians. I hear it remarked that Wilson's conduct of affairs has lamentably failed to reach the level of his speeches. Why did he not begin in Paris by declaring that America could pay no regard to the secret Treaties, and that she would insist on a strict application of the fourteen points? He could have done it.

May I venture to ask you to read, and give me your comments and criticisms on, a study I have written on the working of democracy in America for my book on Modern Democracy?

To Charles W. Eliot

Hindleap,
Forest Row,
Sussex.
3rd October, 1919.

Do I understand you to say that Commission Government has not proved useful in the greater cities, and is that so because it does not suit their conditions? Is there no improvement visible in Philadelphia, Pittsburgh, Chicago, St. Louis, Cincinnati, and Boston, which, I suppose, are too big for that form of government? English Labour leaders are probably better educated, and with slightly wider minds, than yours; but they are generally fearful of appearing to oppose or mitigate class demands and class sentiment even when one fancies their better judgment would lead them to do so. Some few have all the ferocity against the "bourgeoisie" which belongs to many Continental Socialists, but they are not so much influenced by Communistic theories and they are not anti-Christian. Nobody among them has so wide an influence as Gompers.

There is little or no evidence of any repentance among the German men of science and learning, nor among the theologians. We have been sadly disappointed with men like Harnack, Dryander, Deissman, and Eucken. I gather that you think American men of learning are not yet generally willing to resume friendly relations.

To Mr. James Ford Rhodes

Hindleap,
Forest Row,
Sussex.
October 4th, 1919.

Thank you for your cheering account of the Eliots. It is fine to see him throwing his energy into the economic problems of to-day, and all the more a pleasure because one can agree with his views, which I never could do in educational matters, in which he carried the Elective system much too far.

As to Mommsen, I asked him in Berlin in 1898 why he did not continue his History of Rome down to Constantine or Theodosius; but he raised his eyebrows and said "What authorities are there beyond Court tittle tattle?" For his book on the Provinces of the Empire he had at least materials in the inscriptions and in antiquities, and it is a very valuable book, though doubtless dry. His views on the South African War may have had some needless bitterness towards England, but they were substantially correct. Nearly everyone in England now recognises that it was a gross blunder, highly discreditable to those who made it. After all, Mommsen and Ranke were the two greatest historical figures since Niebuhr; we have nobody to compare with them. Perhaps Macaulay and Carlyle might have been comparable with the same diligence as M. and R., but neither of them made such contributions. Of course as "Litterateurs" our men shone more brightly.

We are here in the middle of a revolution, though as yet a bloodless one; for the action of the railway executive, directed not against companies but against the government, is an attempt to coerce the nation, essentially the same as if tried by means of an armed force. Whatever the merits be, the method is a blow struck at Parliamentary Government, and indeed at Democracy.

In reading my proof,[1] as you are kind enough to do, please do not trouble yourself to do more than note any errors of fact, and let me know how far you think the general impression presented truly represents the trend of events and the decline in political methods which went on till the seventies, and began to be then replaced by an upward movement, which happily still continues. The idea is to show that abstract ideas and party methods made things steadily worse, and public opinion with a conscience is now making them better.

To Dr. Charles W. Eliot.

Hindleap,
Forest Row,
Sussex.
11th October, 1919.

First of the great Railway Strike. The Railways have been in the hands of the Government for more than three years. Wages, which were said to have been rather low before the war, have been repeatedly raised to more than double on an average, but more in the higher ranks of the work then in the lower. As prices also have risen the real advance in some cases comes to very little. The workmen demanded a large further advance, and the Government wished to stipulate that if prices fell the wages should be sensibly reduced. The railway men, though it had been agreed to make no change till the end of the year, suddenly struck, hoping to extort terms from the dire need of the country. Whatever the merits of the case, this was a revolutionary action — an attempt to take the country by the throat so that the Government should have to yield. Fortunately the

[1] Of *Modern Democracies.*

Government were prepared, and the classes above that of the wage-earners, *i.e.* clerks, shopkeepers, farmers, etc. encouraged the government to resist, and to a large extent gave personal help — especially the well-to-do. It was a plan to supersede Parliament, and, except that the means were not violent, resembled one of the mediæval insurrections when people took up arms to get their own way. The other Trade Unions sympathised generally, some threatened to join, and probably some would have joined had the conflict continued. It was almost like a class war — the Unions on one side, the rest of the nation on the other; the most alarming thing we had had for many years. Both sides claim the victory, but the Railway Union had become frightened and obtained very little except saving their face. They perceived that every class but their own was against them. But the curious thing is that, among the upper class comparatively few seem to feel as they ought the violent and unconstitutional nature of the method employed — an evil omen for the future.

The other event has been the threat of the Coal Miners' Union — more or less backed up by the Engineers and the Railway men — to call a general strike unless the Government recalled all the troops from Russia and dropped any intervention there. The same threat is made of striking unless the Government promise to propose the nationalisation of the mines. This is called Direct Action — *i.e.* extra Parliamentary — unconstitutional action, a transference of the seat of authority from the elected Legislature to the wage-earners, acting through their Union. This threat has made thinking people "sit up," and is condemned by some of the moderate Labour Union men. Enclosed is a cutting from an article by the ablest of them — a working man in Parliament named Clynes. These two incidents will show you how arrogant the Unions have become. We seem to have suddenly passed into a new phase of political life. The normal balance of men's minds has been disturbed by the war, and the contagion of Bolshevism counts for something. Its undoubted crimes are either denied or made light of, and that by crowds of educated people who ought to know better. You will regret as I do that Profit-sharing wakens little interest here. The Unions do not like it, and the public-spirited employers who ought to try it are few. Socialism continues to spread, though not in its extreme or Marxian form; nor is it, as on the Continent, anti-Christian.

Mr. James Ford Rhodes

3, Buckingham Gate, S.W.,
14th November, 1919.

A thousand thanks for your criticisms upon the proofs, which are most helpful to me. By way of apology for some mistakes which you have corrected, I will say that there were points upon which I felt some doubt, and had hoped to look up. You have kindly saved me the trouble of doing so. I am possessed with the fear in my elder days of losing the sense which ought to be uppermost in every writer's mind of accuracy at all hazards. When one is in haste, as one must be on reaching a certain age, one is particularly liable to this danger.

Before I come to your comments let me say that Mommsen and Ranke were very interesting illustrations of different kinds of historians, who had only this in common, that they were unwearied in their labours and had a high sense of the need for accuracy. Mommsen sometimes erred, as when he spoke in his history of Ohio as a slave state, but he was a man of extraordinary force and industry. When he came to Oxford he rose at six every morning and worked until the Bodleian Library was open for him at nine, standing on the doorstep till it, the door, opened. On the other hand he had not Ranke's fairness of mind and wish to see characters from every side. He allows his passion for Cæsar and dislike of Cicero to pervert his view, at any rate as regards the latter. In this respect he resembles Carlyle, though the defect does not seem to prevent Carlyle's "Frederick" from being an extremely valuable book in its picture of Frederick's civil administration as well as his campaigns. Carlyle took infinite pains and one can discount his pernicious doctrine of force. It did injure the Prussians, but after all they would have been just the same without it, and it helped to make Froude even worse than nature had made him, but that was a small matter. Probably there never was any country which had two historians of the same transcendent merit, living at the same time, as Ranke and Mommsen.

The impression made by Governor Coolidge's conduct in the police strike is a fine sign of the readiness of your people to value courage coupled with integrity. The time has now come when courage is the quality most wanted in rulers. I wish we had more of it here among those to whose wavering hands chance, helped by intrigue, has committed the fortunes of Britain.

The next letter illustrates the anxiety with which Bryce was following the fate of the Covenant of the League during the protracted debates (June 10, 1919, to March 29, 1920) of the American Senate. The two main objections taken by the opponents of the draft were first the six votes accorded to the British Empire in the League Assembly, and second the provisions of Article X, which were represented as likely to draw America into foreign wars. The Republican 'reservations' popularly known as the Lodge reservations dealt with these points; they laid down that no state should have more votes than the United States and that no obligations were assumed under the Covenant to defend the territorial integrity or political independence of any state save with the specific authority of congress. The President, however, would have no such reservations and the cause of the Covenant was defeated.

To President Lowell

Hindleap,
Forest Row,
Sussex.
19th Nov., 1919.

The news from Washington seems to imply that the League of Nations may fall through if the reservations are insisted on, and if it falls through the project will fail; for we are the only nation in Europe who cares about it. It is a thousand pities that Wilson did not take the advice that you and we pressed upon him to prepare in conjunction with you a proper scheme before he went to Paris. Many of the grounds on which the Senators have been now attacking the League might have been removed or reduced if this had been done. I wonder if you have seen Edward Grey? He has a difficult position, having come in just when the Republican Senators were smashing the League, and there was no champion in Congress capable of defending it when Wilson was *hors de combat*. We are doing our best here to try to keep the flag flying, but you can imagine what a discouragement the action of the Senate has been.

To Dr. Charles W. Eliot

Hindleap,
Forest Row
Sussex.
21st Nov., 1919.

We guess but cannot prove, that Woman's Suffrage had much to do with the tremendous Liberal defeat. To the women, five-sixths of whom know nothing about politics, Lloyd George means something for they were told that he had won the war and was going to hang the German Emperor; and Labour meant something, because there were to be higher wages and larger old-age pensions, etc. etc., but Liberalism meant nothing at all. Nobody has any confidence in the present government, least of all in its head, and it stands by the weakness of its opponents and the pledges given to it by the Coalition members. The election may not come for more than a year yet.

It looks to me as if the best thing for a restoration of common sense and good-feeling between classes would be a collapse of Bolshevism in Russia. Its continuance keeps up wild ideas here, infecting a large part of our working class. The world has not yet recovered sanity.

I can hardly tell you how much pleasure your letters give me, not merely by their contents, but in the fact that through them I am kept in touch with your life and thoughts; at the age we have reached, when few of our generation are left, the old and tried friendships become doubly precious and helpful, and mitigate the sense of solitude in a time when — despite all one can do — it is hard to enter into the ideas of the younger, some of which seem so far from sound. You have probably been able — as America is less revolutionary — to have more minds round you in sympathy with your own, but you can understand what I mean. To enter into your mind and feel its hopefulness is delightful to me, and I thank you every time. We rejoice in the goodness of your wife's better health.

To Mr. M. Storey

3, Buckingham Gate, S.W.,
27th Nov., 1919.

Thank you for your letter with its remarks upon the position of the League of Nations scheme, and the effect of the Reservations proposed to be introduced. It seemed to me so relevant and important that I ventured to show it to one of my friends here, who has been most active in the League of Nations project, Lord Robert Cecil, and he has sent me the following remarks — placed on a separate paper — representing the result of a conversation he had with another friend actively interested in the matter. I believe with you, that if the American people really understood what is involved, and the matter had not been clouded by some honest misconceptions, and some dishonest misrepresentations, they would insist that the League of Nations should be adopted in all its essential principles, although they might request a re-drafting, or an authentic interpretation of it in some points in which it is obscure or ill-expressed, or goes beyond the interests of the cause. It always did seem to me an ill-drawn document, and what one would like would be to see it simplified and the points of difficulty better treated, but one recognises how hard it would be now to throw the whole thing again into the melting pot, and, therefore, one wonders whether the principal states could be got to agree upon an interpretation of the obscurities which would remove most of the difficulties, and could refer certain points to a Committee, which would recommend alterations. I fear, however, that that would not get over the fundamental objection which the Senate takes, and which seems to have had much effect in the United States viz — the objection to the United States binding itself to take action except by the consent of Congress. This would mean that there would never be any certainty of the United States taking action at all, *id est* the alliance would be one carrying no obligation with it. Unless your people are prepared to pledge themselves, as the other nations will have to do, in a positive and definite way, the League cannot have the power which is essential. Do you not think that the people might be brought to undertake such a pledge?

It is most regrettable that the Paris Conference should have sanctioned many injustices, because this makes it the easier to say "why should we bind ourselves now to a guarantee to territories the frontiers of which have been unjustly drawn?" But this argument, which weighs with us here, who know how grave are the errors which the Conference has committed, does not seem to have been much used in America.

Although the news in this week's papers seems to indicate that the case for the League is almost lost, I cannot but believe that there must still be a chance, sharing your feeling that if the foundations of the plan and the need for it were properly understood, it would win the support of American opinion. I need hardly say that the arguments in your letter as regards the effects of Reservations carry legal conviction to my mind. What a pity that there is no strong man in the Senate, or in the Cabinet, to handle the subject effectually while the President is disabled? It has always been a weak point with him that he does not get sufficiently able men round him.

To President Lowell

3, Buckingham Gate, S.W.,
29th Nov. 1919.

A crisis in the Armenian question is at hand. The Powers are going to take up the Turkish treaty immediately. The French want to restore the Turk to all his dominions, except Syria and Cilicia, which they want for themselves. They expect to take the place of the Germans as the controlling influence, getting mining and railway concessions, and various other good things for those big financiers who control French politics. Our Government does not wish that, but has no solution for the future of Armenia, now it seems unlikely that the United States will accept a Mandate. Two questions arise:

(1) Will the United States bear a part in settling the Turkish question? There seems to be some doubt as to the policy of the United States Government. Its Paris Delegation is sick of the Conference altogether; and it is of course alleged that as the United States was not at war with Turkey, it need not take part in the Settlement. But without the United States the designs of France will have a better chance of prevailing. Cannot your Administration be pressed to bear its part? Cannot United States opinion be aroused against any settlement that will let Turkish power back into the regions it has filled with bloodshed and cruelty?

(2) If the United States refuses a Mandate, cannot it be induced to make a grant of money for some few years to help some of the Minor Powers (*e.g.* Norway or Holland) to take

and work a Mandate, which it could not do from its own resources? Of course England and France would also be expected to contribute. It seems to me your people might, as a salve to their conscience, be persuaded to go so far as this. Is it even impossible they could send a force, or allow one to be raised by voluntary enlistment, of some thousands of men to hold back the Turks for some months till the final arrangement is made for the country? Anyhow, the main thing is that the United States should support our Government against the French scheme for reinstating the Turk.

To Mr. James Ford Rhodes

Hindleap,
Forest Row.
Sussex.
Dec. 6th. 1919.

One thing strikes me in the present struggle at Washington. The American people does not seem to have had the real case for the League of Nations, and the real gist of the Covenant, properly put before it, unless Taft did that in speeches which we have not seen. Whatever Wilson's faults and blunders, the Republican leaders seem to me to be sinning against the world in depriving it of the best chance for bettering its condition that has appeared for centuries. Without the United States the League of Nations will come to little. Nobody now has a good word for the Paris Conference. Instead of reducing the causes of war, it has multiplied them, making fresh injustices. The Congress of Vienna was at any rate true to its own bad principles. This Conference has sinned against the light.

To Dr. Charles W. Eliot

3, Buckingham Gate, S.W.,
18th Dec. 1919.

The class war, although preached fifty years ago by Marx, has only lately become really formidable. Here, though apparently not yet in America, it has taken two forms. One is that of a general strike over the whole country of all the workers engaged in one of the large industries upon which the industrial life of the country, and even the private life of individuals, depends. A railway strike stops everything. If the late railway strike here had been joined in, as seemed possible, by the Transport Workers generally, and by the coal miners, there would have been no way out except surrender on the part of the nation, or else civil war. This is the result which might have been foreseen, but was not, of those developments of modern science which have made us dependent on skilled workers. As soon as the skilled workers organised it was evident they would hold the community at their mercy, and we do not see the way out, for it is impossible to suddenly replace the switch men and some other skilled classes on railroads, and in the case of a coal strike it would be quite impossible to turn unpractised men on for work in the mines.

The second development is that the dictation of a particular trade or group of trades is being applied to questions which are properly political, not even labour questions, such as wages and hours of work. This, which they call "Direct Action" has been repeatedly threatened in connection with the proposal to nationalise railroads and mines, and we may have it any day in England. They have even threatened to apply it to such a question of foreign policy as the official recognition of the Bolshevik government in Russia, and the conclusion of a treaty of peace with it. This is, of course, a direct blow at the authority of Parliament. In fact, it is an attempt at revolution, none the less so because it does not involve an armed insurrection. Things spread so fast from country to country that you may very possibly have a like attempt in America, but you are better able to deal with them than we are since the working class is not as here, the largest element in the population. Practically we are now in a position where democracy has been tried and found wanting. The Labour Unions try to override the constitutional expression of democracy, and democracy seems to have no way of dealing with them. The Unions could in many constituencies return any members they liked, and the weight of those members in Parliament would prevent Government from dealing firmly with the strikes. The one point that is not quite certain is how far the unorganised trades would side with the organised trades who are striking. Of course the middle classes, including the clerks and shopkeepers, are hard hit by the strikes, and indignant, but they are the minority. I should like to have your reflections upon this situation and the chances of dealing with it.

Agreeing with your views that the best remedy for labour troubles generally is to be found in a system of profit sharing, and also in a system, where practicable, of some participation in the management of an industry by the workers in it, I see, regretfully, that the leaders of the Labour Parties do not want profit sharing. Many of them do their best to oppose it. The Socialists are largely in control of that party here, and they look upon it as a dangerous rival to their own schemes.

Central Europe, and especially Austria, is threatened with starvation. We shall have to come to its help, and hope America will join us. This is partly due to the harsh terms which the fears and vindictive sentiments of France have imposed upon Austria. People have now come to see what a hideous failure the Paris Conference has been. The heads of States had never so great an opportunity for setting the world right as the Paris Conference gave them, and never has an opportunity been more deplorably misused. Hardly anybody here is found to say a good word for the five men who ruled the Paris Conference, and ruled it in secret, and I grieve to say that although I believe Wilson's intentions to be entirely good, he managed so badly as to deserve a large part of the blame.

To Mr. M. Storey

3, Buckingham Gate, S.W.,
22nd Dec. 1919.

Every Treaty can impose only a moral obligation, *id est:* there is no means of legally compelling its performance, but where the moral obligation is solemnly undertaken by a nation, its duly authorised obligation is deemed as strong as a legal one, because it involves the national honour. In the United States that obligation is entered into by the President and Senate conjointly, binding both. Every Treaty for mutual defence is based on the assumption that the obligation will be fulfilled. The Covenant of the League is just such a treaty, no more and no less, as any other treaty of alliance. The United States does no more to bind itself for the future by the Covenant than by any other treaty to which a term of years is not fixed, and which is, therefore, understood *prima facie* to be of perpetual duration. In what respect, therefore, is the Constitution violated, or the rights of the Senate infringed in this case more than in that of any other treaty? Of course the moral obligation rests upon the Senate as well as upon the President, both being jointly bound as parties, but it is not less strong upon the Senate because the President is also a party. Why therefore should the Senate insert a reservation entitling it to withdraw any more than the President would be entitled to do so? The real question, therefore, is whether the benefits to be expected to America and to the World are sufficient to justify the acceptance of the obligation. To me it seems that America stands to gain as much by the Covenant as any other country, and to have as little danger of suffering in any respect, because her great power and her detachment will give her exceptional weight in the Council of the League. So I still venture to hope that an arrangement will be made, for without the help of the United States there will be no prospect of success.

To Mr. M. Storey

January 9, 1920.

England has during the last eighty or ninety years abolished all the practical grievances that Ireland had to suffer from: first the exaction of tithes, then the Land grievances by successive steps, then the Protestant Episcopal Church Establishment,

cisms? I ought, perhaps, to except Stopford Brooke's. Do you know them? I agree, however, that Shakespeare has far more of the highest qualities of poetry, a greater richness of thought, and a forceful splendour of expression, than Goethe ever attains to. It is only Homer and Dante who approach him.

The rise and fall of Wilson are almost like a Greek Tragedy; but of course his illness, which is a sort of accident, interferes with the ethico-political significance of these four years from 1916–20. You in America seem to be badly off for great men, but so are we, so is France, and all Europe. The best one who has come up seems to be Mazaryk in Bohemia — the most simply engaging, Paderewski — the most amiable and adroit Venizelos. You will have seen a book that has made a great sensation here containing sketches of Wilson and Lloyd George in Paris, by a Cambridge don named Keynes, an economist.

To Dr. Charles W. Eliot

3, Buckingham Gate, S.W.,
5th Feb. 1920.

There may not be less of intellectual power now than there was fifty years ago, but it is less concentrated in a few leading figures. We have no person who is admired, honoured, and trusted as some men were then, such as Peel, a little earlier, and the Liberal constellation, among whom Gladstone shone out. There is a great deal of aspiration, a great deal of sentiment, and a good deal of moral purpose, but much of it is visionary, too vague and too sentimental to be in touch with the facts and capable of dealing with existing evils. One is constantly reminded of the contrast between aspiration and sentiment on the one hand, and the want of honesty and practical ability on the other, which marked the French Revolution. There is no sign of a higher level of morality in the mass of the people. During the last three years morality has been going down, and causes alarm; so at least I am told by those who ought to know. Education or rather, the habit of reading, which is a different thing, has its faults as well as its merits. To strike the balance between them is not easy.

The most significant change at present is the wild rush of a large part of the well-educated but sentimental and unthinking youth of both sexes towards socialism; the results of the wide extension of the suffrage have begun to be felt. Organised workers are intoxicated with the sense of their power and are prepared to overthrow the foundations of society. The middle classes are suffering heavily in income, and are being squeezed out between the new rich and organised labour. Nothing is too absurd to find adherents among the working class and the large section of our youth to which I have referred. My alarm was first started not only by the Feminist movement, but by the extraordinary tolerance, to say the least of it, with which the outrages perpetrated by the suffragettes, (1907–12) were received by the respectable classes, who did not seem to feel that when one class of persons, whatever sympathy might be felt for their aspirations, were openly violating the law in every direction, the spirit of lawlessness would grow. It has grown. Those who ought to lead the middle class by their intelligence have mostly gone over to what is called Labour, but is really revolution.

We have been trying for many years to break up large estates and create a large body of small land-owning farmers, but hardly any progress has been made in that direction. The large estates are now being sold by the old country gentry, but they are passing into the hands of the new rich, who have all their faults and few of their virtues. They belong largely to the class which made fortunes out of the war, and is called here "profiteers." But however disappointed one may be with the turn things have taken during the last thirty years, one must always remember that there are ups and downs in the moral as well as the economic prosperity of countries, and the elements for a return to better things are a new development of the moral forces coupled with a cooler and more penetrating intellectual perception of what is possible and of what is impossible, because opposed to human nature. What strikes one most is the continual recurrence of a belief that human nature will be different from what it has been. I do not mean that it is not susceptible of improvement. We have seen some improvements, but the old sources of evil are not extirpated, or likely to be in any future we can foresee, and there will always be fountains sending forth bitter water.

The extinction of intoxicating drinks all over a continent is one of the most surprising, and, on the whole, most encouraging phenomena of our time. There is no apparent likelihood of any such change here, but then, nobody believed twenty years ago in America that a prohibition bill could have been carried. We are anxiously waiting to see whether it is effectively enforced. If it is, the triumph of a sense of the general good over individual propensities will be well vindicated.

We are, of course, grieved that the United States should step back out of the part she was playing in world politics, because we believe that she could have done much infinite good in helping to re-settle this distracted Old World. Do you see any chance that if a broad-minded President, with high ideals, comes in a year hence, he might induce the people to take up again their duties in relation to humanity at large? America has higher ideals and more conscientiousness than any Old World people, and can do more to set an example of disinterested philanthropy.

As regards the Conference at Paris, some of the American delegation, such as Henry White, could tell you much more than is known here. The only revelations we have had about Wilson will be found in the book by J. M. Keynes, "The Economic Consequences of the Peace," which I mentioned to you already. You should look at it. As I said in my last, the picture he represents is very different from what Haskins gave in his lecture, and, I fear, nearer to the facts. Since I wrote last the desired recognition has been given, *de facto*, to the Armenian Republic at Erivan, and the question now is, how much territory of what was Turkish Armenia will be allotted to this

Republic. It is not fit to stand alone. There must be some sort of mandate or guidance by the League of Nations, and I still continue to hope that the United States will at any rate grant a pecuniary subvention.

To Dr. Charles W. Eliot

3, Buckingham Gate, S.W.,
2nd March 1920.

(1) I am afraid that I must have badly expressed myself in some of my letters if I have led you to believe that I am doubtful about the value of a League of Nations. On the contrary, from 1914 onwards I have been advocating it on every occasion, and you will remember in 1915 that I sent you a draft of a scheme prepared here by a small group here to which I was Chairman, containing an outline for such a League. I still think it is the only chance of peace for the future of the world. The Covenant of the League is faulty in many respects, and if Wilson had taken the advice which Taft and Marburg and I among others, gave him in 1917, to take great pains to have the best heads in America prepare a good scheme, which he could bring with him to Paris, some, doubtless, of the faults in the present Covenant might have been avoided. Unfortunately, Wilson refused to listen to us, and came unprepared to Paris. But whatever the faults of the Covenant, it is better than nothing, and we here would have accepted it gladly, with all its defects, for the sake of making a beginning. Most of the objections taken by the Senate seem to me either frivolous or based upon a misunderstanding of the meaning and aims of the Covenant. We should have desired acceptance without Reservations, but now we should desire acceptance even with Reservations, so far as they do not knock the bottom out of the whole thing. If we cannot get the League, then I agree with you that the next best thing is to have a permanent union between England and the United States whether or not by a formal treaty. England is the only great power in Europe that really cares

about the idea. Meanwhile, the Bolshevist propaganda goes on and does immense harm all over Europe, and, indeed, in Asia also.

(2) I entirely agree with you about the strikes in Government services, and that is the general view of all sensible men in this country, but our Labour Unions are very powerful, and our Government is very weak. It has completely lost the confidence of the country; I could say much more about it and its leading figures if I had time at this moment. I remember none worse, and none so utterly discredited.

(3) There is a certain amount of Socialism and even of sympathy with the Bolshevists among the younger people in this country, including the students at Oxford and Cambridge, and even the younger Clergy of the Church of England; many of the young liberals are drifting into the Labour Party. It is becoming almost as hard as it is in the United States to obtain domestic help. What is called "feminism" is still active, and unthinking. The House of Commons has just passed a Bill for immensely extending Woman Suffrage, so that the majority of voters in this country will be women, and nobody seems to realise how great a difference that will mean to the steadiness of our Government.

(4) Prices of food, coal, and all other necessaries, have risen to more than twice what they were before the war. This is partly due to want of shipping to bring articles from abroad, but it is also due to the combinations of big firms, which are keeping prices at an inordinately high figure. Many enormous fortunes have been made during the war at the expense of the people. Here, again, the total incompetence of the Government has been made manifest. They have had no foresight and no firmness. There is, however, hardly any actual hardship here, and the real sufferers are not the working people and the poor generally, but the poorer section of the clerks and the professional class, especially the latter, who have no means of raising their incomes. The Clergy, for instance, especially the Clergy of the Church of England, and elderly people living upon their

savings, are much to be pitied, and a great deal of quiet, uncomplaining suffering goes on.

We are distressed over the Armenian situation, and don't know now what can be done, since the President has washed his hands of the whole business. We have been fighting hard for the freedom of the Eastern Christians, but the French want to give back to the Turk all they can of sovereignty, retaining economic privileges for themselves. What is to become of Cilicia? The French say they have not troops and money to occupy it, so want the Turks back. The Turks meanwhile are starting fresh massacres. Wilson had led the Armenians to believe he would secure justice for them, and now America stands aloof. We — I mean the friends of the Eastern Christians in England, are doing our best, but there is no power to take a Mandate unless with the help of a pecuniary subvention. Could not Congress be induced to grant one for the next seven years till the country can find its feet?

To President Lowell

3, Buckingham Gate, S.W.,
2nd March 1920.

I have always agreed with you in thinking that Article 10 of the Covenant went too far. It would be monstrous, for instance, to expect America to take up arms in order to maintain the Italian rule over German-speaking Tyrol, a thing which the Paris Conference should never have agreed to, or the rule of Serbia in Macedonia, equally a blunder and injustice, and a Reservation which enabled America to refuse to give its support in such a case would be quite legitimate. I hope and believe that public opinion in England would not permit us to support that those who are best informed, know to be an injustice. But some of the Reservations went a good deal further than this. What most mortifies us is the feeling that the American people has never had the case for the League of Nations properly put before it. If that had been done lucidly and tactfully I cannot but believe public opinion would long ago have insisted upon

America's entrance into the League. Meanwhile, we hear with the greatest concern that there has been a marked growth of ill-feeling towards England, due, I suppose principally, to the action of the Irish. Can anything be done to stem that tide?

To Dr. Charles W. Eliot

3, Buckingham Gate, S.W.,
25th March, 1920.

I will at this moment say only one thing to explain the object of the two chapters[1] which I sent to you. My aim has been to be entirely "objective" as the Germans say, *i.e.* to avoid expressing any opinion of my own. Hence I have neither discussed nor exposed the folly of the Communistic theories, neither have I in any way entered into the economic arguments regarding socialism or communism. If I did so I should be involved in controversy, and I should lessen any persuasive value my book may have by appearing to take a side. What I want is, first and foremost, to state the facts and to raise questions on which my readers may think for themselves. This line I have taken right through the whole book, believing that any good it may do will be done by helping people to think for themselves. Hence, I have neither described nor propounded remedies. The book has already grown to a thousand pages, and if I were to enlarge it by entering into controversy it would become far too big for any reader.

As respects my article upon the Near East settlement which you have read, it was written primarily with the view of showing the necessity for turning out the Turks. That is the one thing that we have now to think of here. Once it is certain that that will be done, I shall write again to state my views as to the arrangements to be made for the future. I do hold strongly that in the interests of the future peace of the whole East, the Trans-Caucasus countries — for it is to them and not to the Balkans, as you seem to have thought, that I am referring in speaking of the safety of Persia, Afghanistan, and India — it is essential that

[1] Of *Modern Democracies.*

the Turks should not be allowed to be in territorial contact with the Muslim countries of Mesopotamia, Syria, Persia, and Turkestan, where a pan-Islamic propaganda of the most dangerous character is being already carried on by the Turks in conjunction with the Bolshevists, and with certain disaffected Muslims in India and Egypt. I am not thinking merely of British interests in India, but of the peace of the East altogether. A factitious agitation about the Khalifate has been worked up, to which our Government has most unwisely yielded, and the anti-European revolutionaries in the Near East as well as in India, are bent on mischief.

You are quite right in thinking that socialism and communism have gone much further here than they have in America. England has not recovered from the disturbance of men's minds which was due to the war, and our working men are far more permeated by anarchist or communistic ideas — in fact by a sort of Bolshevism — different as these are between themselves, than your people are in America. To this subject also, however, I must return again.

To Miss D. Neill Raymond

3, Buckingham Gate,
London S.W.

My best thanks are due to you for your gift of your book on "British Policy" during the Franco-Prussian War of 1870–71 which I am reading with lively interest, well remembering the events of that time. They seemed tremendous then, but small now, compared to those of 1914–19. When the war broke out British popular sympathy was predominantly with Germany, because Louis Napoleon was regarded as the constant menace to European peace. We thought that if we had sympathized, as France herself had done, with Italy's efforts at unification, we might properly sympathize with Germany's efforts also. J. R. Green, whom you quote, and E. A. Freeman and Goldwin Smith, a leader of University thought, were among the warmest partizans of Germany, three of our leading historians. The tide began to turn when France suffered one defeat after another, and when it was plain that the Third Empire was dead and gone. It turned distinctly when the German Government demanded Alsace and part of Lorraine. We thought then, and I think now, that Gladstone and Granville deserved the greatest credit for saving Belgium then from what Belgium suffered in 1914.

Gladstone, though he distrusted Louis Napoleon, was not personally antipathetic to France. He liked her on the historic and ecclesiastical side much better than Germany.

P. S. I was in N. E. France in April 1871, and found the German Officers very bitter against England in respect of the sale of munitions to France. But it would have been, in the rules of international law, almost an unnatural act to forbid that sale. It was constantly done. The Germans have done it since.

To Mr. James Ford Rhodes

3, Buckingham Gate, S.W.,
20th April, 1920.

I need not say that we are beyond measure distressed at the apparent total failure to settle the question of the Treaty and the entrance of the United States into the League of Nations. It is a misfortune that such matters should have to be discussed at the Presidential Election. I am most curious to see how the candidates are selected. Of the Democrats named the best seems to me to be your Ambassador here, who has acquitted himself admirably since he came.[1] His speeches are models of tact, diction, and excellent sense. Hoover is certainly a man of force and independence, but, apparently, the politicians do not want him. Remembering U. S. Grant, I am almost as much afraid of a man who had had no experience of politics as of one, who like Blaine, had too much. President Butler's chances seem to have been destroyed by the fact that he is a College President, which would have helped him three years ago. To me President Wilson's critics seem unjust, because they forget that

[1] Mr. J. W. Davis.

he really has been during the last eight months not in a normal condition. The work at Paris overtaxed his physical strength, and his mental resources. His mistakes were, of course, tremendous, but we can none of us escape from our physical condition. Is it true that Napoleon lost the Battle of Leipsig from the indigestion caused by the bad cooking of a leg of mutton? Diaz lost Mexico because bad bridge work had been done upon his teeth. Your knowledge will enable you to multiply instances. The Peace Conference continues to add to the number of its mistakes. They are now going to make a treaty with Hungary which cannot stand and does not deserve to stand, in spite of the warning which their atrocious failure in the case of Austria has given. Friends who have just come thence tell me the Hungarians are arming and will put up a fight. Considering how monstrous are the terms being imposed on them one can't be surprised. If you can find time to give me now a fair judgment — and no judgment any where is fairer than yours — upon the action of the Senate, I shall be grateful. To me it seems worse than one likes to think, because, though they had a good case, they seem to have spoiled it by party resentment and personal vindictiveness, and want of respect for their own position. This pandering to the Irish vote would hardly have been seen forty years ago.

To Dr. Charles W. Eliot

3, Buckingham Gate, S.W.,
20th April, 1920.

People's minds are so excited here, and so full of vague sentiment, ready to grasp unworkable schemes, that what is generally wanted is to get them to *think* of realities, and deliver them from the dominion of words and phrases. There is far less reason and common sense, especially among the younger folk here, than I think there is among you in America. I find sons of my old friends drifting, out of discontent with present conditions, into labourism or some form of socialism. The amount of sympathy which these detestable Bolshevist ruffians have

and has not encouraged the French commercial interests to try to squeeze out British competition and take undue advantage of their political control. The tribes of the Atlas are still restless, but the Germans entirely failed in their efforts to create an insurrection and the Pan Islamic propaganda has made no progress. Whether France is well advised in her large expenditure on roads — excellent roads — and harbours seems very doubtful, considering her financial difficulties, for it must be a good while before the capital sunk in these ways will give a return. But almost the same criticism applies to our occupation of Mesopotamia, as to which the country has never been consulted. It will cost more to protect than will Morocco, which has no neighbour except poor old Spain, which seems as incompetent in its administration, as it was fifty-five years ago, when I first visited it.

To President Lowell

3, Buckingham Gate, S.W.,
15th June, 1920.

Thank you very much for your letter, which I have just found on my return from Spain and Morocco. It arrived on the very day when the news came of the result in the Chicago Convention, and the thought came at once to my wife and myself, that if you were not President of Harvard University, you might make a fortune by starting as a prophet of political and sporting events, for your forecast made so long ago as to what was likely to happen at the Convention has been exactly verified by what has happened. Unfortunately, the senatorial Republican group, with some other shrewd members of the National Committee politicians of the old familiar type, has gained control and manipulated the delegates. It never seemed to me that Wood would be chosen, but I had some hopes for Lowden, and knowing him to be a straight and sensible man, thought he would make a fair President. Harding had not emerged when we left Washington, and I don't remember to have ever met him.

He would seem to be a man, more or less, of the familiar Ohio type, though not exactly either a Hayes or a McKinley.

Needless to tell you how distressed we are at the Anti-British feeling which has arisen and the likelihood that it will be cultivated during the campaign by the desire to capture the Irish vote. There will, I fear be nothing to choose between the two parties in that respect, but the Democrats could hardly go further than the Senate went in the way in which it has behaved about Ireland. Fortunately, there has been less irritation here than might have been expected, and the offensive things said about the United States have come only from contemptible sources, such as the "Saturday Review," and a man called Bottomley, who is our nearest counterpart in vulgarity to W. R. Hearst.

The state of Ireland has been steadily going from bad to worse, and people have settled down here into a sort of despair. The Government has made every conceivable mistake, and the Sinn Feiners have behaved in a way for which the only excuse is that they are practically mad. But indeed there is plenty of lunacy everywhere in Europe now. We all say to one another the war was bad, but this sort of peace is worse. Indeed, what peace is there when Western Asia and Eastern Europe are still in flames?

To Mr. Bayard Henry

3, Buckingham Gate, S.W.,
17th June, 1920.

Thank you for your letters, which I have found on my return from a long journey in Spain and Morocco. Much has happened since they were written, and by the time this reaches you the Democrats will have probably chosen their candidate. Do you think they will have a chance? Harding is not personally known to me, as he did not emerge until after we had left Washington, but I gather that he is a respectable man, who might make a good President. We are sadly afraid that both parties will be tempted to play for the Irish vote and thereby increase

To President Murray Butler

3, Buckingham Gate, S.W.,
2d Dec. 1920.

There never was a crisis in the world's history which so much wanted first rate men as that which began in 1914, and there has not been in Europe a single man equal to the occasion, and the series of blunders is, perhaps, without parallel in history.

Your suggestion of a movement for the neutralisation of great international waterways is excellent. It is just the kind of project that the League of Nations might undertake, but could not be done without America's co-operation, and this seems still a good way off. The League of Nations Assembly seems to have been doing some good work but many of the States represented are quite ignorant, and, therefore, liable to be carried away by plausible speech. The so-called Latin nations, who have to be addressed in French, are, I hear, completely swayed by the eloquence of Viviani. Many of them ought not to have been admitted to the League, but that was one of Wilson's countless blunders.

To Mr. M. Storey

Hindleap,
Forest Row,
Sussex.
January 4th, 1921.

Thank you for your interesting letter of December 20th — I will try to answer your questions about Ireland categorically.

(1) The Sinn Feiners demand independence, but many — probably most of them — would be content with less: *i.e.*, very wide Home Rule under the Crown.

(2) A majority — I think a large majority of the people do not want independence. The Roman Catholic Church does not want it, nor the commercial class, nor the farmers who export dairy products and cattle to England.

(3) England could not concede independence, and if the Protes-

tant North East was left as part of Ireland civil war might be expected.

(4) There is now no serious grievance in Ireland from unjust laws.

(5) Whether Ireland could get on financially alone would depend on the policy she might attempt. She could not maintain an army or navy.

(6) Most of my Irish friends say that an offer of Dominion Government, *i.e.*, Canada plus British control of Army, Navy, and Foreign Policy, would be accepted if a secret popular vote, freely given, could be taken.

(7) There is no body of men to represent the Irish people. The Sinn Feiners have the sympathy of the large majority of Roman Catholics, but that is partly because the present government in Ireland has made itself hated and despised.

The way to settlement is to offer the widest Home Rule that can be safely given; *i.e.*, Self-government, minus Army and Navy, and with the retention of the *legal* supremacy of the United Kingdom Parliament, with the understanding that it would never be used save in a very extreme case. The greatest difficulty has been the Protestant minority in the north-east corner, small but resolute and pugnacious. It has now, by the act just passed been given a Constitution and a Parliament for itself; and in order to avoid bloodshed that new Constitution ought to be respected and the North East corner left severely alone. They would probably come in before long for commercial reasons, especially if the other five-sixths of Ireland managed their business fairly.

The League of Nations Assembly at Geneva accepted Austria, Bulgaria, and Albania, and developed a certain amount of cosmopolitan spirit. May we not hope that if it is able to show some good results there will be a return of sentiment in your people, towards some sort of *effective* combination of nations to avert war? There is surely more of a true love of peace in the United States than anywhere else.

one can again feel about America as men felt in the days when yours was the one country which set an example of constitutional freedom.

To President Lowell

3, Buckingham Gate, S.W.,
9th May, 1921.

The miners' strike has imposed grievous hardships and frightful economic loss upon the country. It is essentially more revolutionary, and even more communist than other countries seem to have realised. I am daily amazed at the extent to which quasi communistic principles have spread among the educated and well-to-do classes. Even the Bishops are permeated by them, and still more the average clergy, even of the Church of England.

CHAPTER XXXI

MODERN DEMOCRACIES

The propensity to obey is at least as strong as the sense of independence, and much more generally diffused.

BRYCE

A quoi bon vivre si ce n'est pour s'instruire, c'est à dire pour modifier sans relâche sa pensée.

MELCHIOR DE VOGUÉ

SOME six or seven years after their marriage the Bryces began to look about for a small house in the country where they could spend the week-ends and some weeks in the vacations. The site must be peaceful and remote, yet easily accessible from London, high above sea level and commanding open views. These requirements were not rapidly satisfied. Eventually, however, Mr. Douglas Freshfield, an old friend and a fellow mountaineer, came to the rescue with the offer of a site (about 650 feet above sea level) on the edge of Hindleap Warren in Ashdown Forest. It was a wild larch plantation with a few Scotch firs and a few groups of Douglas pines, but commanding fine views of the Weald of Sussex and the Forest and the middle distance of cultivated lowland with the rounded shapes of the South Downs beyond. Here then the Bryces determined to build and here from the summer of 1898 onwards they made their English

often spent hours of railway travelling in thinking out a subject and noting it down. He would frequently also dictate letters to me as we travelled. He would usually work nearly up to lunch time, getting a breath of air at the last moment. After that, he would take a little time off, read the paper (or have it read to him) and smoke a cigarette or two, which he always rolled himself, having learned the habit in Spain many years ago. He seldom smoked while he wrote. Then he would work on for most of the afternoon, and he always put off taking his walk as late as possible, often till it was dark, in order to make the most of the daylight for work. His eyesight was extremely strong and good, but he found that reading and writing by artificial light was apt to be trying to him. He seldom did any serious work after dinner, though he would sit and think over a subject. I usually read something to him, and he often wrote his letters late in the evening and read a little. I think he had a natural habit of sitting up late from his youth up, and this was confirmed by twenty-seven years in the House of Commons, in the days when they sat up to all hours. He retained the habit to the end of his life. The last thing at night it was his custom to go out for a few minutes to look at the stars and take note of the weather and breathe the night air, wherever he was — by the sea or in the mountains or on deck on an ocean voyage. He had great interest in meteorological things and had a keen eye for all weather signs, and he had a record kept of the rainfall at Hindleap from the beginning, sending up the records each year to the Meteorological Office.

In his work, when he had once thought out his subject he would write fairly quickly, but he was very fastidious in his method of expression and corrected both his manuscript and his proofs remorselessly — so much so that, when I read manuscript for him it was sometimes hard to get at the subject through the maze.

He took immense pains in collecting his information and also in testing its accuracy. He corresponded for this purpose with men all over the world who could supply what he wanted or correct what he had already received, and this entailed an enormous amount of work over and above his own writing; but the result was that in very few cases, and only on minor points were his main statements and conclusions contradicted or disputed.

He himself had great power of steady thinking and he always declared that people as a whole did not think nearly enough. They read too much and thought too little.

During the later years of his life, and more particularly from 1918 to 1921, Bryce's spare energies were largely employed upon an elaborate study of modern Democracies for which he had begun to make collections as early as 1904. Here was a theme to which an experience of the working of political institutions in many lands was clearly contributory. What an experience it was, varying from the little Republic of Andorra where in 1873 he had seen the head of the Republic, "a stalwart old peasant in a red flannel shirt threshing his own corn" to the brand-new Parliament of China with its queer miscellany of frock coats and pigtails which he had visited in 1913! His practical knowledge of Parliamentary life in England, his pro-

civilization in 1909 than he had been twenty years before. In the work of his old age, however, he definitely set himself "to repress the pessimism of experience." He knew that he stood in danger of painting too dark a picture, and that this must be guarded against; and so we have in *Modern Democracies* an estimate wonderfully balanced and steady, and wholesomely free of the besetting proclivity of old age — the tendency to disparage the present in comparison with years gone by. What, however, is clear is that the certainty of assured progress has vanished. Bryce did not exclude the possibility that "an ice age might await the mind of man."

The belief that the book, though "every generalisation now made is only provisional" might be a contribution to sound thought and action in the sphere of practical politics gave momentum to his pen; and the creation of seven new democratic States in Europe after the Great War encouraged him to believe that the lessons to be derived from the experience of the older democracies might be turned to useful account by the statesmen of the new European republics.

Sometimes however, it seemed to him that his book was addressed rather to a past than to the present generation. "That generation busied itself with institutions; this generation is bent rather upon the purposes which institutions may be made to serve." It is certainly true that a world, excited to the tremendous issues of the great war and by far-reaching schemes of social regeneration was in no mood to listen with quiet attention to an author whose conspicuous merit was a close and subtle appreciation of constitutional agencies in the State.

Yet this work of Bryce's old age is a wonderful legacy of political wisdom. Whether he treats of France or Switzerland or Australia he handles his facts with a keen sense of their significance, pressing no conclusion too far, but always holding in his mind counterbalancing or limiting considerations. New experiments naturally attract his special interest such as the referendum and initiative in Switzerland, the reforming movements in the United States, the socialistic legislation in Australia and New Zealand. He analyses the qualities of the Swiss mind revealed in the working of the referendum and finds them to be independence, parsimony, dislike of officials, jealousy of the Cantonal government and suspicion of novelty, and after a cautious summary of the results of the referendum concludes that it is specially suited to "small areas and to small populations not dominated by party spirit." It would not then be reasonable to infer that because the system of direct popular legislation has succeeded in Switzerland, it would do equally well in other countries. "Such success as has been attained in Switzerland by the method of direct popular legislation is due to the historical antecedents of the Swiss people, to their long practice of self-government in small communities, to social equality, and to the pervading spirit of patriotism and sense of public duty. No like success can be assumed for countries where similar conditions are absent." Again opposed as he had always been to the feminist movement as "an amazing departure from ancient and deeply rooted custom with hardly a parallel in the history of society," he is bound to admit, writing of the emancipation of women in the United States (1920) that women

parliamentary assemblies under a democratic régime? Bryce finds that the two defects most commonly charged against legislative bodies in our times were first that they were too little representative of the best knowledge, wisdom, and experience of the country, and secondly that they were liable to fall under the control of one political party disposed to press through class measures in a hasty and tyrannical spirit. The best remedy for these two evils was a properly constituted Second Chamber. Indeed a special section is devoted to the reasons which in our time increase the need for a Second Chamber. What was needed to correct the evils complained of in popular legislatures was a second Chamber not popularly elected or in which the pressure coming from constituents was less heavy than it is now apt to be for the members of the popular House. This, as we have seen, was no new doctrine with Bryce. He had always been a Second Chamber man, and the gathering experiences of a long life had only served to supply fresh support for his early faith.

For the historically minded man there is no such thing as an ideal state suited to every age and clime. Bryce had seen enough of South America to realise how futile it was to confer self-governing institutions on a people unfit to comprehend or use them. A State was the result of history and the mode in which one form of government worked was conditioned and determined by the historical preparation of the people. To grasp this fact was at once to avoid many errors into which the critics of foreign nations are apt to fall. They see a State differing in many respects from their own. They find fault with these differences. They assume that these differences argue some original sin — but the differences are the result of a different historical preparation. When they are understood by reference to their causes they are shown to be natural, to be inevitable, and to be consistent with many honourable and wholesome features of national life. So Englishmen lightly condemn the French Republic forgetting that whereas they were well prepared for democratic government, France lacked all of the preliminary discipline which acclimatises a people to the use of political liberty. Indeed the whole treatment of France in *Modern Democracies* is nearer to the truth and more discerning than that which is to be found in the much applauded volumes in which Mr. Bodley transmitted to the English-speaking world the political philosophy of M. Taine and the prejudices of the Quartier St. Germain. To those who would hastily condemn the French Republic Bryce replies that its Foreign Policy has been more exempt from error and weakness than was that of the Empire and that France is a soil unfavourable to demagogues, less favourable even than England. Once possessed of these two impregnable truths the student of the French Republic recovers his balance.[1]

It is not to be expected that a book written with the hand of extreme old age will reveal any new lights on the character of its author. The Bryce of *Modern Democracies* is the Bryce of the *American Commonwealth*, inexhaustible in toil, zealous for truth, careless of rhetorical effect, interested in minutiae, alert to the play of political forces,

[1] A more authoritative encomium may be found in M. Charles Lyon-Caen's *Notice sur la vie et les travaux de Lord Bryce*, 1925 (*Académie des Sciences Morales et Politiques*).

must be referred. Bryce represented, as no other individual could, all that the Academy stood for, and with the prestige of his Ambassadorship fresh about him, he gave the Academy the status to which such a body was entitled to aspire.

Much of the detail of Bryce's work for the Academy is known only to his colleagues on the Council, who had the benefit of his wise handling of its domestic policy. To the public he appeared as presiding over the reading of papers, to which he could provide fitting introduction and illuminating comment. But in addition to these services, he delivered four Presidential addresses, which will remain as the monument of his tenure of office. The first, after a comprehensive survey of the work and needs of the Academy (which had then, for the first time, received a small grant from the Government — for the foundation of its series of *Social and Economic Records*), ended with some characteristic remarks on the state of learning in the countries which he had most recently visited, Japan, China, Australasia, and South America. The second, delivered after nearly a year of war, is a notable attempt "to note and set down in a spirit of detachment the impressions made upon us by the events which our eyes see and watch as they pass into history." Bryce, while as fervently patriotic as any man, and entirely devoid of that pseudo-impartiality which delights in weighting the scales against its own country, had the training of a historian and the wisdom of a great student of humanity, and his observations on the phenomena of the war, stated *sine ira et studio*, will have permanent value as a reflection of the best mind of the time at the height of the great conflict. He also stated rightly (and the example of the Academy had no little weight with kindred bodies) the position of a learned society in relation to the war: —

"The Council has thought it better not to let these events disturb the even tenor of our way, but rather desirable that we should seek in the pursuit of our studies a measure of occasional rest and refreshment of mind from vexing anxieties and dolorous thoughts. . . . The general feeling has evidently been that the more all learned bodies are kept outside the passions of war the better for them and for the nations. When strife has ended, and a period has elapsed long enough to soften the bitterness of feeling which now exists, it will be for learned bodies to try to link up the bonds of personal regard and intellectual co-operation, now unhappily severed, which have in time past served to bind the great peoples to one another."

From personal recollection of conversations and correspondence I can testify that Bryce's influence was always used to deprecate the proposals which were sometimes made that action should be taken against the Corresponding Fellows who were subjects of the States with which the country was at war.

In 1916 this philosophic survey of the war was continued, and this address is particularly noticeable for its summary of the forces which make for war and for peace. He notes regretfully that nearly all the historic causes of war seem to continue to operate with full force, with the noteworthy exception of religious or ecclesiastical hatred. Among the forces that may make for peace in the future he examines particularly the proposals already under discussion in this country and in the United States for "some kind of federation or league or alliance of nations charged with the duty of compelling disputant Powers

CHAPTER XXXII

LAST VISIT TO AMERICA

But — a stirring thrills the air
Like to sounds of joyance there
That the rages
Of the ages
Shall be cancelled, and deliverance offered from the darts that were,
Consciousness the Will informing, till It fashion all things fair!

THOMAS HARDY. *The Dynasts.*

THE last year of Bryce's life was signalised by the appearance of one of the most brilliant of his smaller pieces, a lecture on the Study of American History delivered at the Mansion House, London (June 27th, 1921) to inaugurate the newly founded Sir George Watson Chair of American History, Literature and Institutions. With the object of this foundation, which was to serve as a permanent memorial of America's loyal partnership with the British Empire during the war as well as of the historic ties which unite our two peoples Bryce was, of course, in profound sympathy. A very great part of his life-work had been directed to the very purpose of improving the mutual understanding and friendship of the two peoples and here he was enabled in bare outline to supply what had been noted as an omission in his American Commonwealth, a general conspectus of the history of the United States.

There are few better examples of the art of elucidating in simple language and in a small compass the salient features of a nation's history than this masterly little treatise, in the course of which Bryce incidentally referred to his favourite thesis that the separation of the American colonies from Britain in the eighteenth century was not the unmixed blessing which it has been generally represented to be.

"The misfortune was, not so much that independence came, as that it came in the way it did. . . . In 1776 things might have happened otherwise and happened better. Independence, virtual and legal, ought to have come gradually and peacefully as the natural result of America's growth. Coming as the result of a war it left bitter memories behind, which poisoned the relations of peoples for generations thereafter."

And then he proceeds to speculate upon what might have happened if the controversy under George III had been peaceably adjusted as the wisest statesmen in England desired. Perhaps the French Revolution would have been averted. Perhaps the economic development of America would have been slower and for that reason more wholesome. Perhaps the example set in 1834 by the mother country of abolishing slavery in the West Indies and South Africa would have influenced America to adopt a policy of gradual emancipation! Such speculations may be dismissed as unsubstantial, but they are at least valuable as rousing the historic optimist from his dogmatic slumbers.

Later on in the summer Bryce crossed the Atlantic with his wife to pay a last visit to the United States. He had

represent and express the convictions and wishes of the people? The citizens of democracy can do everything if they express their united will. The raindrops that fall from the clouds unite to form a tiny rill, and meeting other rills, it becomes a rivulet, and the rivulet grows into a brook and the brooks as they join into one another swell into a river that sweeps on its resistless course downwards into the sea. Each of us is only a drop but together we make up the volume of public opinion which determines the character and action of the State. What all the nations now need is a public opinion which shall in every nation give more constant thought and keener attention to international policy and lift it to a higher plane. The peoples can do this in every country if the best citizens give them the lead. You in America are well fitted to set an example in this effort to the European peoples smitten down by the war and painfully struggling to regain their feet. They will gratefully welcome whatever you may do now or hereafter by sympathy and counsel or by active co-operation in efforts to redress the injustices and mitigate the passions which distract most parts of the Old World. Your help, your powerful and disinterested help will be of incomparable service in any effort to rescue your brother peoples from the oldest and deadliest of all the evils that have afflicted mankind."

Before leaving the States the Bryces paid a visit to their old friends Dr. and Mrs. Charles Eliot at Mount Desert on the coast of Maine. The fine rock pinnacles in this favourite summer resort were well known to Bryce for he had long ago scaled them all, but there was an island visible from the coast which he had never visited. An expedition was accordingly planned for Bacon Island, about half an hour's sail. The party landed and while the Eliots and Mrs. Bryce sat on the shore, Bryce rambled over the island and returned having discovered all that was to be known about it, including the fact that the three families who constituted the island society were not on speaking terms with one another. On the return journey he sat in the prow facing a glorious sunset, saying nothing and keeping his head rigidly fixed for more than twenty minutes, while he watched the changing hues on rock, sky, and sea. Then he turned round and said decisively, "Eliot, that is the most beautiful landscape in the world which can be taken in at a single glance."

A last public engagement was arranged for him in New York on October 9th, when addressing the Merchants' Association he returned to the central theme of Anglo-American relations. He opened with a reference to the war and the disappointments which had followed in the Peace, but added that if the war had not brought the moral regeneration which was hoped for, it had done one great thing for America and for England — "It had revealed the presence in both nations of those great fundamental virtues, courage, self-sacrifice, devotion to a cause, which are the fundamental qualities on which the life of every nation reposes and which have been the glory of the stock to which we belong in both its branches — the glory of that stock for more than a thousand years." He then spoke of Ireland and of his confidence that a settlement of the Irish difficulty would be effected. "The vast majority of the British people desire it. There is hardly a man in England who does not desire, with all his

CHAPTER XXXIII

LAST DAYS

Εἰ δ' οὕτω, τὸ ανθρώπινον ἀγαθὸν ψυχῆς
ἐνέργεια γίγνεται κατ' ἀρετὴν, εἰ δὲ πλείους
αἱ ἀρεταὶ, κατὰ τὴν ἀρίστην καὶ τελειοτάτην,
Ἔτι δ' ἐν βίῳ τελείῳ.

ARISTOTLE.

But if so, human good is an energy of the soul in accordance with virtue and, if virtues be plural, according to the best and most perfect virtue, and further in a complete life.

WHEN Bryce returned to England from America in the late autumn of 1921, he found a sudden and to him unexpected change in the Irish situation. The miserable revolver war which had caused nearly as many casualties as one quiet day on the Western Front had shown to the more reasonable section of the Irish Secessionists that if the British Government was unable to rule Ireland, it was powerful enough with only a slight expenditure of force to prevent an independent Republic from ruling; while it had likewise exhibited to the British Government the odium attaching to the prolongation of a guerilla struggle which was necessarily degrading to both sides. At the same time the opening of the Ulster Parliament by the King confronted the Irish leaders with the accomplished fact of partition. An opportunity was thus opened for negotiations on the basis of a full concession of Dominion rights to Catholic Ireland within the Empire; and in the end and with infinite pain a Treaty was struck despite the opposition of an implacable section of Republicans on the one hand and of Die Hard Conservatives on the other.

The debate on the Irish Treaty in the House of Lords was memorable for the speeches of two veterans, who had experienced every peripety in the Anglo-Irish drama since first Mr. Gladstone launched his policy of Home Rule forty years before. Lord Morley was drawn from his retirement at Wimbledon to move the adoption of the Treaty and made on that occasion to a House crowded from floor to gallery his last public utterance. Later on in the debate the Peers listened to a speech from Bryce marked by a return of that spirit of hope, which the disappointments of political life, severe as they had recently been, had never been able to extinguish. He welcomed the Treaty as a sign of better times, pointing out that in a society of peasant proprietors, such as now existed in Ireland, there was no danger of Communism, and that there was more friendly feeling between Catholic and Protestant than was usually supposed. He regretted that the offer had not been made sooner, but confessed that the Treaty had gone further than five years before he thought he should ever himself be able to go. In conclusion he expressed in a few eloquent phrases his hope that "the people of Ireland may attain to a unity of hearts and purposes which will express itself in a respect for law and in attempting the long-deferred task of constructive statesmanship." These were his last words addressed to the red benches.[1]

[1] Lord Lansdowne wrote in terms of warm approval of this speech, June 18.

In the tranquil atmosphere of the House of Lords, where the keenness of party difference is muffled by a long tradition of stately courtesy Bryce attained to a position as a speaker which had never belonged to him in the Lower Chamber. "There was," said Lord Curzon, "scarcely a subject on which he was not qualified to address us with authority and few which he did not adorn. The range of his knowledge, the inexhaustible fertility of his mind were such that the words of the poet in their best connotation leap to our lips!

> "'A man so various that he seemed to be
> Not one but all mankind's epitome.'"

Whether he was discoursing on Children's Magistrates in the United States, or on the comparative aptitude of Indians and Chinamen for Self-Government, or on the precedents for the trial and execution of the Sovereign of a hostile State (the latest, not an encouraging example, was apparently the judicial murder of Conradin in 1268), or on the proposal to federalise Great Britain, he was always easy, abundant and full alike of good sense and knowledge. If his estimate of the political situation was not invariably exact, he brought into every discussion in which he took part a width and serenity of outlook as well as a wealth of relevant information and experience which were always of value; and having a ready command of pure and unaffected English, he was listened to with pleasure as well as with respect.

Despite the burden of his years he was still full of projects. In the winter recess 1921–2 he was busy with the preparation of a volume of his *Memories of Travel* which was to be followed by the long delayed Life of Justinian, for which fresh material was to be collected in Rome at Eastertide. In January he and Lady Bryce went down to Sidmouth for sea air and sunshine. He had become thinner in the last few years but showed little abatement of his physical and none of his mental powers. He enjoyed exercise as usual, walking six miles over hilly country to attend a service on Armistice Day 1921, and had lost no part of the relish which attended the operations of his eager and unresting mind. An article about Troy and Ithaca about which he had been corresponding with Dr. Walter Leaf in April, and for which a sheaf of pencil notes remain, was occupying his thoughts on the last day of his life. Once more he had plunged into the times depicted by the Homeric poems, the delight of his boyhood and the solace of his age. Then when he had accomplished the tale of work for the evening he said to his wife that he would go out and look at the stars. These were his last words, for on that soft winter night with the stars shining brightly over sea and coast he died quietly in sleep.[1]

A week before he had expressed the hope that he might soon complete a catalogue of the Flora of Ashdown Forest, his country home.

There is nothing to lament in the close of a life so crowded in activity and so rich in achievement. Yet in the manifestations of regard which were provoked by the

[1] He lies in the Grange Cemetery at Edinburgh where his parents and his sister Kathleen are also buried. From the grave the hills round Edinburgh, Arthur's Seat and the Salisbury Crags on the one hand and the Pentland Hills on the other, are in the field of vision.

news of Bryce's death there was something distinctive, marking them off from the tributes which are ordinarily paid on the departure of old and famous men. First there was the impression of extraordinary goodness and elevation of character, and second the rare spectacle of a life dedicated amidst much political and scientific activity to the advancement of great human causes. "He did as much," wrote Bishop Gore, "as any man of our time, to keep up the moral level of national life and to promote the fellowship of mankind." "He occupied," wrote Lord Cecil of Chelwood, "a unique position in the esteem of his fellow countrymen. He was, as it were, their moral referee, and his judgment on any question of public morality was accepted without question. His position was due not only to his wide experience, his extraordinary knowledge and natural impartiality. It was, I suppose, the deep moral purpose which directed every thought and every action of his life." It was felt that a citizen not of one country but of the world had passed away, the friend of the weak and the oppressed in every quarter of the globe, a sage whose verdict upon perplexed and controversial questions appeared to many people in many lands to be the oracle of absolute justice. The vastness of the geographical area over which these sentiments were experienced was very remarkable and probably unprecedented.

In Britain he received the honours usually accorded to illustrious public men. The King wrote of him as "an old friend and a trusted counseller to whom I could always turn, confident in the strength and wisdom of his advice," and alluded to the love and respect in which he was held not only in his own country and in America but among all English-speaking peoples. Memorial services were held in Westminster Abbey, at Lincolns Inn, of which society he was a Bencher, and by Trinity and Oriel Colleges, of which two bodies he was at the time of his death an Honorary Fellow. But even more striking were the expressions of gratitude which were evoked by the recollection of his devoted service to the cause of the Christian peoples in the East. The Armenians held special commemorative services in the Chapel Royal, London, and in Constantinople. The Greeks paid their tribute in the Greek Orthodox Church in Bayswater. "There is no Armenian," said Mr. J. S. Malcolm, speaking at the Armenian service in the Chapel Royal, "whether in our home lands or in our dispersion who does not couple the name of Lord Bryce with that of Gladstone, whose mantle fell twenty years ago upon his shoulders. Whoever has failed us, these two great hearts never failed." They felt also that the loss was irreparable, and that there was no one to fill his place.

To the Greeks also, whether of the Greek Kingdom or of the dispersion, his was a name to be ranked with the names of Byron and Gladstone. "To those of our nation," said Sir John Stavridi, "who are still under bondage, the news of Viscount Bryce's death . . . will cause widespread grief and even despair. His name had become known throughout the Near East as that of the greatest champion of the oppressed and he was loved by them on account of the successful appeals he made on their behalf to the conscience of mankind. More lives have been saved by his pen and his voice than even he realised and it is a notable fact that after every denunciation by him of the outrages perpetrated on the Christians in the East, the massacres immediately ceased."

To the Jews also he appeared "as a true and lifelong friend." "Lord Bryce," says a writer in the *Jewish Chronicle*, "came into close contact with the Jews of the Tower Hamlets Division which he represented in the House of Commons and gained an estimate of our peoples which as he himself more than once observed, impelled him, apart from all else to champion the Jewish cause." But what was more striking, because it would not so easily have been surmised, was the impression which he had succeeded in making in China and Japan. Here he was regarded as the savant who had revealed the true anatomy of modern democratic government as it was practised by the white races in both hemispheres of the globe. The secret which the Far East desired to understand and to apply, if necessary, to their own uses, was to be found in the books of this British sage. To the Chinese and Japanese students of political phenomena the *American Commonwealth* and *Modern Democracies* were the last authoritative deliverance of Western wisdom. They were read and commented on; and when the intelligence of their author's death was received, it was felt that a great teacher had passed away, from whom China and Japan had learnt much and had yet much to learn. Early in 1923 a young Japanese came to pay his respects and to pay condolences to Lady Bryce in Buckingham Gate. Having ascertained that a bust standing in the drawing-room represented the Master, and that the grave was not in London but in Edinburgh, he silently proceeded to open a little parcel he had brought and produced a small enamel bowl in which he placed thin stalks of some aromatic plant (somewhat like lavender). He then placed a small table in front of the bust and on it he set the enamel bowl, having lighted the stalks which began to smoulder and curl away in smoke, in the manner of incense. As the smoke rose he stood behind the table facing the bust and made two very low bows to it. All this was done with great simplicity and reverence, and it was obvious that it was a homage to the Spirit of the departed. Then he came back to Lady Bryce and said very gravely — "That is what we do for our own people."

In the United States the sentiments provoked by the intelligence of his death were sincere and universal. President Harding's Conference on Naval Disarmament was sitting at the time in Washington, and when the Committee on the Pacific and Far Eastern Question met on the morning of January 23rd, the news having been received late in the previous night, speeches were delivered in Bryce's honour by Mr. Hughes, the Secretary of State, by Mr. Elihu Root, by M. Jusserand and by Mr. Balfour, the British Delegate. A cartoon by Rollin Kirby in a widely circulated paper representing Uncle Sam laying a wreath before the picture of James Bryce represented in a pictorial form the general impression that the United States had experienced a national loss. In New York, where he was much beloved, a great assembly was gathered at the impressive Memorial Service held in St. John's Cathedral to listen to addresses by Bishop Manning, by Mr. J. W. Davis, and by Mr. Henry Fairfield Osborn. The American Press was unanimous in its recognition of his goodness, his scholarship and his services to the American people. "No scholar," wrote the *Boston Evening Transcript*, "ever wore the graces of learning more lightly or revealed them with less sense of vanity or care of conscious possession." As an example of the hold which he had acquired over the affections of the American people, it was recalled how frequently the hope had been expressed during the last two or three years of his residence at Washington that he might be induced to accept the Presidency of one of the great Universities of the United States and thus spend the remainder of his days in the New World. Perhaps, however, the most eloquent testimony to the position which he held in the United States is the brief inscription on the walls of the British Embassy at Washington, set up by the Commissioners of the city in his lifetime. "In this house lived from 1907 to 1913 James Bryce, the author of the *American Commonwealth*."

The coloured population shared the general emotion which the news of his death evoked in the United States. They recognised in him a friend. Had not the British Ambassador and his wife stayed at Tuskeegee with Booker Washington and more than once received the champion of the African race at the Embassy? Had he not shown his interest in the measures which were being advanced for the education and social improvement of the coloured people? Was he not the determined opponent of racial hatred, injustice, and violence? The coloured men were right. Bryce was no theoretical egalitarian. He was strongly of opinion that it had been a mistake to concede the franchise to the men of colour, and that from this false theory of equality hastily adopted much political corruption and dishonesty had flowed. But he held with Booker Washington that there was a sphere of useful economic labour for which the coloured races were well adapted and that within that sphere they should receive an economic education calculated to give support to all that was most wholesome in the African character, without exciting political ambition, which could only lead to general bitterness and strife.

Though he worked with a great variety of English public men for many years and was in most friendly intercourse with them he was not altogether of them either by race or in his deepest affinities. On his father's side he was, as we have seen, of pure Scottish blood; his mother was Northern Irish with a Celtic strain in her composition. Though actually born in Ireland he grew up and was educated in Scotland up to the age of nineteen after which period he passed his life in England, at an English University, at the English bar, in English journalism, and in Parliament at Westminster. This mixture of Scottish and Irish blood gave him on the one hand the cautious sobriety and shrewdness of judgment which belong to the Scottish temperament, and on the other the ardour of spirit and gift of imaginative sympathy which are part of the best Irish inheritance. In their turn these Scottish and Irish characteristics were greatly affected by his English environment and he became a blend of all three races. His intense interest in the various nationalities and peoples of the world and the ease with which he was able to get into touch with them and to see through their eyes may be largely attributed to these circumstances. He usually refused to call himself either Scottish, Irish, or English, and when asked on one occasion what he was, he replied, "I think that I am a citizen of the world."

To those who were most intimate he presented the impression of a character, proud, sensitive, independent, somewhat detached from the ordinary life and drawing upon deep inner reserves of thought and feeling. His nature was pure and simple, deriving strength from deep spiritual convictions which ran like a thread through his whole life colouring his ideas and determining his attitude towards the world and his fellow-men. With great powers of enjoyment and an unusual capacity for forming and retaining affectionate friendships he combined a keen sense of the frailties and imperfections of human nature (his own included) and this gave to his mind, which was at once complex and contemplative, recurring shades of melancholy. On matters of principle and conduct he was stern in judgment and yet while he condemned the sin would often feel compassion for the sinner. His opinions, which were reached only after much thought and deliberation, once formed were held with tenacity, however much they might commit him to the furtherance of causes unpopular and even forlorn. Liberty was his watchword. His belief in Liberty in its widest sense, and in every sphere of thought and action, was deep-rooted and remained unshaken through life. Though the forms which Liberty might take might sometimes be evil, he regarded it as the guiding star for men and nations in their progress through Time.

There are unending stories to illustrate his omniscience. Professor Gilbert Murray recounts how in a literary discussion with Stopford Brooke, Bryce not only abounded with quotations in support of his own theory but also supplied his adversary with all the facts and quotations, which he was endeavouring to recall but could not quite remember, to buttress up the opposite contention. On another occasion some naturalists were discussing South African antelopes and more especially two closely related species which it was almost impossible to distinguish. Bryce intervened and said that there should be no difficulty in distinguishing Antelope A from Antelope B because in the case of A the spiral of the horns wound from left to right whereas in the case of Antelope B, it wound from right to left.

All this miscellaneous learning was allied with a quite unusual measure of simple goodness. "There was no one," writes Lord Lansdowne, "quite like him. His boundless knowledge, unspoiled by any taint of pedantry, his wonderful modesty, his infinite patience with people less learned than himself, all these helped to make him a singularly lovable and interesting personality." In the blaze of his intellectual eminence one was always surprised to find, in Sir George Trevelyan's words, "what a very good fellow he was." Besides his vast correspondence on matters of business and in satisfaction of his learned curiosity he would often write to unknown young men in the United States and in other parts of the world as well, who desired his help and direction at some crisis of their lives. Youthful scholars never appealed to him in vain. He would reply in his own hand and with great promptitude to their enquiries. Thus, in addition to his enormous personal acquaintance, there was a large circle of people in every part of the world who, though they had never seen him, were indebted to his kindness.

If one feature were to be singled out as specially marking his career as a public man it would be his fierce detestation of cruelty. The thought of the prevalence of cruelty in the world was a continual distress to him and an urgent call to action, and there is nothing finer in his long career than the unshaken persistence with which he advocated the cause of the suffering Christian populations of the Near East and endeavoured to stir the conscience of civilised men and women to a sense of the horrors which were being enacted under Turkish rule. Thus he became the acknowledged champion of oppressed and downtrodden people all the world over, and hateful as the idea of war was to him, and strongly as he was opposed to the notion that war was a purifier of character and in certain circumstances a power for the regeneration of society, a crusade on behalf of Eastern Christians would at any time have appeared to him to be a legitimate assertion of the empire of moral ideas over men.

It may seem strange that emotions so quick and painful should have played so large a part in the life of a man whose published work is characterised by a patient accumulation of facts and a long-sighted refinement of statement — qualities which seem to indicate an unemotional nature. For Bryce, however, the imaginative and ratiocinative elements of the human soul were blended in not unequal proportions. If he was a man of scientific method with a passion for exact mensuration, he was also the practical idealist dreaming dreams and seeing visions, and battling for generous causes which appealed to the common heart of man. As with Mr. Gladstone, a strong vein of Christian feeling entered into his attitude towards public questions. Consciously or unconsciously the conduct of public men or the propriety of high transactions of state was brought to the bar of an ethical judgment rooted in the soil of Christian belief. Thus it was not because he thought British policy towards the Transvaal Government lacking in positive justification that he condemned it, but because, from the standpoint of Christian chivalry, it seemed to him to fall short of the measure of clemency and consideration which a strong and civilised Power should show in its dealings with a small and backward people. The ideal Christian statesman would, in his view, have acted with more patience and forbearance.

Perhaps a life of political combat is not well suited to a man so conspicuous for tenderness of feeling and so easily saddened and exasperated by the spectacle of wrong. Had Bryce spent himself less eagerly in chivalrous causes he would probably have made a greater impression upon his Parliamentary contemporaries, for the House of Commons listens most readily to men of moderate views and highly disciplined emotions and is constitutionally averse from displays of philanthropic sentiment, however genuine. Moreover, the causes which Bryce had most nearly at heart were remote from the knowledge and experience of the ordinary member. A tragedy in a slum in Aberdeen or a miscarriage of justice in a London police court makes a greater impression upon a British audience than the report of the massacre of an alien people in the distant highlands of Anatolia.

The ingrained caution of his nature was carried to a

point which unfitted him for political leadership. He was never the man to take swift and dangerous decisions, not because he was afraid of unpopularity, or infirm in adherence to principles, but because his mind was of the scientific and balancing order, as fertile in suggesting arguments against any particular line of conduct as it was ingenious in presenting a case for it. Thus for some time he hovered in uncertainty as to whether it was his duty to offer an opposition to the Government over the South African War, being drawn in one direction by his personal liking for Cecil Rhodes and his feeling that the Government of President Kruger had been obscurantist and oppressive, and in the other direction by his resentment at the Raid, by his sympathy with small liberty-loving Republics, and by his conviction that the situation had been handled with a lack of tact and patience on the British side. A similar spell of hesitation affected him at the beginning of August 1914. On both occasions he hovered for a day or two in genuine division and perplexity of spirit when the born leader of a political party would have darted forward in full confidence and with flying pinions. It is true that when his course was once taken, he pursued it with energy and without deviation but in politics, as in war, the moment is all important and the art of leadership consists in seizing it. The crisis which throws gifted and perspicacious men into torments of conscientious doubt finds the leader of a party unruffled and unperplexed.

For a man of his singular activity and reach of mind, Bryce was curiously exempt from metaphysical misgivings and scruples and indifferent to much that most interested his contemporaries in the region of philosophical speculation. This must not be taken to mean that he was not alive to what was being said or thought upon such subjects as the criticism of the New Testament or the relations between Science and Religion or the ultimate constitution of matter, but that philosophical speculation possessed no attraction. Any tormenting doubts as to the deepest matters of Faith which may have assailed him were either vanquished early or resolved in secret. Once when Leslie Stephen was pressing the agnostic case with his habitual force, Bryce asked him in tones of unaffected simplicity and earnestness to break off the argument on the ground that it gave him pain to hear it. Again when allusion was made to some books tending to humanise the character of Christ which were put out during the Great War, he said with great earnestness to his sister: 'When I read the New Testament I am always struck by its sublimity.' The essential faith of his fathers, robbed no doubt of many of its dogmatic trappings and of the austere exclusiveness which made it incompatible with the highest point of intellectual cultivation was enough for him. He did not then employ his intellect in the examination of the moral and metaphysical foundations of Being. He was a man of facts and feelings rather than of fine-spun arguments about the Absolute, of active rather than of speculative energies. But he had what is most valuable in the conduct of life, a strong and serious moral purpose, so powerful and so present that he was never very far from large thoughts about big subjects. Men who attach, as he did, real importance to the simple verities expose themselves to the charge of being platitudinous. Such an allegation may be fatal to the reputation of a philosopher: but for the thinker in action it is no drawback to feel the authentic force of the simple moral truths which lesser men accept and circulate on hearsay.

Of religion itself he spoke seldom, practising the reticence of the truly wise. Yet he succeeded in communicating to men, far removed from him in the plane of political or religious conviction, the distinct impression of an essentially religious nature. One of his friends at Oxford in the days of his Civil Law Professorship was Edward Talbot, then Warden of Keble and afterwards Bishop of Winchester. Dr. Talbot was a High Churchman and a Conservative, Bryce a radical Presbyterian and a vigorous opponent of Church Establishment in any form. Yet the Anglican Bishop writes thus of his old Oxford examiner: "While he held the Chair at Oxford and came up for short visits from his busy London life, I think he was glad to find us, from circumstances, less purely academical than some residents. If I am to say anything more distinctive it would be this. He came into Oxford life at a time when things were rather strained between parties ecclesiastical and academical and 'Liberals' seemed often to those who were not of their number to carry something in their manner a little scornful. Bryce never had a scrap of this. I always connected the difference with his Scottish origin, and the sturdy seriousness which he inherited. To put it in another way, he gave one the convincing impression that the positive side of his convictions was uppermost rather than the negative and critical, however combative he might have to be. His was a very human and hearty nature with eager energy, chivalrous sympathies, gracious instincts, warm affections. There was nothing cynical or chilling about him. What were the deepest roots of all this I am not in a position to say for I did not, so far as I remember, talk to him about the deepest matters. But I shall not be surprised if it does not come out in his biography that what we saw and heard had its springs in very strong though reticent religious convictions."

It would be an affectation to claim for Bryce that he is among the first of English writers, for apart from the fact that his contributions were rather to the literature of knowledge than to that of power he worked too rapidly to achieve supreme perfection of form. But within his own wide sphere of history, travel, politics and law, he reached a very high level of excellence. Few better or more enjoyable books of travel have been written than *Transcaucasia and Ararat. The Holy Roman Empire* is a classic which no future historian is likely to dethrone; and such is the reputation of the *American Commonwealth* that more than thirty years after its publication there are few High Schools in the United States which fail to make it the basis for the study of political institutions. When it is also remembered that the *Studies in History and Jurisprudence* and the two volumes on *Modern Democracies* are continually in the hands of academic students who occupy themselves with the problems of political science, the range and fecundity of his contribution to the instruction of his age will be appreciated. In all that he wrote there is evident the candour and charm of a real savant, a mixture of humility and power and a gift of easy, flowing and perspicuous expression not often found in alliance with such learning as his.

In a letter to a friend he expressed the view that Gibbon's perfection of style had secured him a greater reputation than his historical gifts really deserved, for Gibbon often failed to ask the right questions. From this defect, which is noticeable in the Historian of the *Decline and Fall* as soon as it has been pointed out, Bryce was singularly free. He had a genius for asking the right questions, whether he was handling mediæval chronicles or the miscellaneous company in the smoking car on an American train. Thus all his historical work, however summary, shows the hand of the master who knows what is important and what is not, and can seize with unerring precision the essential characteristics of a man, a policy or an age. Though he wrote comparatively little history, historical writing, as the *Holy Roman Empire* shows, was the true line of his talent. Clio, however, is a hard task-mistress and no one engaged in active political work can aspire to serve her.

Is it really to be regretted that Bryce did not settle down to the production of a great historical work on the scale of the *Decline and Fall?* The question will be answered differently by different persons. Some will regret his lack of concentration. Others will maintain that in an age of minute historical specialization a man of wide horizons has a special value. And Bryce was a man of the widest horizons. He had a planetary mind. It would perhaps be no exaggeration to surmise that in his knowledge of this planet and its inhabitants he stands first so far among the descendants of Adam. Let it be remembered that he had travelled in every part of the globe save the Malay Peninsula, Borneo, and Java, using his eyes and ears all day and a great part of the night, and employing every available opportunity for learning what the best authorities had to tell of the lands through which he voyaged, that he was geologist, botanist, historian, lawyer, politician, mountain climber, that his memory was of extraordinary strength and vividness, that he lived with faculties unimpaired to the age of eighty-three, that his circle of friends and acquaintances in all civilised countries, more particularly in the United States, was very large, so that he had probably in the course of his long and strenuous life seen more places, known more knowledgeable people, studied more sciences and read more instructive printed matter than anybody in the modern world whose name readily occurs to us. It may be said that his knowledge of any one civilization was below the standard of the specialist. Sir Alfred Lyall has seen much further into the fabric of Hinduism and Sir Charles Eliot into the beliefs of the Buddhists. Nevertheless his knowledge was never idle information. It had quality as well as quantity; it was accumulated for a purpose and served a purpose, being part of the material which he required to complete his understanding of the world in which he lived.

If there was one subject more than any other which engaged his attention it was the action of political forces in modern democratic communities, an immense topic to which he devoted the greater part of his minute curiosity over a period of fifty years. To interpret democracy to his own age not as an intellectual system but in its actual working in those communities in which most scope had been offered to the play of democratic principles, and to do this not in the spirit of the partisan but in that of a dispassionate naturalist culling and analysing and labelling specimens for his cabinet, this was a task which, as years went on, exercised an increasing attraction for his mind. It was a task, which within the measure to which the analogy between the political and natural sciences may be said to hold, resembled one of those branches of scientific enquiry which are directly ministerial to practical convenience. To know what is really happening in a State is generally the first step towards the amendment of that which is amiss and the corroboration of that which is wholesome. To American democracy, with all its points of strength and imperfection, Bryce was content to hold up the mirror, hoping that in so doing he might help the good citizen not in the United States alone but in every community in which democratic rule is practised, to realize the dangers to which modern democracy is subject and to work for their removal. Thus his books upon political science must not be regarded as mere academic exercises, but as disinterested contributions to the improvement of Democratic government throughout the world. How far this aim has been accomplished does not admit of nice assessment, but there will be few men acquainted with the course of recent history in the United States who will deny that the *American Commonwealth* has exercised a wide influence for good and that it has proved to be a powerful auxiliary to those strong moral forces which are working for the elevation of American public life.

More perhaps than most very able men he was influenced by a sentiment of intellectual loyalty to his teachers and friends in early life. From Goldwin Smith and Freeman he acquired a general view of foreign politics which remained with him as a body of guiding principles and helped to shape his public action. That the Teuton was superior to the Latin or the Celt, that French Imperialism was to be profoundly distrusted, that the national movements of the Italians and the Magyars deserved the warmest sympathy, that the Austrian Empire was an injurious, tyrannical, and anomalous structure and that the political boundaries of Europe should be drawn on the principle of nationality, these were ideas common to the school of Liberal historians at Oxford when Bryce was a young man. Long before President Wilson popularised the doctrine, they stood for the principle of self-determination. The despotism of Russia was hateful to them, but far less odious than the presence upon European soil of the Ottoman Turk. That, as Freeman was continually urging, was an offence against Christian civilization and the tradition of Europe which it was the urgent duty of statesmanship to remove. To these guiding ideas Bryce remained persistently faithful.

The bright stars of the nationalist movement, Kossuth, Mazzini, Garibaldi, who had illumined the political prospect in his youth, shone with undiminished lustre amid the storm clouds of his closing years. He lived to see the triumph of national principles in the Treaties of Peace, which gave to Europe a political map closer to the presumed wishes of its inhabitants, if that be a benefit, than any which Europe had yet known. Nevertheless the design of the New Europe was unwelcome. The broad advantages secured by the Treaties were overshadowed by certain palpable defects which caused Bryce infinite

pure et eleganter actæ ætatis placida ac lenis senectus" cannot be quoted here, for there was in Bryce to the end mingled with spaces of quiet thought and contemplation the eagerness and rushing activity of youth.

CHRONOLOGICAL TABLE

1838 May 10. Born in Belfast.
1846 Bryce family move to Glasgow. James Bryce successively educated at the Glasgow High School and the Glasgow University.
1857 Scholar of Trinity College, Oxford.
1858 First Class Honour Moderations.
1859 Writes on Flora of the Isle of Arran.
1860 Gaisford Prize (Greek Prose).
1861 First Class Literæ Humaniores, Gaisford Prize (verse). First Class Law and History. Meets Alfred Tennyson at Freshwater.
1862 Vinerian Law Scholarship. Latin Essay. Craven Scholarship. Fellow of Oriel. Journey to Switzerland, Dresden, Munich, and Berlin.
1863 Arnold Historical Essay Prize on the Holy Roman Empire. Semester at Heidelberg University. Visits Salzburg, Venice, Munich.
1864 *Holy Roman Empire* published. Reads for the Bar and lectures at Oxford. Visits Florence, Rome, Naples, Monte Cassino with C. P. Ilbert, C. Robartes, and Edward Boyle.
1865 Begins life in London, sharing rooms with Kenelm Digby and reading in Sir John Holker's Chambers.
1866 Assistant Commissioner of the Schools Enquiry Commission. In Transylvania with Leslie Stephen.
1867 Called to the Bar at Lincoln's Inn. Schools Enquiry Commission's Report issued. Contributions to "*Essays in Reform,*" *Saturday Review* and other papers.
1868 Practices at the bar. Lectures in Law at Owen's College,

Manchester (1868–70). Holiday in the Dolomites with C. P. Ilbert, K. Digby, and C. Robartes. Speaks for Liberal Candidates at the General Election.

1869 Practises at the Bar. Visit to the Dolomites with C. P. Ilbert and Aeneas Mackay — afterwards to Padua, Bologna, Ravenna, Milan.

1870 Goes the Northern Circuit. Appointed Regius Professor of Civil Law at Oxford. First visit to the United States with A. V. Dicey. New York, Newport, Boston, Cornell, Niagara, the White Mountains, Philadelphia, Washington.

1871 Bar work, teaching at Oxford, Journalism. Visit to Switzerland and the Rhine with C. P. Ilbert and Miss Ilbert and with his sisters Mary and Katharine. Visits Oberammergau.

1872 Visits Iceland with C. P. Ilbert and Aeneas Mackay.

1873 Climbs in the Pyrenees with C. P. Ilbert.

1874 Stands unsuccessfully as Liberal candidate for the Wick Burghs. Visits Portugal on legal business for Messrs. Carver of Manchester. Visits Oporto, Lisbon, Coimbra, Busaco, and travels in the mountains.

1875 Again visits Portugal on legal business — travels through Spain, visiting Santander, Burgos, Valladolid, Avilia El Escorial, Madrid, Toledo, Cordova, Granada da Seville, Malaga, Cadiz, Gibraltar.

1876 Travels in the Caucasus and Armenia with Aeneas Mackay and ascends Ararat. First visit to Constantinople.

1877 Publishes '*Trade Marks, Registration Act and Trade Mark Law.*' *Transcaucasia and Ararat* published. Death of his father Dr. James Bryce.

1878 Prominent member of the Eastern Question Committee. Journey to the Carpathians with Leslie Stephen.

1879 Elected to the Alpine Club. Working on the Eastern Question Campaign. Holiday in Norway, Denmark and Finland.

Chronological Table

1880 Enters Parliament as Member for the Tower Hamlets. Begins contributions to New York *Nation*. Visits Greece and Constantinople.

1881 Refuses post of Legal Member of the Council of India. Work at Oxford and in the House of Commons. Second visit to the United States. Visits the Pacific Coast and the Southern States. Stops at Boston. Visits Tennyson at Freshwater.

1882 Gives up practice at the bar. Holiday in the Alps.

1883 Jan. Visits Rome with Mr. and Mrs. Henry Sidgwick. Third visit to the United States. Trip over the Northern Pacific Railroad to the Pacific (Washington and Oregon) and San Francisco, thence to the Hawaiian isles and the volcano of Kilauea and back to the Eastern States. Lowell lectures at Boston. Begins writing *The American Commonwealth.*

1884 Writing *The American Commonwealth.* Parliamentary work. Visit to Eastern Italy and Umbria.

1885 Elected member for South Aberdeen. Holiday in the Dolomites and Dalmatia. Oct. goes to Belfast to warn Ulster Liberals of the coming proposals for Irish Home Rule.

1886 Under Secretary for Foreign Affairs in Mr. Gladstone's Government (Jan. to August). Defeat of the Liberal Government. Represents the University of Oxford at the Heidelberg Centenary.

1887 Writing *The American Commonwealth.* In Switzerland Aug. Visit to Egypt (Dec. to Jan. 1888).

1888 "*The American Commonwealth*" published. Visit to India (Nov. 1888–Feb. 1889).

1889 Marriage to Miss Marion Ashton, July 23. Journey in the Dolomites, Eastern Alps, Croatia (Agram) Carinthia, Carniola, Adelsburg and Venice. Interview with Kossuth in Turin.

1890 Fourth visit to the United States (Aug. to Nov.). New York, Washington, Ottawa, Toronto, Montreal, Winnipeg, Vancouver, Puget Sound, Yellowstone Park, Seattle and afterwards to Richmond (Va.), Frankfort (Ky.), Nashville (Tenn.) and Massachusetts.

1891 Voyage to the North Cape via Bergen and Trondjhem — thence to Stockholm, the island of Gothland, Lübeck and Hamburg.

1892 General Election. Chancellor of the Duchy of Lancaster in Mr. Gladstone's Cabinet. Member of the Cabinet Committee for drafting the Irish Home Rule Bill.

1893 Resigns the Regius Professorship of Civil Law at Oxford. Long fight over the Second Home Rule Bill. Journey to St. Jean de Luz and the Basque country. Visits to Tarragona, Barcelona, and Majorca.

1894 Retirement of Mr. Gladstone. President of the Board of Trade in Lord Rosebery's Cabinet. Chairman of Commission on Secondary Education. Visits Siena in the autumn.

1895 Report of the Commission on Secondary Education published. General Election. Defeat of the Liberal Government. Journey to South Africa — Cape Colony, Orange Free State, Bechuanaland, Matabeleland, Namaqualand, the Portuguese Territory, Natal, the Transvaal.

1896 Journey to North Africa. Tunis, Susa, El Djem (Thysdrus), El Keranan, Biserta.

1897 Spring holiday in Normandy and Touraine, bicycling. Fifth visit to the United States. Attends meeting of British Association in Toronto. Publishes '*South Africa*.'

1898 Bicycles with E. Bowen in Germany (Hanau, Jena, Weimar, the Black Forest). Goes into residence at Hindleap, Forest Row, Sussex.

1899 Beginning of the Boer War. Elected President of the Athenaeum Club.

1900 Protests against handling of the South African negotiations by the British Government. Bicycling tour in Southern France (with E. Bowen) in the spring. August and September in the Alps.

1901 Publishes '*Studies in History and Jurisprudence*.' In Burgundy with E. Bowen in the spring. Death of Bowen. Sixth visit to the United States *en route* for Mexico, Cuba, and Jamaica. Sees President Roosevelt at the White House.

1902 Takes a prominent part in the debates on the Education and Licensing Bills. Visits the Orkney and Shetland Isles and tours through N. W. Scotland.

1903 Publishes '*Studies in Contemporary Biography*.' Delegate to the Historical Congress in Rome (Easter). Death of his mother (aged 90) in August. Visits Sicily (November), ascends Etna.

1904 Visits Corsica (April). Seventh visit to the United States (Sept.-Oct.). Gives an address at the St. Louis Exhibition and delivers the Godkin Lectures at Harvard and Columbia. Stays with President Roosevelt at the White House.

1905 Tour in Greece — Smyrna and the Greek Islands (April). Journey in the Balkans (Sept. and October) via Vienna, Buda Pesth, Bucharest, and Belgrade to Salonica and back through Bulgaria. Visits the birthplace of Justinian near Uskub. General election (Nov.) Chief Secretary to Ireland in Sir H. Campbell Bannerman's Cabinet (Dec.).

1906 Chief Secretary for Ireland.

1907 British Ambassador at Washington (Feb. 21, 1907 to April 24, 1913).

Mar. New York. Pilgrims' Dinner.

April Jameston (Va.) Tercentenary Celebration of first English Settlement.

May St. Louis and the State of Oklahoma.

June Chicago — the University Commencement.

Aug. Provincetown (Cape Cod) for foundation stone of Puritan

in settlement of Pecuniary Claims outstanding between the two countries.

Sept. Oct. Nov. Took double leave: journey round South America.

Dec. Returned from Brazil by way of England and reached New York on January 1st, 1911.

1911

Feb. Treaty signed between the U. K. and U. S. A., respecting measures for Preservation and Protection of the Fur Seals. Gave an address on Washington's Birthday at Johns Hopkins University (Baltimore) and received a Degree.

Mar. Gave addresses at Trenton (N. Y.) and at the City Club in New York. Also addressed the New York Legislature in joint session at Albany and spoke at the University Club. Spoke at the St. Patrick's Day Dinner at Baltimore.

April To Detroit: gave address at Ann Arbor University (Mich.), also addresses to Board of Commerce and the University Club in Detroit. On the return journey, went to London (Ontario) to address the Canadian Club, and to New York, to speak at the St. George's Day Dinner and at the Celebration of the Tercentenary of the translation of the English Bible.

May An official visit to Canada. Stayed at Government House, Ottawa and with the Lieut. Governor of Ontario at Toronto. Addressed the Empire club at Toronto, and the Canadian Club at Hamilton (Ont.). Delegates from Canada to the Behring Sea Seal Conference and the Commercial Conference met at Washington.

June Gave an address at the Union College, Schenectady (N. Y.).

July The Pecuniary Claims Agreement finally signed and settled. Also the "Fur Seal Convention" Agreement signed. Moved the Embassy up to Seal Harbor, Mount Desert.

Aug. 3rd Signed the Arbitration Treaty between the U. K. and the U. S. A., at Washington (which the Senate later refused to ratify), in the presence of President Taft, with Mr. Knox as Secretary of State.

Oct. To Pittsburgh to address the Alleghany Bar Association. To New York to dinner of British Schools and Universities and gave an address on Thackeray (Centenary); also address at Rutgers College (N. J.).

Nov. Spoke at dinner of New York Chamber of Commerce and at the Brooklyn Institute.

Dec. Official visit to Canada: stayed at Government House, Ottawa, with Duke and Duchess of Connaught. On return journey, went to New York to speak at Dinner of the Canadian Society.

1912

Jan. The Duke of Connaught came to Washington to see President Taft — stayed at the Embassy (Dinner and Reception).

Feb. Address to the Southern Society on Washington's Birthday. Published "*South America.*"

May Took "double leave": crossed the Pacific from San Francisco and visited Tahiti, the Cook and Society Islands, New Zealand, Australia, and Tasmania, calling on the way back at American Samoa and Hawaii (which he had first seen 30 years previously). In New Zealand and Australia he made a number of public speeches, addressed the Universities of Melbourne, Sidney, Adelaide, and Brisbane in Australia (received Hon. Degree at Adelaide and Brisbane), and saw a great deal of these countries. He travelled in both the North and South Islands of New Zealand; and through Victoria, South Australia, New South Wales and Queensland in Australia, visiting the "back blocks," the mountain districts, the sheep stations, and the Bush in turn. He also crossed over to Tasmania and stayed at Hobart, where he addressed the University. Landed in San Francisco on September 12th, 1912.

Sept. In 1912 effect was given to three Treaties — (1) The Protection of the Fur Seals (between the U. K., the U. S. A., Japan, and Russia. (2) The Settlement of Pecuniary Claims (between the U. K. and the U. S. A.) (3) The North Atlantic Fisheries (between the U. K. and the U. S. A.).

Oct. Addressed the Economic Club and the American Antiquarian Association at Worcester (Mass.). Also addressed a Missionary Conference at Baltimore.

Nov. Addressed the Law Students at the George Washington University at Washington. Also spoke at the Meeting of the Archaeological Institute of America in Washington and at the Civic Convention in Baltimore. Also at the Y. M. C. A., in Washington and the St. Andrew's Society Dinner in New York.

Dec. Spoke at the Dinner of the "Housing Congress" in Philadelphia; also at the Dinner of the Canadian Society in New York, the Dinner of the Committee on "Hundred years of Peace," and at the Dinner of the Pennsylvania Society in New York.

1913

Jan. Gave two Lectures (under the Page Barbour Foundation) at the University of Virginia (Charlottesville).

Feb. Attended the County Bar Dinner and the Harvard Law School Alumni Dinner in New York, and the Dinner of the Trans-Atlantic Society in Philadelphia.

Mar. Made an address on "The Beautifying of Washington" and also addressed the Scientific and Philosophical Societies in Washington. Paid a final official visit to Canada. Published "*University and Historical addresses*."

April Preparing to give up post: trying to settle the Panama

Canal Dues question with President Wilson before leaving. Took final leave of the President and the Secretary of State on the 24th April and presented papers of recall. Quitted the Embassy on the 25th April for New York and was entertained at a Dinner (Mr. Choate in the chair) of the Pilgrims' Society that evening. Left New York for San Francisco on April 28th and sailed thence for Japan on May 3rd.

May Gave up the post of Ambassador on April 25th, within a fortnight of completing 75 years of age.

1914

Jan. Went to the House of Lords.

Feb. Bencher of Lincoln's Inn. Member of the Clothworkers' Company.

Mar.–Apr. Journey in Palestine (Jaffa, Jerusalem, Hebron, the Dead Sea, the Jordan, Jericho, Nablus, Samaria, Nazareth, Haifa, Acre, Galilee (Tiberias) and Petra. In Syria: Damascus, Baalbec, Beyrout, and Sidon. Ascended Mount Carmel, Tabor and Hor.

Aug. The Great War
Chairman of the Inquiry into Alleged German Outrages in Belgium. Working on a Committee to promote a Scheme for a League of Nations.

1915 Report of Inquiry issued.

1916–1917 At the British Front in France, July 28th to 31st. Went over part of the Fleet at Rosyth.

1918 Chairman of Second Chamber Conference.

1918 to 1921 At work on "*Modern Democracies*," Published in March, 1921.

1919 To Switzerland in connection with work on "*Modern Democracies*."

1920

April–May Journey in French Morocco and Spain. Gibraltar, Seville, Cadiz, Granada, Cordoba, Toledo, Madrid, El Escorial, Aranjuez, Vigo, and in French Morocco,

Casa Blanca, Rabat, Fez, Mekhas, and back by Tangier to Gibraltar.

1921 "*Modern Democracies*" published. Last journey to the United States. Lectured on "International Relations" at Williamstown Conference. Speeches at Harvard, Princeton, Washington, and New York.

Dec. Last Speech in the House of Lords on the Irish Treaty. Last Address: an Appeal on behalf of the Armenians at the Mansion House. Speech on unveiling the portrait of Lord Reay at University College.

1922

Jan. Last Address to the Historical Association in London. "*International Relations*" published.

Jan. 22nd Died Sidmouth.

APPENDIX I

In Memory of

William C. G. Gladstone

d. 1915.

Speech delivered at the opening of a Memorial Ward in Chester Royal Infirmary.

April 15, 1916

"It is most fitting, in a time like this, of such effort, such suffering, and such grief as our country has never known before, that when we wish to commemorate those who had been associated with events of the war, who had played a part and given their lives — such commemoration should take the form of some institution for the relief of suffering. And I think it is specially appropriate it should take this particular form, because among the many forms of suffering which the war had brought upon those who had fought in it none was more common, and none was more melancholy, than injury to or loss of sight. These wards will be remembered in connection with the honoured name now attached to them; and those of you who are now the youngest will, when you come to be old, and when those who are younger ask you about the time of your youth, and you tell them of the awful ordeal through which Britain passed in these years wherein we stand now, you will remember, and point out, that among the things by which the war was commemorated, there were works of beneficence and mercy, works which were intended to show our sympathy with suffering, and our gratitude to God who is supporting us through these terrible days.

speak of him because I had the privilege of knowing him well when he served as an attaché in the Embassy at Washington some years ago. Everybody there became fond of him at once. No one, I think, in the whole diplomatic corps more quickly became popular in the society at Washington and was more valued, and liked there for his amiable qualities. I saw, even then, how anxious he was, in every way, to do his duty. He had, I think, no ambition for himself; no ambition of the sort that seeks for personal favour or distinction, but he had a strong sense that he was somehow called upon, in respect of his father and his grandfather, to enter political life, and when the opportunity for entering political life came he took it. He entered Parliament, and I have heard from all those who knew him in Parliament how quickly he made his way there, not by obtruding himself, but by his simple genial ways, by his innate desire to know what was true, and to do what was right; and when he spoke, which was not too often, he always spoke with an evident desire to help things forward, and to reach that which was true and right. As you know, he became Lord Lieutenant of this county. He was very diffident about accepting that post, and he consulted me about it, as he consulted, of course, his uncle and his other friends, and I had no hesitation in advising him to do it, for I felt perfectly certain that, young as he was, the innate strength and dignity of his character would fit him to fulfill the duties of that high office. As you know, he devoted himself, when war broke out, to the duties of that office with the utmost energy and earnestness. He did all that he could to induce people to enlist, and he took the greatest pains in the organising, and all the work in connection with recruiting, and the care of recruits, and it was in the course of his doing so that it was borne in upon him that when he was urging others to come forward to help their country, he ought not to stay behind himself. He was a member of Parliament with his duties at Westminster; he was Lord Lieutenant of Flintshire with his duties here, but he felt, and he rightly felt, that, at such a moment as this, it might be expected of him that he should set an example, and that he ought to do so.

He felt it to be his duty to his country; he felt it to be his duty to God. As you know, he trained himself to be an officer. He went as a Lieutenant to France, and within a fortnight his end came. So he lived and so he died! — pure and tender, upright and gracious. And it is well when we grieve for those who have gone from us that we should feel when we are grieving for them, that we have nothing in their life to grieve for. What more can we think in praising any one, than that their life's course should have given us nothing to regret? I daresay you remember the lines in one of those poems of lamentation I have mentioned to you — the lines of Shelley, where he says: —

> 'From the contagion of the world's slow stain
> He is secure. . . .
> Heaven's light for ever shines, earth's shadow fly.'

"His life was short, but it was long enough to show what he was. It was long enough to enable him to set an example. As he said himself, 'It is not the length of existence that counts, but what is achieved in that existence, however short it may be.' In that short life he set an example not only to those who were around him here, but to all of us — an example of devotion, an example of earnestness, an example of unselfishness. He was one of the many who answered the call which the nation made. How many have answered the call, and how many have gone? Never was there a time when so many of our best and noblest young men have gone from us — gone from us willingly because they felt it their duty; and never was there a time when their parents have shown such a noble example of uncomplaining patience under the loss that to them was the greatest that any loss could be. We may well feel proud, not only for the children, but for the parents in this time of ours, that they have willingly given their children, and that they have borne their loss with Christian dignity and patience and faith.

"These young men who have gone have set us a noble example, but they have done even more than that. They have given us a proof of what our country can produce. The old spirit of devotion is alive again in Britain. It is again the old England of ancestral fame! Some had thought that England had degenerated. But never has England shown herself worthier of the greatest traditions of her greatest days than she has done in these last months! An England that can do this is an England worth fighting for. Is not that the thought that thrills in all our breasts? Let us, who remain, be worthy of those who have gone! Let us, who remain, be worthy of the country that could rear such children. They have revealed to us the soul of the nation, the inner spirit, and life which is what counts in a nation. It is by its soul, far more than by its wealth or its prosperity, or its material strength that a nation lives, and while the soul of England lives, England will maintain her greatness. Let us then remember these young heroes who have gone from us — not altogether with sorrow, but also with a sort of solemn thankfulness — thankfulness to God who has strengthened them to do their duty, thankfulness to them who have strengthened and helped us all by the way they have done their duty. Not in vain have they given their lives for their country which is fighting for a cause to which honour and justice call her, a cause as righteous as any nation has ever sustained. The memories of these young heroes will, for us and for those who come after, shine like lights in the world, lights that will burn for ever, set up around the altar of patriotism and duty."

APPENDIX II

Degrees

Great Britain & Ireland

Oxford.
Cambridge.
Manchester.
Edinburgh.
Glasgow.
Aberdeen.

	St. Andrew's.
	Belfast.
	Dublin.
Holland	Leyden.
Germany	Jena.
	Leipzig.
Hungary	Buda Pesth.
U. S. A.	Harvard.
	Yale.
	Princeton.
	Columbia.
	Johns Hopkins.
	Chicago.
	California. (State University)
	Illinois. (State University)
	Michigan. (State University)
	New York University.
	Washington University. (Missouri)
	Grinnell University. (Iowa)
	Williams College. (Mass.)
	Schenectady. (New York)
	Rutgers College. (New Jersey)
Canada	Toronto and Montreal.
Australia	Adelaide and Brisbane.
South America	Buenos Aires.

Continental Societies

France	Member of the Institut de France.
Italy	(1) Member of the Royal Academy of Turin.
	(2) Member of the R. Accademia dei Lincei. (Rome)
	(3) Member of the Societa di Storia Patria. (Rome)
	(4) Member of the Royal Academy of Naples.

Belgium	Member of the R. Academy of Brussels.
Sweden	Member of the R. Academy of Stockholm.
Russia	Member of the Imperial Academy of Sciences, St. Petersburg.
Spain	Offered the Membership of the Royal Historical Society, but Lord Bryce died before it could be conferred.

Membership of English Societies

The Royal Society.
The British Academy (*President*).
The Royal Geographical Society (*Honorary Fellow*).
The Geographical Club.
The Royal Historical Association.
The Society of Roman Studies.
The British School at Rome.
The Society of Hellenic Studies.
The Classical Association.
The Sociological Society.
The Royal Economic Society.
The Society of Comparative Legislation.
The Commons and Footpaths Preservation Society.
The National Trust.
The Empire Parliamentary Association.
The Glasgow and Lanarkshire Association.
The Alpine Club (*President*).
The Swiss Alpine Club.
The Cairngorm Club.
The Norwegian Club.
The Pilgrims.
The Anglo-American Society.
The English Speaking Union.
The Sulgrave Society.
The Dante Society.
Trustee of the National Portrait Gallery.

Clubs

The Old Mortality (Oxford).
The Ad Eundem (Oxford and Cambridge).
The Oxford Law Club.
The Oxford Dante Society.
Grillion's Club.
The Club.

APPENDIX III

Portraits of James Bryce

1. Portrait by Arthur Cope — 1880 or 1881. (In the possession of Lady Bryce.)

2. Portrait by F. Wilson Forster about 1899 in Trinity College Hall, Oxford.

3. Portrait by Sir George Reid in Oriel Senior Common Room, Oxford. (Painted 1905.)

4. Portrait by Mons. Delécluse. (In Miss Bryce's possession.)

5. Portrait by Ernest Moore in the National Portrait Gallery, London. (Painted in Washington in 1907.)

6. Portrait by Seymour Thomas, presented by a friend to the National Liberal Club, London. (Painted in Washington about 1912.)

7. Portrait by W. Orpen, in the Aberdeen Art Gallery. (Painted in London, 1914.)

Index

B

Index

Index

Index

Index

Index

Index

Index

H

Index

Index

Index

Index

N

Index

R

Index

Y

Z